IIMA Monograph in Business History – I

Business Communities of India

A Historical Perspective

Edited by

DWIJENDRA TRIPATHI

MANOHAR
2026

The publication of this book was financially supported by the Indian Council of Historical Research and the responsibility for the facts stated, opinions expressed or conclusions reached. Is entirely that of the author and Indian Council of Historical Research accepts no responsibility for them.

First published 1984
Reprinted 2021, 2022, 2023, 2024, 2025, 2026

ISBN 978-93-88540-83-4

Published by
Ajay Kumar Jain *for*
Manohar Publishers & Distributors
4753/23 Ansari Road, Daryaganj
New Delhi 110 002

Printed at
Replika Press Pvt. Ltd.

For the memory of

RALPH W. HIDY,

A TEACHER AND FRIEND

Contents

Foreword

The IIMA Monograph Series in Business History is a part of our continuing effort to encourage the study of the subject in the country. It goes without saying that the knowledge of the past is an essential input for our understanding of the present and insight into the future. And yet, historical research in Indian business has made very little progress. In fact, most of the institutions concerned with business education have paid practically no attention to it; and the history departments of our universities have viewed it as not quite within their domain. To date, this Institute is the only institution of higher learning in India where Business History is included in the formal curriculum.

The task, however, is too stupendous to be accomplished by one institution alone; collaborative effort may pay rich dividends. The IIMA Seminar Series in Business History, started about two years ago, is directed to this end. It provides for a common forum for scholars, irrespective of their institutional affiliation, to deliberate on various themes relating to Business History. Our Monograph Series aims at disseminating the outcome of these deliberations among wider scholarly community.

I commend this effort and hope that the seminar series and the resultant monographs will not only fill the gaps in our historical literature but also give a much needed impetus to historical enquiries in the dynamics of Indian business.

Indian Institute of Management
Ahmedabad
25 March 1984

I.G. Patel
Director

Acknowledgements

This volume has emerged from the first seminar in the IIMA Seminar Series in Business History held from 3 to 7 March 1982. In addition to those whose contributions are included here, a number of other scholars participated in the deliberations and, thus, indirectly, contributed to the quality of these essays. They include Indu Banga (Guru Nanak Dev University, Amritsar), Aparna Basu (University of Delhi), Sudhir Chandra (Nehru Memorial Museum and Library, New Delhi), Mariam Dosal (University of Bombay), S.P. Gupta (Muslim University, Aligarh), David Hardiman (Centre of Social Studies, Surat), Alan Heston (University of Pennsylvania, Philadelphia), Dharma Kumar (University of Delhi), Ravinder Kumar (Nehru Memorial Museum and Library, New Delhi), Jim Masselos (University of Sydney), A.N. Pandey (Indian Institute of Technology, New Delhi), Om Prakash (University of Delhi), V.I. Pavlov (University of Moscow), Ghanshyam Shah (Centre for Studies in Social Sciences), Lakshmi Subramanian (Vishwa Bharati University, Shanti Niketan) and Prakash Tandon (National Council of Applied Economic Research, New Delhi). Some of these, particularly Dharma Kumar, Ravinder Kumar and S.C. Misra, rendered valuable help in the academic planning of the exercise. The doyen of Indian historians S. Nurul Hasan set the tone of discussion by his erudite inaugural address which is the basis of his paper included in this volume.

Financial support for the seminar came from the Indian Council of Historical Research, Indian Institute of Management, Ahmedabad, and the Lalbhai Group of Industries. Shrenik K. Lalbhai and Manubhai D. Shah played critical role in arranging for funds from the last mentioned source.

Kulvinder Chhabra and Priti Misra helped not only in organizing the seminar but also preparing the bibliography appended to this volume. Others who supported the endeavour in various ways include V. Arumugam, who typed and retyped the manuscript and the staff of the Publications Division, the Kasturbhai Lalbhai Management Development Centre and the Vikram Sarabhai Library, Indian Institute of Management, Ahmedabad. Among the colleagues at the Institute, the encouragement given by V.S. Vyas, who was then its Director, must be particularly acknowledged.

To all these individuals and agencies I owe a debt of deep gratitude.

D.T.

Introduction

Considerable debate has centred around Indian business communities during the last thirty years or so. And yet, the existing literature leaves a number of issues unresolved. What do we mean by "community"? How does a business community differ from a business class? What are the antecedents of various business communities in India and what were the stages through which they have evolved? Do they represent a unique feature of the Indian social structure or a stage in the evolution of Indian business system? What has been the social composition of these communities at different points of time? Do they exhibit markedly different approaches to business strategies? If not, is the caste system, which wittingly or unwittingly influences all analyses of social realities in India, responsible for this kind of categorisation? Some of these questions have seldom been asked, much less answered.

None of these and similar other questions is easy to answer. Take for instance the problem of definition. The number of existing definitions of the term "community" is so large and they differ from one another so much that to find the lowest common denominator is an uphill task. A review of almost one hundred definitions sometime ago yielded no better result to an inquisitive author than the harmless conclusion that "beyond the concept that people are involved in community, there is no complete agreement as to the nature of community". (G.A. Hillery, "Definitions of Community: Areas of Agreement", *Rural Sociology*, vol. 20, 1955, p. 119). Some of these differences are due to differences in the contextual basis of various definitions or because of the disciplinary biases of the analysts. The word in the context of a society where primordial loyalties have a preponderant influence on social behaviour may have a meaning different from its connotation in societies where such loyalties are less potent. And the approach of a sociologist may not be the same as the one expounded by a political scientist or a social worker.

But this is not the only source of difficulties. For, myriad definitions may refer to a single social context and a common understanding may still elude us even if we look at the phenomenon through the mirror of a single discipline. All sociologists, for example,—and the sociologists must be credited with greater competence to explicate this concept—do not guide us in the same direction. Even if we disregard relatively minor differences among them, there would still emerge at least two broad categories. Those who emphasise the structural elements would view the community as an aggregation of individuals belonging to a definite geographical area and bound together by certain degree of cultural and economic interdependency. For others, however the geographical affiliation is unimportant; for them the hallmark of a community is the functional elements generating cooperation and collaboration among the members of a collectivity, regardless of spatial boundaries.

It may be argued that the accent on the functional element in the definition is the logical outcome of the process of social change. As the frontiers of collaboration expanded and narrow geographical boundaries crumbled in the face of rapid and far-reaching infrastructural developments, a purely structural basis of the definition became inadequate to explain the dynamics of social formation. The proponents of the structural formulation, however, have lost none of their vigour. The result is that the term "community" signifies both these meanings in the sociological literature today.

One way to reconcile these two approaches is to view a collectivity in the context of its centre of interest at a given point of time. But it is not at all easy to determine the centre of the boundary of a community in whatever sense one uses the term. Is it the economic interest, religious affiliation, occupational grouping, or social division or other collectivities to which the members of a society owe allegiance? If all of these in varying degrees influence the expression of the human desire and need to belong, if the interests flow from more than one centre, then to think of a community is to think of a series of intersecting circles. And since the social situation is seldom static, the boundaries of these circles would always remain fluid and somewhat indeterminate.

If this is so, a proper comprehension of the antecedents and growth of a community requires a historical perspective. Very little attention, however, has been given to the history of Indian business communities because very little attention has been given to the history of Indian business as such. The result is that our understanding of the nature of these communities, the process of their evolution, and their distinctive contribution to the growth of Indian business system is woefully inadequate. If we wish to grasp the social dynamics of Indian business, this gap in the literature must be filled.

The present study does not seek to fill this gap; separate monographs would be necessary for a fuller treatment of each of the communities studied here. Our purpose is to present in one single volume brief historical accounts of some of the most important socio-economic groups which dominate the Indian business scene today. Hopefully, these will generate further interest in the subject. Our starting point is pre-British India so that we can have a fairly good idea of the continuity and change in the social composition and behaviour of the Indian business class over a period of time. It must be stressed, however, that since the volume is a cooperative effort, the papers included here do not have the same emphasis. It must also be conceded that there are significant gaps in the study in as much as it altogether ignores some of the regions and the communities. At the present stage of historical interest in the subject, it was not easy to cover them in the present work.

Even though the volume has emerged as a result of rigorous deliberations among the authors of various chapters and resource persons of considerable competence, their analyses are not informed by a common conceptual framework. That the concept of business community is open to several meanings is reflected throughout the volume. This, again, is understandable for the purpose of the exercise is not to seek agreement but to promote joint thinking, not to eliminate differences but to generate awareness of a variety of approaches. A common element in the conceptual bases of all the chapters, however, is that they do not look at the subject through the narrow vision of caste and culture—a vision that has been very popular in the analysis of Indian business situations until very recently and continues to have strong proponents both in India and abroad. Among a group of scholars, as strong as the present volume represents, even this much agreement must be considered a significant accomplishment. Contradictions undeniably do exist, but they add to the richness of understanding instead of detracting from the main focus. It would have been helpful if the issues thrown up in the course of discussion would have been summed up in a separate chapter. But it was impossible to do so because of the sheer range and variety of such issues.

In spite of the differences in approaches and emphases, however, it can be safely maintained that the studies included in the volume taken together present a more comprehensive treatment of the subject than ever before. The volume does not, however, aim at being a definitive study. If it can inspire more rigorous investigations, its purpose would have been served.

DWIJENDRA TRIPATHI

1

Historian and the Business Communities

S. Nurul Hasan

Over 300 years ago, Bernier wrote that in India there was no middle state![1] What did he mean by this statement? Surely he could never have meant that there were no merchants or businessmen in India. Obviously, he was arguing the case for France when he made this statement that Indian cities were like large military camps; they shrank when the king left with his army; they expanded when the king was there. In other words, the suggestion of Bernier was that the importance of cities was principally and primarily due to the presence of imperial armies and their hangers-on.

But the fact was other way round. Large cities in India attracted the attention of the administrators because they were important centres of trade and manufacture; it was not necessarily due to their political or administrative set-up or military importance that they existed or expanded. Any number of cities can be mentioned from the Mughal period which politically were not major centres. I will deliberately not quote the example of Ahmedabad, because Ahmedabad was established as a political capital. But surely during the 18th century its importance was far greater as a commercial city than as an administrative centre. Its political importance continued because it was a major centre of business. Likewise, Amritsar was never a major political centre. It had its religious importance but apart from it, it continued to be a very important centre of trade and commerce even though it was away from Lahore which was more important politically.

Modern scholars have collected a great deal of evidence to show that the business communities were numerous and trade was flourishing in pre-British India. Debate among historians today seems to be whether this class of merchants and businessmen could have brought about a transformation in medieval Indian society, particularly in its mode of production. In other words, could this class have industrialised India if the British rule had not been superimposed? Even though the contemporary implications of this question cannot be ignored, I hope that the Indian historians have the intellectual discipline to look at it from the point of view of the evidence and theories rather than its implications for the India of today.

Unfortunately for us, a very large number of our historians have found it convenient to study only the published records of the European trading companies, particularly those that were either written in English or translated in English, and form their opinions on that basis. No one can deny the value of these records and the immense amount of information that they contain. But because of partial character of these records, an unfortunate impression has gained ground that non-agrarian activity was largely conditioned by the European trade and European trading communities. As more and more records are becoming available to us, most Indian historians are coming round to the view that external trade formed but a very small part of the mercantile activity of the Indians. Today it is no longer a controversial issue among Indian historians that European trade formed only a small part of the total volume of trade or the total manufacture in pre-British India. If we are observant a good bit of evidence is available in our traditional economies. Only we have not always looked at our source materials as carefully as we ought to have done.

A recent collection of edicts of the Mughal era[2] contains an extremely fascinating *farman* or *nishan* of Noorjahan Begam about a *katra*. What is a *katra*?. It is a word used in relation to innumerable cities, large and small, and date back to the medieval period. The word *katra* has a definite meaning today. But we can assume that it had the same meaning 300 or 400 years ago. The *farman* I have referred to makes it absolutely clear what a *katra* was and what its role was in trade and commerce. If we do not use the English translation of *Ain-i-Akbari* and *Ain-i-Kotwali* but read the original, we can understand much more about the city and how it was governed and what was the marphology of a Mughal city and what was the role that was played by the mercantile community in administering the city. *Ain-i-Kotwali* refers to two very interesting institutions, one is the head of the *Muhalla*, viz., *Meer-i-Muhalla*, and the other is the head of what had been translated as craft guild. Craft guilds are known to have played important roles in the governance of the city in the ancient and the early medieval period, but we do not have enough information about them in the medieval period. When we come across works like *Ain-i-Akbari* we know much more about the organization of the city and the part played by the mercantile community and business classes in civic life.

There are other works which are known and read but unfortunately not adequately utilized for understanding the nature and the role of the business communities. I am referring in particular to a well known autobiographical account written in Hindi by Banarasi Das during the reign of Shahjahan under the title of *Ardh Kathanak*,[3] though there is a some controversy about its exact title. The writer had no pretentions to scholarship although he was a well known and very devout Jain merchant. It is a delightful account. He wrote it when he was 55, signifying the midpoint in his life-span, and the book is supposed to contain an account of the first half of his life. Written in poetic form, it contains great deal of valuable information.

Several other chronicles and memoirs provide valuable information on the position and role of the business communities. Very helpful in understanding this phenomenon is a group of works that were written at the instance of the British for the benefit of the British officials in India. As you are aware, when the English East India Company acquired the rights of *diwani* in 1765, it was very keen to find out what were the rights of different sections of people and what were local customs and institutions. Written in Indian languages, some of these were translated into English which were used by Ranajit Guha to write his delightful book, the *Rule of Property for Bengal*.[4] But I would urge you to have a look at the originals, as the translation does not have the same flavour as the originals; sometimes the sense has undergone a change when rendered into English.

Mercifully the originals are intact. According to these accounts also the merchant community was extremely numerous and economically important. After the British rule was established it, or a section of it, started loosing its importance.

Still more important than these accounts is a class of documents which are coming to light every day and are enabling us to understand the functioning of socio-economic institutions. The *Khatapatras* located in an Ahmedabad library belong to this class. Recently an interesting study on the *Nagarsheth* of Ahmedabad based on these documents has been published.[5] Likewise, S.A.I. Tirmizi has published some documents relating to the Jagatseths.[6] They indicate that when Jagatseth the second died and his successor was recognized as Jagatseth the third by the British, he wanted the title of Raja and the Governor General was inclined to oblige him. But the question arose whether the Governor General had the right to confer the title. The right was vested in Shah Alam. Now, Shah Alam by 1793 was not the most powerful sovereign that the world knew. Even though his sway did not extend beyond Palam, a suburb of Delhi where we have the aerodrome today, it was he, and not the powerful Governor General, who, according to the time honoured custom, could confer the title.

I have myself had the occasion to see the du Jardin Papers in the Bibliothèque Nationale in Paris which I have briefly introduced in the form of a paper.[7] Originally I thought that the du Jardin Papers comprised eleven volumes. Now I have gone through 23 volumes and still do not know whether I have seen the last of the volumes. One of the volumes contains *taqavi* documents. *Taqavi*, as you know, is a form of agricultural credit which in the 18th century was given in accordance with the principle of *Sood Sawai*. That is to say that for a hundred rupee loan one had to return, possibly in kind but not always in kind, a quarter per cent more at the next harvest. So if the *taqavi* was taken at the beginning of a *rabi* season, that is to say that if it was taken in November, it was to be repaid some time in April or May. The rate of interest, thus, worked out to be more than 50 per cent which by any standard was exorbitant. It is commonly believed that the *taqavi* was given by the state. But in these papers it becomes quite clear that neither the *Hakim*, who represented the state, nor the Raja of

Etah gave the *taqavi*. It was given by one Daniel du Jardin, a French merchant settled in what are now the districts of Aligarh and Etah.

These papers cover the period from 1778 to 1788, that is just before the British rule was established. These regions had certain dealings with Farrukhabad which started coming under the British domination around 1785. The British did not take kindly to du Jardin and he had to pull out. Finally what happened to him is not known to me because all documents ceased after 1788 though Aligarh itself did not come under the British control until 1803. One of the volumes deals with *hundis* and we have several volumes of *bahis* and *Khatas* which in modern terminology would be equivalent to journals and ledger books. These records also tell us about a number of other features—what was the type of insurance, what was the type of business and so on.

I have tried to categorise the type of functions that the businessmen performed not only on the basis of the du Jardin Papers but on the basis of other evidence that I have found elsewhere. The first was *malsamini*—standing surety—for the payment of revenue. This was a very important function of the business community. Precisely how much commission or *batta* they got for *malsamini* is not known to me. My suspicion is that it would have differed from time to time, from area to area, and according to the personality and the credit-worthiness of the person for whom surety was undertaken.

The second was agricultural credit; *taqavi* in some cases, in other cases direct credit by the comparatively well to do village headman—*Mukhia* or *Mandal* or *Patel*, or *Patil* or *Desai*. If the *Khudkashta* was large, the credit would be given to the person who actually cultivated the land or who got the land cultivated or arranged it to be cultivated. The merchant community granted credit when large amount of liquid cash was needed which neither the *Hakim*, the representative of the state, nor the *Zamindar* was in a position to advance.

The third major function was *ijara* or revenue farming which was a common feature of the medieval economy. Beginning with the twilight years of the Mughals, however, we find a new feature emerging in this age-old system. The merchants themselves started sowing cash crops on land taken on *ijara*.

To put it differently, the merchants used the *ijara* land for growing cash crops and thereby making profit. In fact, increase in cash crops was by and large accompanied by the increase in the *ijara* land and most of the persons taking *ijara* were people belonging to the business community. Some of these, in course of time, became *zamindars* and gave up their mercantile pursuits. I know some families who from the time of Farrukhsiyar became pure *zamindars* and gave up all business activities which their ancestors had pursued. It seems to me that the mercantile class started taking *ijara* around the middle of the 18th century.

Then the next important function of the business communities was grain trade. Approximately 50 per cent of the grain produced in a village was given away to others in one form or the other. A sharecropper had to part with 50 per cent of the produce to the owner of the land; a portion of it would go to various hereditary village officials like the *chaudhris*, *qanungos* and so on, and to the *jagirdar* or the state. The process entailed conversion of produce into cash as has been pointed out by several scholars. Although Akbar gave full freedom to the taxpayer to pay the revenue in cash or in kind, more often than not the payment was made in cash. Now, if the revenue was to be paid in cash then the produce had to be sold fairly near the place of production; and if it was to be paid in kind then also it would be sold. Whatever the circumstances, it is the merchants who brought the grain and carried on trade in it. So the trade in food-grains was an important source of their wealth. The du Jardin Papers indicate that their margin of profit was considerable. I do not want to cite figures because I am not quite certain about the accuracy of these figures but the margin of profit was undoubtedly considerable. It would amount to hundreds and thousands of rupees per year in a single *pargana*.

Another source of merchant's profit was exchange. The revenue could be paid in any currency but it was to be deposited in the imperial treasury in the standard currency. For changing the money into standard currency the merchants were allowed *batta* or commission. Then there was the question of transmitting money from one place to the other not only for imperial expenses but also for trade. In some of these documents

I have seen the actual *hundis* through which the money was transmitted. This was another very important function that was performed by the merchant communities. Yet another function that the merchants performed was to provide for the supplies to the armies in the event of expedition. In fact, the entire Mughal system or medieval system depended on the capacity of these people to meet the needs of the military.

The merchants also gave advances to handicraftsmen. There is plenty of evidence in original records of the advances that were given by the businessmen to the artisans. And it was the responsibility of the merchants to market the goods produced by the artisans. In fact, the artisans accepting the advances were required to sell their goods to their creditors. If an artisan tried to do otherwise disputes inevitably arose, as several documents bear out. So in the process of production and distribution, the merchants played a very important role. Finally, they acted as *comprador* of foreign companies. They acted as their *gumastas*, and served as their interpreters or *dubhashis*.

While dealing with the past of the Indian business communities, one should be very careful in interpreting certain words in the documents for the words may have different meanings in different regions. For instance, the word *mahajan* denoted an association of merchants in Ahmedabad, playing crucial role in the life of the city, while in north India it referred to an individual merchant. It seems to me that in the latter sense also the *mahajans* were so called because they performed important economic functions. They enjoyed some concessions also. They were taxed lightly in order that they did not run away. Those who were called "*saraf*" or "*shroff*" or *sheth*, likewise, performed some specific role. Today, any businessman of substance is called "*sheth*" or "*seth*", but I have a suspicion that the *sheth* in the past discharged some administrative or economic function. The basis of my suspicion is that the word "sheth" is used whenever administrative duties are mentioned, whether it is *nagarsheth* or *jagatseth*. It is probable that other common nouns such as *gumashta* and "*purchunee*" and "*Pansari*" had different connotations. It seems to me that a distinction was always maintained between the wholesaler and the retailer and the retailers carrying on the trade in different objects were known by different names.

All this suggests that historical enquiries into the antecedents and growth of business communities would unfold several aspects of our socio-economic life about which we still know very little. There is a great deal of materials which remain unused or which have been used only partially. To use them with profit and to use them with care is both a challenge and an opportunity to the historian.

NOTES

1. F. Bernier, *Memoirs* (London, 1672).
2. S.A.I. Tirmizi, *Edicts from the Mughal Harem* (New Delhi, 1979), 29-30.
3. Banarasi Das, *Ardha Kathanak* (Bombay, 1970).
4. Ranajit Guha, *Rule of Property for Bengal* (New Delhi, 1981).
5. D. Tripathi and M.J. Mehta, "The Nagarsheth of Ahmedabad: History of an Urban Institution in a Gujarat City" in Indian History Congress *Proceedings*, 39th session (Hyderabad, 1978), 481-96.
6. S.A.I. Tirmizi, *Indian Historical Vistas* (New Delhi, 1979), 29-30.
7. S. Nurul Hasan, "du Jardin Papers: A Valuable Source for the Economic History of Northern India, 1778-1788", *Indian Historical Review*, Vol. V, Nos. 1-2 (July 1978-January 1979), 187-99.

2

Theoretical Framework for the Study of Indian Business Communities

N.R. Sheth

Theory and theoretical framework are among the more diversely used terms in social sciences. I should therefore state my own understanding of these terms before I use them explicitly or implicitly in this paper.[1] A theory consists of a set of propositions defining the pattern of relationships among chosen variables comprising a social phenomenon. The propositions constituting a theory should enable the observer to predict events in the relevant field of social existence and should help him to integrate apparently dissimilar observations. The propositions should also allow the possibility of the theory being modified or disproved. A theoretical framework consists of either an integrated set of interrelated theories on a social phenomenon or a schematic approach to the task of building theory on such phenomenon.[2] In this sense, a theoretical framework for the study of Indian business communities should help us in identifying the distinctive social characteristics of these communities in India vis-a-vis the rest of Indian society, the process of emergence and growth of business communities in specific social settings and the nature of interaction between these communities and the other segments of society. The observable diversities among them should provide a significant backdrop for comprehension of their common attributes with predictive value.

Unfortunately, not enough theory-based studies of Indian business communities are available to enable us to attempt a comprehensive theoretical model about their social behaviour.

I shall therefore try to raise questions regarding the social behaviour of these communities that may contribute to the formulation of social theory about them. Specifically, I shall address myself to the following questions: (1) What do we regard as business communities in India? (2) What is the main social foundation of these communities? (3) What role do these communities play in the wider society?

The Concept of Business Community

The term 'community' has been conventionally used to refer to "a territorially bounded social system or set of interlocking or integrated sub-systems (economic, political, psychological, religious, ethical, educational, legal) serving a resident population plus the material culture or physical plant through which the sub-systems operate.[3]" Territorial proximity and social completeness (fulfilment of all psychological and social needs of members within the territorial group) are thus the major hallmarks of a community. In this sense, only small socio-geographical units such as a tribal settlement, a small village and relatively self-contained sub-units of urban centres would qualify to be covered by the definition of community. In complex societies, however, some of the most important and conventionally regarded attributes of community such as a sense of belonging, a body of shared values, consensus and collective action are often absent or insignificant among members of small territorial groups (village, suburb, etc.). On the other hand, these attributes characterize the network of social relationships among territorially dispersed groups, namely, castes, extended kin-groups and linguistic and religious groups. Thus, for example, groups such as the *Patidars* of Gujarat, the Gujaratis in Madras, the Muslims or Christians in an Indian town, the Indian immigrants in Britain and the Jews in different parts of the world are indentified and treated as communities. Such communities are usually bound by multiple interests including social interdependence and a shared sentiment of exclusiveness among members, common moral or religious values and joint socio-political action to preserve the community identity in the event of external threat. However, a large number of groups formed around limited interests tend to develop the major characteristics of community. For instance, as Weber argues:

> Specialized professionals, particularly, now maintain webs of intimate contact with other professionals, wherever they may be. They share a particular body of values; their roles are defined by the organized structures of their groups; they undoubtedly have a sense of belonging to the groups; and, by the nature of the alliances, all share in a community of interests. Thus, these groups exhibit all the characteristics that we attribute to communities except physical propinquity.[4]

Groups such as students, farmers, congressmen and businessmen can thus be regarded as communities of people sharing limited interests. The traders in a small town constitute a community across caste and local divisions in so far as they have an association, a code of conduct, programmes of social interaction among members and a collective approach to transactions with municipal and government administration. Similarly, people engaged in trade, commerce and industry at any local or regional level as well as at the national level can be regarded as business communities. Indeed, the term business community is freely used in common parlance to refer to such groups of businessmen. Organizations such as the Ahmedabad Grain Merchants Association, the Gujarat Chamber of Commerce and the Federation of Indian Chambers of Commerce and Industry represent the business communities at their respective levels.

A body of businessmen at any level, however, rarely constitute a community in all its major aspects. While all businessmen are likely to share an approach to issues such as excise, taxation and government control, they tend to be divided in terms of variables like volume of business, content of trade or industry and business environment. Thus, while all businessmen in Ahmedabad loosely represent the business community of Ahmedabad in the eyes of non-businessmen, there are few common interests, for instance, between the major textile houses and the petty traders in consumer perishables such as food-grains. Thus there are often sub-communities within business communities at all levels. In some respects, this division within a business community assumes the form of class division. In spite of the many-splendoured variety of meaning and usage of the term "class", it emphasizes essentially the social and economic exclusiveness of the people sharing an identifiable level of social existence and some amount of antagonism or conflict vis-a-vis people at other levels in a hierarchical social order. Indian social scientists have, however, often used the term 'class' for socio-economic interest groups across caste and other ethnic groups regardless of the degree of class-consciousness and antagonism in relation to other groups.[5] In this sense, people involved in large business whether in trade or commerce or industry, tend to occupy an exclusive status in the social, political and economic hierarchy in their respective local areas. They carry several symbols of social exculsiveness such as luxurious houses in elite residential areas, membership of exclusive clubs and distinctive food and recreation habits. In large urban centres, one can identify several business classes within the business community, ranging from petty hawkers to multi-millionaire industrialists. Each class may have an exclusive status, exclusive status symbols and awareness of a separate social identity. The Hawkers' Association in Ahmedabad, the Naroda Industries Association (representing the interests of small industrial employers) and the Ahmedabad Textile Mills Association represent distinct classes within the local business community.

A class of businessmen in large business centres, on the other hand, may be divided into regional or ethnic groups. Large businessmen in places like Bombay, Calcutta and Madras recognize social differentiation among Gujarati, Marwari, South Indian, British and similar groups among themselves. In fact, rival associations of businessmen and social clubs have existed at some places to symbolize ethnic divisions within the upper class which is but one section of the business community as a whole.

The concept of business community would therefore apply to different social entities in various social situations. It may include the entire spectrum of businessmen in relation to government or other segments of society. Or it may refer to a specific class of businessmen as against other strata of the wider business community. Or it may refer to a compact social unit within a class of businessmen.

I am aware that in the preceding analysis I have confounded the terms, class and community. This apparent confusion, however, may have arisen from the fact that groups of businessmen, as perhaps other social groups, in India possess the attributes of class and community at the same time. Such confusion in terminology is shared by researchers in Indian social history. For instance, Sharma's paper included in this volume[6] refers to the Marwaris as an Indian capitalist class. On the other hand, Morris elsewhere[7] prefers to identify the Marwaris as a community in statements such as "... one invariably finds reference to the various great south Asian business communities—Gujarati, Marwari, Bania, Chettiar, Muslim, Jain, Parsi, etc." Clearly, while one scholar is interested in examining the class aspect of the Marwaris, the other emphasizes the community aspect of the same group in a different context. As some papers in this volume illustrate, the researcher interested in the structure and process of business groups which can be identified with specific caste or regional groups tends to stress the concept of community.[8] On the other hand, the scholar interested in the relationship of socially heterogeneous business groups with the rest of society tends to stress the class aspect of such groups.[9] This point is explicitly made by Tripathi and Mehta in the statement: "... occupational affiliation transcending socio-cultural barriers and collaboration to safeguard economic interests as distinct from socio-cultural interests are characteristics of class. ... Gujarati business community was in fact a business class."[10] In their conventional sense, therefore, class and community may prove inadequate labels to capture the social reality of Indian business groups. Any debate on whether businessmen constitute a community or class in an exclusive sense is likely to be unproductive.

The inclusion of all sizes and categories of business groups in the above analysis may need to be explained in view of the general trend among scholars in entrepreneurship to restrict their attention to relatively large business and industry. It is obvious that the socio-economic origin and functions of a major commercial or industrial enterprise would be qualitatively as well as quantitatively different from those of small traders and hawkers. At the same time, the process of capital formation and development of enterprise in large and small business is likely to be based on similar social and economic forces at their respective levels. Thus, for instance, the unwillingness of large trading families to invest in industry or of small traders with surplus capital to diversify their businesses may be, at least partly, rooted in comparable cultural and economic factors. A comparative socio-historical study of business enterprise at different levels will prove to be of considerable theoretical and practical value.

The Social Foundation of Business Communities

A simple functionalist view of Indian business communities would suggest that groups of businessmen arise and engage in social action to protect and promote their own collective interests in relation to the wider society whose needs for products and material services are met by them. A business entrepreneur or business community may thus be regarded essentially as a social product generated by the existence of demand for various goods and services. However, it is elementary to note that business not only responds to existing demand but also creates demand in the wider society. The logic of business enterprise includes well-known attributes such as thrift, calculation, investment, organization and innovation, aptly incorporated in the phrase "the spirit of capitalism." These attributes may be viewed in terms of individual personality traits. Hence it may be argued that a businessman is the product of a combination of personality traits among individuals. Ideally, it is possible to assume a uniform distribution of such traits in a given population. Business communities may then be seen as communities of businessmen possessing psychological traits relevant to business enterprise. Some psychological and social-psychological studies of entrepreneurship have emphasized the motivational aspect of enterprise. McClelland's famous studies[11] explaining entrepreneurship in terms of achievement motivation among individuals in various cultures provide an outstanding example of such psychological theories.

Enterprise in India, as well as in other societies, has however not arisen evenly among all segments and strata of the society. Some socio-economic groups have shown consistent leadership in business enterprise, while others have shown hardly any interest in such economic activities. The spirit of enterprise, therefore, needs to be explained in relation to social and cultural factors rather than in terms of psychological variables.

Business and trade, along with farming and animal husbandry, were reserved for the *Vaishya* class in the classical Hindu *Varna* system. As the *Vaishyas* occupied the third position in the four-fold *Varna* hierarchy, business seems to have held a relatively low status in the social hierarchy. For the past few centuries, however, the classical *Varna* system has remained merely as a model. The social reality of India across its length and breadth has for long been quite different from the *Varna* model. The occupational basis of caste has progressively become more flexible over the centuries, although a loose connection between the two has continued all along.[12] This connection, along with the supposedly other-worldly Hindu ethic, led scholars such as Weber to argue that the spirit of capitalist enterprise in India was jeopardized by traditional institutions such as caste and Hinduism.

Weber's thesis regarding the religious-cultural barrier to development of capitalist enterprise in India has been questioned by historians and sociologists with the help of concrete evidence. Trading and commercial groups have existed in India since early historical periods and have performed their tasks with considerable social acceptability and respect. As Gadgil suggests,[13] the emergence and growth of business enterprise had to depend on some important environmental factors: (i) availability of enough surplus in agriculture to support non-agricultural activity; (ii) existence of urban centres to provide the necessary demand and infrastructure; (iii) availability of trade routes for transport and communication; and (iv) political stability to create security and support. India has contained through history urban centres of various sizes inhabited by caste-groups that were mainly urban-oriented (such as *Bania, Lohana, Bhatia, Khatri, Chettiar*). Those groups which were traditionally engaged in business seem to have possessed cultural traits relevant to the spirit of capitalism, such as risk and trust, even when transport, communication and security were in primitive conditions. Caste links and religious faith appear to have played an important role in developing the traits of risk and trust. Hence, as Gadgil observes,[14] the history of business in India has been the history of certain social groups (such as particular castes). For instance, Timberg[15] has quoted Tod to indicate that he had identified 128 merchant castes in India.

It should however be noted that the social groups which constituted business communities were not always coterminus with caste groups. Unfortunately, social historians have often treated regional or religious groups as castes. In this respect, Tripathi's[16] analysis of the development of entrepreneurship in India also shows that caste barriers against modern business and industry broke down whenever some social groups saw the opportunity to enter the new activities. These opportunities included demand for new goods and services, concessions in government levy, improved transport facility, political stability and contact with the western systems of trade and commerce. The various opportunities were seized by diverse social groups such as *Banias*, *Parsis*, *Lohanas and Muslims* in Gujarat, *Brahmans* in Bengal, *Khatris* in Punjab, and *Chettiars* in the South. Timberg's study of the Marwaris[17] brings out in detail how this community, which had developed a long tradition of trading skills, attitudes and institutions availed of the business opportunities offered by the Muslims and British rulers. The Marwaris migrated to various parts of the country in response to economic opportunities and dominated the trading, commercial and finally industrial activity in a large measure.

The rapid and successful involvement of groups such as *Parsis* and *Jains* in modern business and industry have led some observers to believe that such occupations tend to attract marginal social groups[18] which have comparatively less opportunity within the main Hindu-oriented social system and also are less under the direct control of this system. However, there is little evidence to ascribe the success of *Parsi* or *Jain* business communities to their marginal status in the wider society. As Desai argues:

> . . . the origins of Parsi enterprise in the nineteenth century are not to be found in their social or psychological characteristics. Being a Parsi helped in emergence as an entrepreneur; but only because a Parsi trader was neither confined to internal trade nor suffered from the depredations of authorities like the Hindu trader and because he did not

have to share the defeat of the Muslim trader by the British East India Company in the eighteenth century struggle for the mastery of the seas. Nor was it enough to be a Parsi; the rich Parsis of Surat declined together with their Hindu and Muslim neighbours. It was the Bombay Parsis that were responsible for the industrial upsurge, and their achievements cannot be divorced from their British auspices.[19]

There is, however, some evidence to indicate that some lower caste-groups with no legacy of entrepreneurship may take to business enterprise to satisfy their urge to rise in the social hierarchy, especially if they are threatened by the attitude of higher castes. Saberwal,[20] for instance, has explained the development of entrepreneurship among the *Ramgarhias* of Punjab, in terms of their collective experience and urge for rise in social status. The *Ramgarhias*, a caste of high-skill artisans, acquired wealth over two or three decades, but suffered hostile stereotypes from the higher castes such as the *Jats*. They then took up the challenge, launched educational institutions for their members and eventually became businessmen. This helped them to reduce the dissonance between their traditional social status and the new status symbols of wealth and education acquired by them. Similarly, a large number of immigrant groups to India from Pakistan after independence successfully met their economic and social challenge by taking to business enterprise.

Owens' study of entrepreneurship among the low-caste peasant community of *Mahishyas*[21] in the Howrah region provides valuable insight into the cultural context of business groups. The low status and peasant background of the *Mahishyas* enabled them to soil their own hands in their factories and to save capital by living modestly and involving kinsmen and castemen in the production process. In this case, caste culture and social deprivation seem to have facilitated entry into business entrepreneurship. On the other hand, Barnett's study of the *Kontaikatti Velalars* (KV) near Madras brings out the obstructive role of caste culture in entrepreneurship. In spite of economic stress and availability of opportunity to enter business, the KVs chose to continue as peasants as their status as a dominant caste in the region and the association of trade with lower castes disallowed them to enter business.

It follows from the above discussion that the emergence and development of business enterprise or business communities are the result of a wide variety of forces. These forces include psychological factors such as motivation; social and cultural traditions, institutions, skills, and attitudes relevant to business; economic opportunities; political stability and support for congenial business environment; contact with contemporary business systems; and exigential pressures generated on social groups during periods of social change. As Tripathi[22] suggests in relation to entrepreneurship, a study of business communities should take into account a constellation of forces rather than emphasizing any single factor as the only or predominant basis for a business community.

The "constellation of forces" approach, in a sense, implies a statement of truism. For, only a naive or biased social scientist is likely to argue in terms of economic, sociological or psychological determinism to explain the evolution and growth of business groups. Social reality in any sphere of existence would perhaps be explainable only with reference to a multitude of juxtaposed or interacting forces. Hence those scholars who emphasize the importance of economic opportunities and congenial political climate for the growth of business enterprise as against the religious and cultural factors stressed by Weber may convey the contention that economic and political factors are significant besides religion and culture. Their contention, however, should not imply that economic and political factors are the only predominantly significant factors and hence culture is irrelevant to the understanding of the growth of business communities in India. In practice, social historians seem to project bias in favour of one set of factors as each study of entrepreneurship perhaps needs to overstress some factors to counterbalance the significance of other factors overstressed by earlier studies In this context, the argument that a constellation of forces have given rise to business enterprise provides a useful perspective to researchers. At the same time, it is important to recognize that the constellation of forces is not likely to have acted uniformly at different places and times. The social historian's main burden may then consist in identifying the specific set of forces responsible for the growth of enterprise in a given situation and the relative weightage of each of the relevant set of forces. This is illustrated in a perceptive comment by Singer while analysing the evidence of greater degree of entrepreneurship among low-caste *Mahisyas* in comparison with higher-caste *Kayasthas* and *Brahmans* in Howrah.

> In fact, the Mahisyas, entrepreneurs and non-entrepreneurs alike, tend to have a lower level of "n achievement" than the non-Mahisya entrepreneurs. Nandy's explanation of this apparently paradoxical finding is that the greater number of successful entrepreneurs among Mahisyas than among the upper castes is the result of supportive community self-image which gives meaning, value and status to an entrepreneurial career. Among the upper castes, on the other hand, the community self-image gives no support to the entrepreneurial role, so the threshold of "n achievement" for going into business is higher than among the Mahisyas, where to go into business is to conform to a community norm. As Hoselitz points out in his comments, these studies need further validation of the demographic and economic magnitudes involved before the psychological conclusions can be confirmed. It seems important to point out, however, that these conclusions stress social and cultural psychology rather than individual psychology. The functional equivalents of the "spirit of capitalism" and a "Protestant ethic" in Howrah may be a *community* "spirit" and "ethos" among the Mahisyas, and an *individualistic* ethos among the members of upper castes who go into business and industry.[23]

A scholar wishing to study the forces generating and sustaining business enterprise in a given situation would of course need to keep in view the entire constellation of "possible" forces, collect evidence on the effect of each of these possible forces on entrepreneurship, eliminate irrelevant forces and, finally, assess the relative significance of relevant forces. For instance, in one situation a group of highly motivated individuals may create economic opportunities for business enterprise in the face of an uncongenial religious and social tradition. In another, an elitist culture may inhibit the members of a social group from entering business enterprise in spite of accumulated wealth and economic opportunities. Each of the main forces comprising the constellation may be viewed in terms of its facilitating and obstructive effects. A study of entrepreneurship may, thus, have to take into account the following aspects and the analysis in tabulated form may take the shape given below.

Type of Factor	Facilitating Effect	Degree of Significance	Obstructive Effect	Degree of Significance
Socio-cultural				
Economic				
Psychological				
Political				
Exigential				

Such an approach may help us to analyse the social history of a business community in terms of the emergence of the capitalist spirit in a complex social environment and its movement (or stagnation) through the opportunities and hurdles posed by the various forces in this environment.

Business Communities and their Role in Society

One does not need researchers to appreciate that businessmen and business communities play a vital role in the society of which they are constituents. Obviously, they make a significant contribution to the nature and degree of economic growth, satisfaction of wants and availability of jobs. At the same time, business groups constitute a large part of the foundation for concentration of wealth in small segments of a community or the society at large. Apart from this, business groups, as going concerns, evolve among themselves an exclusive culture, including mannerisms of speech and writing, styles of dealing with government and the public and rituals and supersstitions relating to business. This economic and cultural distinctiveness provides to business groups the identity as a social class whether or not they are bound by caste, religious or regional background. As far as I am aware, social historians have so far studied the cultural traits of business communities essentially in terms of the culture of the dominant caste, religious or regional groups constituting the specific business groups under study. Perhaps the underlying assumption is that business activities are grafted on a group or groups sharing non-economic (ritual, religious, geographical) affiliations. Consequently, the existence and role of a business community as a community *per se* seems to have been undervalued and hence understudied.

Dasgupta's analysis of the Indian merchants during 1500-1800[24] shows deep insight and provides a valuable lead in the study of business communities as business communities. He stresses the functioning of the Indian merchant essentially as a lone operator and examines his involvement in the familial, social, economic and political networks linking him in a variety of interactions. He notices the absence of class-consciousness among merchants in spite of occasional pursuit of exigential common interests. Similarly, Misra's paper on the medieval trader[25] deals with a "merchant society" existing as a part of several distinct but interlinked worlds such as family, caste, market and polity. Such studies, in my view, illustrate the need to study business groups in their discrete socio-economic identity and not as mere extensions of family, caste, religion or linguistic groups.

Although a business enterprise survives and grows by adapting itself to changing environment, business communities are typically traditional in many respects. They are usually interested in maintaining and strengthening joint family bonds as these bonds help businessmen in retaining a tight control over their resources and management. It is not uncommon for businessmen to consolidate their family strength by marriage ties with other business houses. Often their westernized children manage to fall in love with children of other businessmen of equal repute. This inward-looking character of business communities may at times make them a closed group in relation to the wider society. Also, the special stress on family and community bonds may create blocks in the career path of professional managers and administrators associated with business houses. There is still a widespread tendency for family-dominated business corporations to reserve top managerial positions for members of the business communities, although highly competent professional managers may be available for more effective management.

At the same time, the traditionalism of these communities may in some respects be instrumental in the success of business enterprise. As Timberg mentions, the particularistic values of the Marwaris have led them to adopt several measures of mutual social help and economic support as well as educational, recreational and other facilities for their fellow-businessmen and community. These measures earn the business houses considerable support and goodwill among the community members. Such community bonds are forged and continually reinforced within most prominent business communities in all parts of the country.

Most business communities have deep moorings in their religious beliefs and practices. They usually demonstrate intense faith in Hindu or Jain (or other) values with all their stress on truth, philanthropy, honesty and renunciation. However, as Singer suggests,[26] businessmen reconcile their world of religion with their world of business by a process of compartmentalization in behaviour. This means that businessmen follow the apparently incompatible code of religion and code of business in their respective spheres without letting the one interfere with the other. In fact, religious values often provide the much-needed forbearance and reassurance in relation to the psychological and social vagaries of business. Conversely, business enterprise and its human as well as material resources are often used to sustain and reinforce social and religious bonds. As Morris argues:

> The firm becomes the vehicle through which more attention can be paid to the financing of socially visible religious activities. Charitable endowments can be established to finance priestly functionaries who help maintain or restore the religious merit that otherwise might be lost or to undertake educational activities which may be particularly useful in a modernizing society . . . most Indian entrepreneurs seem to achieve via the use of all the legal, fiscal. and financial mechanisms developed for the operation of the modern sector precisely the extensive intermeshing of business and religious administration, control, and financing that

makes the adaptation to modern requirements a relatively easy matter. The entrepreneur can be a religious patron not only of what he sponsors in his home but also of what he sponsors through his enterprise. The devices, I am sure, vary greatly. The big businessmen use trusts; the smaller ones must find other mechanisms.[27]

Indian business communities, especially in the western region, have had their trade guilds for several centuries. These guilds functioned primarily as trade unions to protect and promote the interests of their members. However, in an important respect, these guilds developed a strategy of negotiations and bargaining in resolving their disputes with government or other agencies. This strategy has become institutionalized in regions like Gujarat. It is important to note that when industrial workers in Ahmedabad formed a trade union under Gandhi's leadership in 1918, it was designated as *Majur Mahajan* following the *Mahajan* (guild) legacy of business communities in the region. Apart from the choice of relatively peaceful means for settlement of disputes, the *Mahajan* legacy also implied community welfare as one of the major objectives of the trade guild. The traditional business *Mahajans* in Gujarat contributed from time to time to programmes for health, sanitation, education and general walfare of people in the local community.

One wonders if the *Mahajan* tradition had economic and political significance beyond community welfare and resolution of internal disputes. Shirin Mehta throws some light on this issue in her account of the functions of the *Mahajans* among traders and the *Panchs* among artisan communities in Ahmedabad.[28] She argues that the relationship between these two forms of guild was characterized by class-conflict as the artisans used the *Panch* to dictate terms to traders to promote their economic interests. Apart from this economic role, the *Mahajan* and the *Panch* are unlikely to have played any significant political role as perhaps the political system in the past was politically irrelevant to the business communities. It may, however, be worthwhile to explore this matter at various stages in the social history of Indian business.

NOTES

1. I benefited greatly from the comments I received on an earlier version of this paper from Professor D. Tripathi and other participants in the Seminar on "Business Communities of India: A Historical Perspective".
2. I am grateful to Professor Sasi B. Misra for helping me in clarifying my thoughts on "theory" and "theoretical framework". He also shared with me the propositions he has documented and published in a different context.
3. J. Bernard, "Community Disorganization", in David L. Sills, (ed.), *International Enclyclopaedia of Social Sciences* (London, 1968), Vol. 3, p. 163.
4. Melvin M. Weber, "Towards a Definition of the Interest Community", in P. Worsley (ed.), *Modern Sociology: Introductory Readings* (London, 1971), p. 302.
5. A typical example of the sociologists' usage of class is provided by A. Beteille, *Castes : Old and New* (Bombay, 1969).
6. G.D. Sharma, "The Marwaris : Economic Foundations of an Indian Capitalist Class," Chapter 11 in this volume.
7. Morris D. Morris, "Value as an Obstacle to Economic Growth in South Asia : An Historical Survey", *Journal of Economic History*, vol. XXVII, No. 4, (December 1977), pp. 603-604.
8. For instance, R. Mahadevan, "Entrepreneurship and Business Communities in Colonial Madras, 1900-1929 : Some Preliminary Observations." Chapter 13 in this volume.
9. For instance, G.D. Sharma, "The Marwaris . . ." n. 11 and V.D. Divekar, "Business Elements and Bunsiness Class in Maharashtra : A Historical Perspective." Chapter 7 in this volume.
10. D. Tripathi, and M.J. Mehta, "Class Character of the Gujarati Business Community." Chapter 9 in this volume.
11. D.C. McClelland, and O B. Winter, *Motivating Economic Achievement* (Glencoe, 1969).
12. See G.S. Ghurye, *Caste and Class in India*, (Bombay 1957), Chapters 3 and 4.
13. D.R. Gadgil, *Origins of the Modern Indian Business Class*, (New York, 1958), pp. 1-16.
14. *Ibid.*, p. 16.
15. Thomas A. Timberg, *The Marwaris* (New Delhi, 1978), p. 11.
16. D. Tripathi, "Indian Entrepreneurship in Historical Perspective : A Re-interpretation", in *Economic and Political Weekly*, vol. VI, No. 22, May 29, 1971, pp. M-59-M-66.
17. Timberg, n. 15, pp. 41 ff.
18. For a discussion on marginal groups, see Timberg, *ibid.*, pp. 26-27.
19. Ashok V. Desai, "The Origins of Parsi Enterprise", *Indian Economic and Social History Review*, vol. V, No. 4, December 1968, p. 317.
20. S. Saberwal, *Mobile Men* (New Delhi, 1976), pp. 89 ff.

21. R. Owens, "Peasant Entrepreneurs in a North Indian Industrial City", in M. Singer (ed.), *Entrepreneurship and Modernization of Occupational Cultures in South Asia* (Durham, 1973).
22. D. Tripathi, n. 16, p. M-65.
23. M. Singer, (ed.), n. 21, p. 7.
24. A. Dasgupta, "Indian Merchants in the Age of Partnership, 1500-1800" Chapter 3 in this volume.
25. S.C. Misra, "The Medieval Trader and His Social World." Chapter 4 in this volume.
26. M. Singer, *When a Great Tradition Modernizes: An Anthropological Approach to Indian Civilization* (New York, 1972), pp. 320 ff.
27. Morris D. Morris, "Economic Change and Occupational Cultures in South Asia : Comments on Ames, Owens and Singer." In M. Singer (ed.), n. 21, p. 290.
28. Shirin Mehta, "The Mahajans and Business Communities of Ahmedabad." Chapter 10 in this volume.

3

Indian Merchants in the Age of Partnership, 1500-1800

Ashin Dasgupta

David Hardiman writing in a recent issue of the *Economic and Political Weekly* put forward the suggestion that the premier Mughal port of Surat declined in the early 18th century, not because of the breakdown of the Islamic Peace in the western Indian Ocean upon which its prosperity had been founded, but because conditions had been created by the intervention of the northern European Companies in the maritime trade of the area which made the continuance of such prosperity impossible. Since this idea can be seen as a revival of the Eurocentric view of the Indian Ocean and a sowewhat eccentric reformulation of it, and since I shall be maintaining positions which are directly opposite to it throughout this paper, I would like briefly to refer to it as my point of departure.

The Eurocentric vision, of which W.H. Moreland has been the most persuasive exponent, has argued for the relative importance of the European factor in Indian maritime trade, playing down the role of Indian merchants and shipping. It has never been, as far as I can recall, the view of such historians that European intervention destroyed the prosperity of Indian trade. If it had done so, such destruction must have occurred in the 17th century when the prosperity of ports like Surat, Hooghly and Masulipatam was in fact marked. All evidence indicates that during this time the European made his home in the traditional Indian ports and the wealth he earned in the trade of the Indian ocean contributed to the well-being of these ports. With the exception of the monopoly established by the Dutch in the trade of Indonesian spices, there are no indications that European controls affected Indian trade adversely or that the Indian merchant was driven from the Indian Ocean in commercial competition. At the turn of the 18th century Indian shipping fully held its own against the English and Dutch vessels.

The European factor became considerably more important in the 18th century, especially in the later 18th century. The rise of the Calcutta fleet from about 1715, especially after the 1770s, combined with the political control over Bengal and expanding areas along the coast altered the situation fundamentally. Indian shipping in Gujarat and Bengal had, however, declined *before* this alteration and I know of no evidence that the Indian vessels were driven out of business by European competition. The decline of the Indian ships based at Masulipatam probably occurred at the same time and the reason was Indian and Asian political decline. The competition of the British private merchant from the 1720s onwards was a real adverse factor for Indian merchants and Indian carrying trade. But this competition really accounts for the non-recovery of Indian shipping after the withering earlier and has, of course, to be seen as an addition to the persisting adverse political climate along the Indian Ocean littoral.

Once the British were in control and wherever they were in effective control, the rules of the game changed basically for all merchants. Each British-Indian port would have a dominating group of British merchants, usually the top officials of the British Company. Any trade to be done at that port could only be done in such a manner as would not affect the interest of this group adversely. In theory, the Company's interests came first but in practice the dominating merchants served themselves before anybody else. Put differently, the British used political control systematically to further their commercial interests; if not always the corporate interests of their organization, invariably the personal interests of the men locally in power. This may seem a time-worn nationalist cliche but I wish to make it emphatically to point the distinction between the Mughal dispensation and the British system which followed.

The Mughal manner was distinguished by what can only be

called in this context, a quality of freedom. High officials of the state were often interested in trade but normally they were themselves *not* merchants as were their 18th century British counterparts. The result was that their trading ventures were managed by men who were merchants and such men knew and respected the norms of the system. Merchants and producers had the inalienable right to sell to the highest bidder. Even contracts could be broken if a higher bid came along, provided the money taken in advance was returned. Shippers were free to run their vessels anywhere they wished; no shipping lines were the monopoly of any man or any group. Occasional attempts at monopoly in particular commodities were known but they were frowned on and had no lasting effect. The system of production and distribution knew a large number of interdependent functionaries and each had his place, his function and his rights. Neither money nor power could set aside the meanest broker in the smallest village.

I wish to distinguish between the two orders sharply, accepting the risks of over-simplification, as I wish to argue that till the assumption of control by the British, Indians and Europeans were 'partners' in the traditional system. This system remained firm from the 16th century to around the middle of the 18th, and anyone trading in maritime India accepted it. Europeans accepted the system just as the Indians and Asians did, and by their commerce strengthened it. Partnership did not mean friendship; it did at times mean murderous competition. But it did mean sharing the rules of the same game and these rules were not twisted to the advantage of any particular group throughout the period.

The reason why I wish to emphasise this fact of 'partnership' is that a number of historians have tended to assume that the Europeans had 'an impact' on native trade as a result of which the Indian mercantile structure altered significantly even before political control was assumed by foreigners. Surendra Gopal, whose important views appear to have influenced Hardiman's position, has seen the emergence of the comprador and the collaborator in the 17th century and discerned a drain of wealth from India due to European trade at the time. If that is true, then the notion of 'partnership' must be abandoned and the Indian be seen as already a subservient factor within a structure dominated by Europeans. I do not think there is any evidence to establish such conclusions, and I shall spend some time explaining how such notions may arise and why they should not be entertained.

The notion of European dominance before empires were in fact established is based on two considerations. First, upon the vast trade of the European companies (although, it is interesting to reflect that no one brings this allegation against the Portuguese). Second, on the undoubted naval prowess of all the Europeans compared to the Indian and Asian. Both these notions in the present context are dangerous half-truths. The trade of the companies, however important for certain areas at certain times, did not alter the Indian structure. The carrying trade of the Indian Ocean was never monopolized by European vessels, and, if anything, partnership is clearly demonstrated by the trades being shared and even in the shipping being shared by all concerned.

I am not here concerned to examine how vast exactly the European trade was when compared to Indian and Asian trading. Obviously the relative magnitude would vary according to time and place. Pearson has suggested that in the early 16th century Portugal's Europe trade from Goa formed no more than 3 per cent of the total trade of Gujarat. I have myself seen evidence which suggests that at the turn of the 18th century, European companies at Surat carried no more than one-eighth of the city's maritime commerce. The evidence about Bengal would, however, indicate a much greater relative importance for the European factor, especially in the late 17th century, and this was also very likely the case with southern Coromandel. Masulipatam may well have been, like Surat and Calicut, was more or less free of European presence.

Even in areas and during such periods as saw considerable relative importance for European trade, the structure of Indian trade evolved no new forms. The stumbling block for most historians has been the broker who managed the trade of the companies. In him we have the *comprador* and the collaborator, and it would be well to remember that this broker was not invented by the Europeans. It was a traditional institution with which Indians carried on their trade. Every large merchant had a broker of the type the Europeans used. In the case of foreigners, the broker was also the *wakil,* the man responsible to the local Mughal authorities for their good behaviour. This was essential because the foreign merchant often borrowed money—as indeed every other merchant did; and sometimes the foreigner left the Indian shore without remembering to repay the debts. The Mughal authorities wished naturally to have someone of the city to fall back upon in such cases. Besides, there were foreigners who 'created trouble'. The English were troublesome, so were the Dutch but they were not the only ones. The Arabs of Muscat who were annual visitors at Surat in the later 17th century seldom left without a riot. The broker was the man to go for on such occasions. Haidar Quali Khan, governor of Surat in 1718, when told of an English plan to blockade the port, remembered that the English had a Parsi broker, and offered to blow every Parsi in town from his guns as an amiable tit for tat. The broker was a useful man, and not merely for his principals.

Why can we not call this man a comprador? I confess I do not know fully what a comprador's duties entail, but assuming that this was a merchant who was dependent on his principal and made his money as a kind of rake-off from his principal's major operations, there is no reason to think of the traditional Indian port-city broker in this light. True, the broker was dependent on his principal, but so was the principal dependent on the broker. No one coming from abroad could trade in a Mughal city without a broker properly accredited to the local court. The broker had the choice of many principals. If some trading arrangement did not work out, he would make others. If one lot of visiting merchants proved disappointing, there were many others. A certain quality of freedom, as I have said, characterised the Mughal milieu, and the kind of dependence I associate with the notion of a comprador cannot arise within it.

For exactly the same reason, the notion of a collaborator is unacceptable, if anything even more so. This word, I take it is a Second World War coinage from the experience of occupied Europe and is clearly a loaded political term. In the world of the merchant it would under any circumstance be somewhat inappropriate, and if we are to use it at all, we must look to the British Indian ports for, I imagine, a fairly brief while in the late 18th century, when the Indian merchant had no choice but to fall in with the trading of small dominating groups of Britishers. I myself know little of this phase, and if we are asking what alternatives the Indians had and how they in fact opted, I doubt whether anybody does.

The position in southern Coromandel deserves our special attention. What we know of this coast suggests that the two European ports, Madras and Pondicherry, but particularly Madras, dominated the trading of the area from the latter half of the 17th century. This is quite exceptional as elsewhere the Indian port cities—that is, centres under the Indian administration—like Surat, Calicut, Masulipatam and Hooghly—held their own till well into the 18th century. It is, therefore, possible that conditions which we associate with later 18th century elsewhere would be present a century earlier in southern Coromandel. I think such a position is reasonable and can be accepted only with the reservation that we know next to nothing about the Indian ports of southern Coromandel, like Tuticorin, Negapatam and Pulicat, other than some scrappy Dutch evidence.

The European domination of southern Coromandel even in the age of partnership may have led to some changes in the world of the Indian merchant. There was a time when S. Arasaratnam and Tapan Raychaudhuri both were enthusiastic about the 'joint stocks' which the English and the Dutch introduced in this region and saw in it 'a growth-oriented impact'. Such ardour, I believe, has cooled with the years and we know now that this kind of joint stock was unacceptable elsewhere where the Indian mercantile communties were strongly entrenched, and even in southern Coromandel it did not work the miracle it promised. After all, it was no more than an insurance for the principals against bad debts. Maritime trade all along the Coromandel coast tended to fall away in the course of the 18th century.

More importantly, Indrani Ray has argued that the partnership between the Bania and the British merchant, which has been a favourite of many a recent monograph, did not in fact work in structures like that of Madras where British domination was already established. I would accept this early emergence of the ties of dependence in Madras as a likely enough phenomenon, would expect it later in Bengal and later still in Gujarat where enough elbow room was however left for older forms to continue.

The point that I have so far been making is that the world of the Indian merchant was not changed in any significant manner by the trading of the Europeans till empires were established. The possibility that some alterations may have begun early in the southern Coromandel does not affect the validity of this general conclusion. Now, when I speak of 'the world of the Indian merchant', I have three things in mind. First, I am thinking of the economic network of trade, secondly of the social organization within which the merchants functioned and thirdly, of the relationship between the merchant and the state. Needless to say that the world of the merchant comprised many things besides, and some of them like the physical setting where they functioned, the technological infrastructure of transport, minting and the like with which they were supported, were quite important. I am not, however, concerned with these in this paper.

I would like now to set out some of the more important characteristics of this mercantile world which remained more or less stable throughout the three centuries I am discussing. And the thing which comes to mind first is the network of trade itself with its divisions between the shipping merchant, merchants in general trade, brokers, commodity merchants and money-merchants, which in its turn meshed with the networks of production. I have discussed this structure elsewhere, and I shall only content myself with saying that from whatever evidence we have this network was already full blown by the time the Portuguese arrived and there was no change in it except towards the later 18th century when in the areas under British political control the salaried cadre of the merchants of port cities were replacing the earlier free merchants and Travancore where the salaried employees of the state had displaced the coastal merchants altogether.

The Indian merchant who functioned w thin this structure was throughout and everywhere an individual operator. We may think of someone very rich like Mulla Abdul Ghafur of Surat or we may think of someone rather middling like Mathuradas of Hooghly or we think of any of the myriad pedlars who plied their coastal boats between any two points we are always with men who are taking risks for themselves and claiming whatever profits may be earned. Sharing of particular voyages of course were known, but these were *ad hoc* arrangements, and were dissolved once the ship was home. Members of a family occasionally shared their trading for years but the evidence invariably is of an eventual break up into single components as, for example, with the Paraks of Surat. Professor N.K. Sinha gives several examples from early 19th century Calcutta, and I am sure the evidence is the same all along the coast. The emphasis on the individual was so strong that ship-owning was unpopular among the merchants as ships were costly and a loss at sea would be a crippling blow from which a middling merchant may in fact not recover. It is interesting to note that for about two hundred years Europeans operating from the same ports set examples in shared ownership of vessels to no effect.

The fact that the Indian merchant was invariably a lone operator made him weak and vulnerable. We must remember that the markets he supplied were small, unstable and unpredictable. Any long run of good seasons even in the most favoured market was most unlikely. Mercantile fortunes, therefore, were not lasting and affluent merchants even in the most prosperous port were few. Historians normally invoke the Mughal to account for the brittleness of mercantile property. I believe we should do better to study the Indian Ocean market which was more ruthless than any oriental despot. Disputes within the family often accounted for the dispersal of an accumulated fortune. I do not know whether the evidence culled from the records of the Calcutta High Court and relevant to the early 19th century presents an exaggerated picture, but I have the feeling that the inability to keep the family together in trade was there all the time.

Nonetheless, next to the individual, we have to consider groups of merchants from the same family or groups of near relations sharing commercial concerns. There are many examples of particular Bania families monopolizing the brokerage of the English and the Dutch companies at their several factories. The sense of community was strong among the merchants and we have migrations along the coast or across the ocean of large segments of, say, the Kapol Banias to Mocha and, earlier, of the Saraswat Brahmans to Goa and Calicut. The reason for this was important and explains a basic strength and a fundamental weakness of the Indian merchant.

Each community had its peculiar customs and members of a group were at home in them. It was therefore easier to share commercial risks with a member of ones own community than to choose a partner outside. If the merchant had any effective protection it was from the community, which we must unfortunately leave undefined. To be sure these 'communities' were social groups but they could as easily be defined in geographical terms. Thus, we come across the 'Gogaris' of Surat, that is to say merchants from Gogha, taking up the cause of a Gogha *tindal* whose boat had been seized by the Dutch. There was undoubtedly some strength in thus sticking together, but it made men disinclined to move out of the group which remained a real limitation for Indian trade.

The simple form of the 'community' was of course the caste. Now it is best to explain that I am lifting this word from contemporary European documents, without taking any further responsibility for it. The English speak of 'cast/caste' and the Dutch speak of casta; and I accept even though, this might not be the way that they would come through in my kind of documentation. The caste exercised a general supervisory function over the behaviour of its members, settled their disputes and helped them in distress. There are instances of merchants, failed in business, living upon the charity of their caste. The records of the Madras Mayor's Court which are published as well as some unpublished records of the Bombay Mayor's Court I have seen, all of the early 18th century, are replete with cases of disputes being in the first instance referred to the caste and the disputants looking elsewhere only when dissatisfied with the verdict. I hasten to add that this was not necessarily a British impact on Indian society, as the merchants in a Mughal town were free to take the case to the local *darbar*, if they were prepared to pay the 25 per cent fee normally charged upon the settlement.

The supervisory function of the caste has, to my mind created a great deal of trouble, tempting historians to se, European guilds in Indian cities. I have said this elsewheree and I would like to say it emphatically once more, that a caste when it came to monopolize a profession, say brokerage in Surat city, exercised great powers over its members, guaranteeing honest dealings, and in emergencies, calling strikes. This, however, does not make a caste into a professional guild; birth still is a more important fact in India. Now, it is true that several castes if they are similar—for instance castes of Hindu and Jain Banias—can be members of the same professional *mahajan* but that does not affect the argument. The contention will be overthrown if, but only if, it can be shown that Hindus and Muslims belonged to the professional mahajan. I am yet to see an instance of this kind.

The fact that most Gujarati cities had their *nagarsheths* similarly does not turn them into European cities. The *nagarsheths* were normally regarded as the head of the Hindu and Jain merchants of the city and as the principal of the majority naturally represented the city in emergencies. A *nagarsheth* could be a Muslim; a *nagarsheth* could be chosen by the Mughal administration, and there could be similar other complications, but a *nagarsheth* would never be a mayor of the city, knowing and guarding continuously the rights of his citizens, clearly laid down in charters.

Organizations like the *mahajans*, institutions like the *nagarsheth* had a curious kind of limited functioning built into them. Indian merchants never evolved a consciousness of being men of the same calling and therefore men with the same interests which demanded defence. This does not mean that on occasions they were not aware of it or that they would not act for it; they never built institutions to enshrine this awareness and shield them from sustained adversity. The merchants I have discussed belonged to the maritime fringes of a subcontinental society, and they earned their bread basically alone. Insecurity was fundamental in the way they worked and the milieu in which they worked, and what little comfort they drew from social support never assured them historical longevity.

A BIBLIOGRAPHICAL NOTE

The paper was written more as a presentation than an article, and reading it after a lapse of time I find that it has the quality and the limitation of the spoken word. I have, therefore, decided to bolster it up with a bibliographical note. There is virtue in this necessity in as much as I use next to nothing of unpublished sources.

There is one reference to a Bohra merchant who spoke of his 'caste' to the Bombay Council and it may be he did not. The reference is to Surat Factory Diary, vol. 32 for 1747-48, at the India Office Records, London, pp. 70-71. I have referred to the unpublished Mayors Court Records of Bombay and the printed series of Madras to suggest the brittleness of mercantile property. The same point can be made from the records of the Calcutta High Court used by N.K. Sinha in his *Economic History of Bengal*, vol. III (Calcutta, 1961) and P. Sinha in *Nineteenth Century Bengal, Aspects of Social History* (Calcutta, 1965), and *Calcutta in Urban History* (Calcutta, 1978). The fact that mercantile property in late 18th and early 19th century Calcutta was as brittle as that under the Mughals cannot be doubted. I wish historians would seriously examine the character of the market which produced this kind of property and stop repeating cliches on oriental despotism.

The other set of cliches I have concentrated on, concern the role of the Europeans in the Indian Ocean. Dr. Surendra Gopal, deservedly well-known for his series of short studies culminating in the book *Commerce and Crafts of Gujarat* (New Delhi, 1975) is, of course, a scholar above cliches. But I have the feeling that Dr. Hardiman, brilliant historian of modern peasants, reviewing my book *Indian Merchants and the Decline of Surat, 1700-1750* (Wiesbaden, 1979) in the *Economic and Political Weekly* (vol. XVI, No. 50 December 1981) was under Dr. Gopal's influence when he ascribed the decline of Surat to the historical role of the north Europeans. The growth-oriented impact of the Europeans was written about by many; not the least T. Raychaudhuri in his well-known book *Jan Company in Coromandel* (The Hague, 1962). An early article of S. Arasaratnam, 'Indian Merchants and Their Trading Methods : (c. 1700), *The Indian Economic and Social History Review*, vol. III, No. 1, 1966, pp. 85-95, indicated an enthusiasm for the prowess of the Europeans which has since yielded place to caution and an ardour for the Indian merchant. Robust Euro-centrism, however, still continues in, e.g. B.G. Gokhale, *Surat in the Seventeenth Century* (Curzon Press, 1979).

To some extent the struggle against the Euro-centric view is akin to shadow-boxing. Not many serious practitioners today would be inclined to espouse it. Considerably more difficult and assuredly far more rewarding is to come to grips with a historian like Professor P.J. Marshall, who in his *East India Fortunes: The British in Bengal in the 18th Century* (Oxford, 1976) has written the history of the Calcutta fleet. It is Professor Marshall's contention that European and Indian shipping shared the profits of an *expanding* trade in the Indian Ocean during the 17th century and as trade *contracted* in the 18th century, European competition drove Indian shipping out of business. With all my evident lack of sobriety I would not venture to deal with this contention in a bibliographical note. But I shall say this for record that the strength of the Calcutta fleet was in an important sense a political one and rested on British ability to maintain its communications in eastern India. On the other hand Indian shipowners at the same time suffered grievously from internal political collapse. Commercial competition was not the most important factor in the decline of Indian shipping.

The British-Indian structure has been written about by many distinguished historians. Professor Holden Furber's *John Company at Work* (Harvard, 1948) first discussed the role of private interests within the facade of the English East India Company. Pamela Nightingale, *Trade and Empire in Western India, 1784-1806* (Cambridge, 1970) and I. Bruce Watson, *Foundation for Empire: English Private Trade in India, 1659-1760* (New Delhi, 1980) are books which readily come to mind. An important study of the same genre, Elizabeth Saxe, *Fortune's Tangled Web : Trading Networks of English Entrepreneurs in Eastern India, 1657-1717* (Yale Ph.D., 1979) is still waiting publication.

I have touched upon the 'freedom' under the Mughal dispensation both in my *Indian Merchants and the Decline of Surat, 1700-1750*, as well as in 'Indian Merchants and the Trade of the Indian Ocean, 1500-1750', in Irfan Habib and T. Raychaudhuri (eds.), *Cambridge Economic History of India*, vol. I (Cambridge, 1982).

The importance of the European factor varied over time and space. M.N. Pearson in his *Merchants and Rulers of Gujarat:*

Indian Response to the Portuguese (Berkeley, 1976) and more recently in *Coastal Western India* (New Delhi, 1981) argues strongly for the insignificance of the Portuguese in the western Indian Ocean. The picture in Bengal is likely to be different. Susil Chaudhuri, *Trade and Commercial Organization in Bengal, 1650-1720* (Calcutta, 1975) is readily available to make this point. Om Prakash's study of 17th century Bengal, based on Dutch documentation will be available soon. The position about northern Coromandel (Masulipatam area) remains very obscure while no one disputes the importance of the European towards the south of the coast. An important book, S. Arasaratnam, *Merchants Companies and Commerce on the Coromandel Coast, 1650-1740*, is now underway and will sum up decades of scholarship devoted to the coast.

4

The Medieval Trader and his Social Words

S.C. Misra

Periodisation is at best no more than an arbitrary label affixed more for the purposes of analysis than for any fundamental characteristics inhering in a certain designated period. For a country like India, vast and multi-dimensional, living at several levels of development ranging from stone age cultures to nuclear ones, this observation is even more applicable. Much of what is said to be past is not past but lives in our being, not as a cultural fossil but as an active ingredient of our social and personal being. Modernity thus is shaped by tradition more often than otherwise; the medieval continues to form the infrastructure of our being.

If, therefore, this paper deals with an age which is said to have ended chronologically by the close of the 18th century, it may not be wholly incorrect to assume that its values and its thought and living are very much with us today. Possibly, therefore, it may not be incongruous to look to the 19th century or even after for corroborative evidence, illustrating a behaviour pattern which possibly in a more unalloyed form signified an earlier age.

With this proviso, I shall try to delineate in this paper a particular facet of an age and a century which can rightfully be regarded as the Mughal century—the seventeenth. The social and economic patterns of this age, though in some disarray in the eighteenth owing to the growing erosion leading to the ultimate eclipse of the Pax Mongolica, formed an essential part of the economic and social structures. It was not the political power of the British alone but the expansion of the railway system in the second half of the 19th century as well that led to serious dents in this socio-economic system for, it was the railways which carried the tentacles of the colonial economy and colonially modified western forms into the deeper recesses of the Indian hinterland, seriously affecting the traditional order.

The Mughal century attained its prime broadly between the middle of the 16th and the 17th century; by the end of the reign of Aurangzeb the glory had begun to fade. Primarily paternalistic in its ethos, it lacked any institutionalisation for what may be called developmental activities; only a limited part of the surplus which was extracted from the land was ploughed back into it. The Mughal ruling circles valued the trader and within their limited means tried to encourage trade and artisan activity; however, with their primary dependence on land revenue for their resources, their efforts stopped short of providing the right environment, the status because of which the body of merchants developed in Western Europe. The most significant failure of the Mughals was obviously on sea; at no point did they try or were able to meet the Europeans on equal terms on water.

It may also be assumed that most of the ravings of the European merchants against local officials—at least in the first half of the 17th century—were exaggerated. Given this, it has, however, to be recognised that the local official, say in Surat or even Ahmedabad, enjoyed a high degree of latitude. Powerful merchants like Shantidas Jhaveri or Virji Vora could influence them or have their way but obviously could not always be assured of an inviting or congenial atmosphere. The vesting of political power in a land-oriented nobility with a highly militarist ethos, their perpetual shortage of cash, financial squeeze, and the possibility of squaring up the matter at higher levels if matters came to a crisis, did not always contribute to an equitable climate for acquiring wealth and even less for displaying it. In Gujarat, thus, in theory the value of the merchants was recognised both by the Sultans and their successors—the Mughals; more often than not, it was possible for the merchants to obtain redress for wrongs done to them by nobles or other functionaries. In the age of Akbar, a crucial dispute in succession was referred to the court for adjudication by the Ismaili Bohoras who began to breathe more freely in this age. But it would not be an overstatement to say that as far as possible the merchants both big and small tried to keep away from the agents of political power.

Political power in this context impinged on the merchant society but by and large as an external agent. Certainly, there were occasions when the political ruler was appealed to for settling acute internal disputes; however, generally he either abstained or tried to provide a well adjudicated answer. Two brief examples would illustrate this point.

The death of Syedna Daud bin Ajabshah on March 5, 1589, in the last quarter of the reign of Akbar, led to an acute succession dispute between two claimants; Shaikh Sulaiman, later accepted as the head by the Sulaimani group and Syedna Daud bin Qutbshah, accepted by the majority, since then known as the Daudi Bohoras.

One of the sons of the deceased Syedna Daud bin Ajabshah filed a complaint at the Subedar's court—the Subedar being Murad, Akbar's second son—against the Da'i Daud bin Qutbshah for a share of his inheritance. The authorities held the Da'i; there was scare among his followers and a scuffle between the feuding factions followed. Daud bin Qutb was released, went into hiding; Shaikh Sulaiman arrived from Yemen to press his claim. It was decided to carry the dispute to the Emperor, not the initial succession dispute but the inheritance claim. Inevitably, the succession problem came to be involved and the plaintiff proceeded to Lahore where Akbar held his court at the time.

The complainants managed to secure the support of Mirza Aziz Koka to lay the complaint before Akbar. The Emperor required the defendant to meet the charge in person. This the Daudi party was reluctant to do since the Syedna was in concealment and his partisans were not certain of his safety. Kamal Khan of Sirohi was asked to proceed to Ahmedabad and escort the Da'i in person. Finally, on the assurance of Hakim Ali Gilani, an Irani and a Shia, and on the safe-conduct furnished by the Emperor, the Syedna proceeded to Lahore.

Syedna Daud met Akbar and was treated with great

courtesy. Before the case could begin, Shaikh Sulaiman passed away, according to Sulaimani authorities because of poisoning. Akbar constituted a tribunal consisting of Abul Fazl, Aziz Koka and Hakim Ali Gilani to adjudicate the case. Certainly, this was a high power tribunal with three of the topmost dignitaries of the realm.

Daudi *rawayats* record with appropriate joy that this tribunal freed their Syedna from any blemish—and that there was no subsequent trouble for them. The significant points which emerge from this discussion are several. First, the political authorities did not intervene or possibly did not even notice the dispute till their own authority was invoked, appealed to initially in a civil suit, but which later also involved the succession dispute. The judicial proceedings were fair; Akbar required the presence of the defendent as an essential condition and if any excesses were committed, they took place because the *Da'i* was unwilling to present himself before the Mughal Emperor and the imperial deputy acted harshly in his attempt to carry out the orders. The tribunal in itself, a high powered one, could be said to have one partisan of Shaikh Sulaiman and one of Syedna Daud and an impartial chairman—an unexceptional proceeding.

The second instance of this kind—but one in which the Mughal authorities refused to intervene—comes from the reign of Shah Jahan. A complaint was made to the Emperor by one of the dissident Jain sects, the "*Mahajans* of the Lumpaka sect" that the *Mahajans* of Shantidas and Surdas had interdicted them by ne ther dining with them nor entering into matrimonial alliances with them and that they should be made to do so. The Emperor opined that such social intercourse was a matter of internal concern for the parties involved and that there could be no external interference.

These two instances indicate that the ruling authorities, by and large, abstained from interfering in the internal affairs of well-knit communities, leaving them to manage their own affairs. In like manner the official action in the *Holi* riot which shook Ahmedabad in 1754 suggests that primary responsibility of restoring harmony was seen to rest with the two respective leaders: Abdul Aziz, the *Ra'is quam-i-bawahir Ahl-i-Sunnat* and Kapur Chand Bhansali, the *Nagarsheth*. The situation worsened because there had been bad blood between the two leaders.

Instances like these suggest the almost unconscious acceptance of what may be called the *enclave system* by the political authorities. The social communities were allowed to regulate their own affairs; the contact between them and the political authorities was not direct but through their *Ra'is* in case of the Muslim communities and the *Sheth* in case of the Hindu. In situations where law and order problems arose, the authorities took action, sometimes quite drastic, but in normal situations the leaders were held responsible for the good behaviour of their people.

The communal inward-oriented psychology was reinforced by the largely residential clusters grouped according to caste. In another paper I have emphasized the role played by these residential unities in the organization of the medieval town, a role which came to be further emphasized when the insecurity of the 18th century converted these *pols* into defensive bulwarks. This mentality was by no means peculiar to India. Writing about the Muslim town in west Asia, von Grunebaum notes: "The loyalty of the townsman belongs to his family group and after this to the ethnic or denominational unit which shared his quarter. The tolerated minorities must occupy their own section of the town, with Jews, for better protection, frequently living in the immediate vicinity of the government area. The occupants of the several quarters will meet typically but in market and mosque; in the market, the minorities may have their place, perhaps not with, but close to their Muslim colleagues, although more often than not, crafts will be traditionally in the hands of the one or other groups, rather than shared."

The medieval merchant, thus, lived within several distinct but interlinked worlds; the primary entity in this complex was the family—the extended joint family with its innumerable obligations—a syndrome which furnished him with one of his major life-goals. Next in order were the social obligations due to the caste and to the faith; merit in this world and salvation in the other was to be gained by fulfilling these obligations, not in a routine fashion but with zeal and enthusiasm. This was the private and the semi-public world, marked off from outside intrusion but obviously not free from internal tension and rivalry.

Related but distinct was the world of the market, the polis. It was in this world that the merchant made money, came in contact with strangers and with powers that were. It was a world of relatively formed mores in large internal markets like Ahmedabad, a world in which a certain degree of stability had been secured. It was, however, a world of frenetic, cut-throat competition and rivalry in cities like Surat where short-term gains were sought and the principal actors in the drama admitted no rules.

These related worlds were, thus, formed of several overlapping "associations". Primary among them was the immediate dimension of the extended family, kinship and marriage which furnished basic affiliations; next was the obligations to the caste and faith.

Distinct but related was the *mahajan* which in Gujarat implied a professional/occupational body, usually but not necessarily monocaste one. As a rule, most trades were followed by distinct castes, known by these occupational appellations; however, castes were not rigid but relatively fluid bodies sometimes with varying compositions. Closely bound up with the caste association and the *mahajan* was the residential *pol* organization, usually but not always overlapping.

I may mention here in passing that a similar structure pervaded the craftsmen communities; only, in their case, the *mahajan* was called the *panch*, a more plebeian appellation. Nevertheless, it would seem that the hold of the *panch* on the community and its productivity was relatively more stringent than that of the *mahajan* on the middle class trading castes.

It has not seemed to me that there was any basic difference between the trading castes on account of religious affiliations. Thus, the generic appellation applied to the trading community within the Hindu fold was Vaishya or more commonly *bania*, or in Gujarat, *vania*. This is the term which the foreign traders used; they could distinguish only between the *bania* and the Muslim trader. But this omnibus term encompassed a host of castes; of these, at least two were major ones: the Jains and the

Vaishnava *vanias*. Among the Muslims, there were at least two, both Bohoras: the Sunni Muslim and the Ismaili Bohoras, the latter again divided among the Khojahs and the Daudi Bohoras.

The similarity and the differences can be illustrated by reference to two nearly pure commercial communities, the Jains and the Daudi Bohoras. Both possess extensive and wide-ranging metaphysical, theological and historical literature, better known regarding the Jains but not so well disseminated regarding the Bohoras.

Among both Jains and the Bohoras, there existed a closely knit communal consciousness, a consciousness which has never been hostile, at least overtly hostile, to outsiders, but keenly conscious of the inner solidarity. As a minority and persecuted community, this awareness has been deeper among the Bohoras than among the Jains; the Jains have relatively been more open, inter-marriages between them and Vaishnava *vanias* of the same caste and status being not unusual.

Linked to the caste solidarity has been a deep family consciousness. Kin obligations have been recognized to have primary claims; business organizations have been manned by the family, the gradations of responsibility being calibrated in accordance with the kin's propinquity to the main figure. In fact, this feature has been so much in evidence that it has been seen as a primary condition to the emergence of Indian business and need not be dilated on.

Equally significant has been the general attachment to the culture bearers and the symbols of the faith. One of the early medieval Jain figures has been Samra Sah who lived at the turn of the 13th century when the Turkish ruler came to Gujarat. The Turkish soldiers damaged the Jain temples of Shatrunjaya to the deep anguish of Samra Sah's aged father; Samra Sah vowed to renovate them, which he did, serving Alp Khan faithfully, gaining his favour, even securing from him the permission to renovate the temples and a handful of gems and precious stones as his patron's contribution towards this task. Proudly did the old Sah lead the *Sangh* to Shatrunjaya and the renovated temples were rededicated. Samra Sah, thus, wrote his name in gold in Jain annals by turning his wealth to good account—putting it to use by serving communal goals and filial aspirations.

Several other instances indicate the favour shown to the Jains and their culture bearers, the Suris, by the ruling powers and their use of this favour to benefit their culture symbols. Sultan Muhammed bin Tughluq, writes Shri Lalchandra Bhagwan Gandhi, showed particular favour to Jinprabha Suri; his successor Firuz Tughluq followed him. Jinprabha Suri used this favour to restore and dedicate damaged Jain temples. When Suri reached Deogir with the Sultan, he was welcomed there by an affluent Jain merchant Shah Jagasinha. The merchant pleased the Sultan as well and thanks to the advice of Jinprabha Suri, travelled with a large *Sangh* to Shatrunjaya.

The influence won by the Nagarsheths of Ahmedabad—a position held successively by the family of Shantidas Jhaveri—is by now well known, and needs no introduction. The founder of this line, Shantidas won his spurs in the Mughal court by his competence and trust-worthiness; his faith had little to do with it. However, he used his influence at the Mughal court to build the imposing Chaintamani temple—and to have it renovated when it suffered owing to Aurangzeb's bigotry. Significantly, one of the earliest episodes by which Aurangzeb sought to make amends after his accession for his earlier error, and to ensure the indispensable jeweller's support to the Mughals in manifold ways, was to confirm by a *farman*, the grant of Palitana to the merchant and his successors.

The deep inclination of the Jain merchants to use their wealth and their influence towards maintaining and reinforcing the cultural and religious ethos and its symbols was sustained by their teachers, the *Sadhus*, particularly the distinguished Suris. These distinguished figureheads provided the basis on which Jain tradition is founded.

In its behavioural aspect, the Jain faith enjoins austerity in those who are dedicated to be its culture bearers. This injunction is further reinforced to require celibacy, continuous travelling, deep learning of the sacred literature and contribution to it and the severest of austerities as a matter of routine. Furthermore, while the "clerics", if that term can be used for such leaders, were dedicated to the faith, for the laity too undertaking fasts and austerities was a virtue meriting public recognition.

The emphasis on austerity, deep learning in the sacred lore and celibacy and dedication to the calling from childhood—the basic requirements for leadership in the domain of faith—served to maintain the inner solidarity of the community. It restricted vagrant individual action even in face of strong temptations to the contrary. Though not recorded, it is likely that there were a number of black sheep in the community, a number of dissidents; but it does not appear at any time that there were secessions on individual personal issues, even when families and individuals held considerable power, influence and wealth. Not only Shantidas Jhaveri, the founder of the *Nagarsheth* line in Ahmedabad, but Virji Vora, the so-called merchant prince of Surat, followed their faith scrupulously, satisfying the demands of the orthodox. In fact, the value-systems had come to be inbuilt in the personality system of these men; they may have used devious means in their struggle to acquire wealth—for Virji Vora there is at least some testimony in foreign accounts—but as the militarist ethos of the landed interests condoned indulgence, the commercial ethos of the trader did not take a hypercritical view of a doubtful practice.

The close kinship links which marked the relationship between members belonging not only to the agnatic sequence but extended to marital relations too is borne out by the history of the *Nagarsheths*, the only family history of its kind written so far. That there were disputes within the family leading to splits is, of course, common, even natural; the more significant fact is that the more afluent of the family group felt a responsibility towards the lesser ones, felt it incumbent upon themselves to build them up.

The information regarding the other community, the Daudi Bohoras, is by contrast limited. Unlike the Jains, the Daudis have been a regional and largely an urban community; their mores have formed in ages when they had to face persecution; one of their own men, Maulana Jafar, turned dissident leading to large scale secessions in the 15th century; the work was continued by another probable secessionist, Maulana Muhammad Tahir in the 16th. These waves of reconversion reduced the original community to a minority status. It seems difficult to share the belief that the rural agrarian communities, known by a collective rubric, the Sunni Bohora, embracing a number of in-marrying castes, who constitute more than half of Gujarat's Muslim population, had originally belonged to the same body which had been converted to Islam by the early proselytizers, who popularised the Ismaili creed. Nevertheless, after the 16th century, the Ismaili community was rendered a wholly urban, trading one; according to one author more than 80 per cent were lost to the Sunni faith.

The ethos formed by persecution was inherited by the community from Egypt and Yemen and was reinforced by its experience in India especially in the 15th century and after. Crucial to the social system which came into being in India, was the role of the *da'i-u-l multluq*, the visible head of the community, the one who not only is responsible to the concealed Imam for the welfare of the community but who also articulates his will in relation to them. The line of the Imam is hereditary, deriving from the prophet's son-in-law Ali. The same law is not applicable to the *da'i* but the nomination, by the *da'i* of his successor has to be clear and unambiguous. In theory, he makes the nomination under inspiration from higher authorities and as such, is the instrument, not the author of this nomination.

Not lineage, thus, but an unmistakable *nas* or nomination and also evident qualifications render a person suitable for this high office. Like the Jains, the Bohoras have placed a high premium on scholarship and learning in the sacred lore and have valuable contributions to this corpus. The *Amils*, the deputies who represent the *da'i* in different areas, have generally been learned figures; known as *Shaikhs*, they have constituted the *Ulema* of the Bohora community and discharged the same duties. Evidently, the intention was to prevent the formation of dynastic sequences at the crucial apex position and thereby prevent an unworthy occupant from coming to power—and to invest the person of the highest office holder with a charisma which would be capable of holding together the community in times of trouble, in ages when it faced persecution and secession. During this era before the British take-over, when the Daudi Bohoras were freed from the gnawing fear of persecution, two major problems tormented them. First and foremost was the hostility of the rulers and more often, their local minions; the only period of relief began with Akbar and ended with Shah Jahan. The second major problem that they faced was succession disputes leading to secessions. There do not appear to have been any major conversions to the Sunni faith after Maulana Muhammad Tahir but independent groups came into being with their autonomous systems.

Apparently, throughout this time the Ismaili Bohoras also kept a low profile. *Taqaiya* or dissimulation for safety's sake, is an accepted Shia practice widely practiced in ages when they were in apprehension. It would seem that for most of the time, the Ismaili Bohoras were by and large shopkeepers and traders. They had large residential localities in Ahmedabad in the 16th century in the age of Akbar; they had other centres in Gujarat like Sidhpur, Kapadvanj and Surat. Outside Gujarat, Ujjain and Burhanpur had sizable clusters.

Yet one does not hear of a porminent Daudi/Ismaili merchant in Ahmedabad, Surat or elsewhere. There is, as far as I know, no identifiable Ismaili Bohora figure in the trading activity which centred in Surat or in Ahmedabad and elsewhere for that matter during the 17th century. Bohora *rawayats* are involved with their internal disputes concerning the Alavi secessions, the renewed persecution under Aurangzeb and with another potential secession; they do not discuss the more mundane affairs of livelihood.

It would, thus, seem that for much of this period the Daudi Bohoras have been shopkeepers, big and small, without venturing into wider fields. In the opportunities opened up in the 19th century when the Parsis entered the China trade in a big way, the only major entrepreneur to emerge was Sir Adamji Peerbhoy who made a fortune as a shipchandler, and that also, in the late 19th century. In India, so far as I know, there has not emerged a major Daudi Bohora industrialist, though large properties have been owned by them, especially the Syedna and his family; in Pakistan too their situation is probably not different, though the Gujarati Memons have developed some major concerns and banks. By and large, thus, the Daudi Bohoras have been shopkeepers and content to be so; not very rich except for a few, but mostly very well off.

Traditionally, as I have mentioned earlier, the Ismaili

Bohoras have been either persecuted community or in imminent apprehension of persecution. They have also been, visibly, a community apart; their dress, their houses, even their speech mark them off. In Surat, which had one of their largest concentration in the 19th century and also Ahmedabad, they lived in their own localities, with only formal contacts with non-Bohoras, their more intimate links being generally within the community. Communal rioting also passed them by; until recently, their affiliations with the rest of the Muslim community were marginal.

What could account for this passivity in ages when fortunes were being made and unmade in cities like Ahmedabad and Surat, when other communities, commercial like Jains and agrarian turned commercial like the Sunni Bohoras, were growing into capitalist entrepreneurs, engaged in high finance? Could persecution be the explanation? Could it be said that the mores formed in ages when the community was living in apprehension were too ingrained to permit innovative efforts?

Until more work is done on Ismaili Bohora history, it is not possible to hazard even a tentative hypothesis on such questions; only a few rather wild guesses may be offered.

It may be conceived that an extreme enclave psychology engendered by persecution created first a rigid pattern which was unfavourable to unfamiliar, innovative activity which might mean undue exposure and consequent risks. That there was an enclave ideology immanent in the caste system itself is of course true; but it was partly compensated by interdependence in the functional context, by the roles ascribed to the several castes, both Hindu and Muslim. The Sunni Bohora trader could operate with more freedom because although he was apprehensive of squeeze from the political side, he could not be marked off as one whose social acceptability was no more than marginal and, therefore, whose transactions if disputed could be prejudicially judged. It restricted the range of trading opportunities for the Ismaili Bohora; it made him unwilling to engage in high profit, high risk endeavours.

A comparison with the Jains might possibly be useful in this context. The Jains shared with the Daudi Bohoras a high degree of respect for scholarship in the sacred lore as seen above; they also had a close-knit social organisation but, unlike the Bohoras, they were without a formal head. They were less secluded in as much as they formed a part of the *vania* world which may have been looked down upon by the tribute and war-oriented militarists but whose functions and rights were recognised as essential for the maintenance of public weal. In times of war, their temples did suffer; but they could make up for it later by gaining the favour of the rulers. At best, they could be looked upon as the goose which laid the golden egg; at worst, they had to be tolerated as a necessity.

The Bohoras—regarded by the Sunni rulers as schismatic, a belief shared by most of the other Muslims and actively encouraged by a host of confirmed proselytizers drawn generally from their own ranks who had gone over to the other side—suffered more intensely. By its very nature, a trading community could not afford to be exclusive, even when its ethos was primarily directed inwards; but distinctive practices practised by the Bohoras led to such exclusion. His reply to his tormentors, though desperate, was hardly the kind to gain any recognition in the eyes of the Muslim world; both the proselytizers, Maulanas Jafar and Tahir, perished at the hands of Bohora assassins.

It has also to be recognised that much of the information we have regarding Ismaili Bohora history—and that history has yet to be written—is based, for the present, on nineteenth century source material, available to the uninitiated and that focuses largely on the political history of the community, the succession and consequent secessions and the persecution its members faced. It does not enlighten us regarding the economic fluctuations and the variations in their occupational life. Nevertheless, since no prominent Bohora merchant is mentioned in other accounts as well, it may be assumed, though with some caution, that there were no merchant "princes" of the dimension of Shantidas Jhaveri or Virji Vora.

And, in any case, even in other communities the bulk of the traders, were petty small businessmen, catering to small often under-monetized communities. Only in bigger marts did large businessmen emerge—in Ahmedabad, in Surat, in Broach probably. Even then, merchants like Shantidas Jhaveri, Virji Vora and Muhammad Ali, were exceptional men; they were the products of their age and their culture but they also had that extra element, that touch of talent, perseverence and ability which made them what they were.

The caste, the extended joint family, the village have since long formed the realities of Indian life, the constellation which provided goals and meanings to individual life and existence. There is an obvious difference, however, in the worlds of the Rajput zamindar, the Kanbi peasant and possibly the Brahman priest—and the Mughal *Jaggirdar*. For the traders, land did not have the meaning which it had for the peasant; they never fought for it as the Rajputs did. It was only reluctantly that the zamindar rendered Caesar his due; and, with his base in the country, recovered when the Mughal fortunes were on the wane.

The trading classes, with profit as their motive and liquid capital as their assets and being mostly urban based, were, on the contrary, in no position to alienate the ruling elite. They needed a relatively stable political system by which law and order was maintained and a regular and reliable system of transport and communication was stabilised. Only thus, could they serve their primary and secondary life-goals, gain resources by trade and commerce and then serve familial and communal culture systems.

A brief note on Surat and its traders is probably called for when medieval traders in Gujarat are being discussed. The Surat and the Cambay commerce is well documented. It goes back to the Gezira Papers of the Jewish merchants which date back to the Solanki accounts of foreign traders and form an unparalleled corpus of material; and in Professor Das Gupta, the age of decline has found an admirable historian. His work reads like a novel and is as informative as an encyclopaedia.

Yet Surat and its merchants who came into contact with the Europeans were certainly atypical, almost unique. Nowhere else do the Sunni Bohoras emerge as effectively from their villages to take to commerce on such an unprecedented scale; nowhere else do these merchants take the political power on with an impunity as daring as that of the Mulla family. Also, nowhere else is found a concourse of merchants as varied as that at Surat—from Armenians to Arabs to Malayas; nowhere else too, do merchant houses show the capacity to defy the suzerain power, the great Mughals, and effectively demonstrate to them where their sway ended. And nowhere else is there the same pattern of competitive *laissez faire* trade with no *holds* barred. The impossible scenario of a merchant prince actually planning to establish an armed bastion at the Piram Island bespeaks of an extraordinary age which could not and did not last.

Yet with all their disorderly working life and doubtful trading activities, the three major communities who held the Indian side of the scene appear to have been deeply traditional in their outlook and behaviour. Muhammad Ali not only raised his own family to a new status but was a known beneficiary of his community; Virji Vora's contribution to the Jain community is indicated by Jain texts. The Parsi contribution is less well known but they at this time were the least of the three. Likewise, it seems that the Mulla-Chellaby conflict goes beyond the confines of economic rivalry and takes on the overtones of a clan struggle.

The descriptions of Surat and its traders in the late 17th century and early 18th century, by authors like Mandelso and Ovington and Stavorinus forcefully suggest not only the power these merchants wielded, especially in the latter days of the Mughal rule but also how deeply steeped in tradition they were. There was no impact of the Europeans on their life-style; rather, it would seem that it was the European trader who was indigenised, at least for the duration of his stay in this land.

It is easy to perceive that the observations, rather the reaction, of the European merchant, to the Indian *Vania* was more often than not biased and unfavourable. There is hardly any attempt to distinguish between the different categories of traders, Jain or Vaishnava; they are termed crafty, deceitful and so on—but a master of their calling. None could deny that the Indian merchant was more than a match for the European on his home grounds; he failed where his rulers failed him.

One could term these European comments as the consequences of the frustrations generated by the peculiar relationship between the European merchant and his Indian ally, the broker. The broker may be fawning, obsequious but he knew the game and the European could not move an inch without him. The European merchant knew this, the broker knew this and the European knew that the Indian knew it and extracted the maximum advantage from it. And this knowledge hurt.

Yet, these business associates knew only one dimension of the Indian *Vania* well, the one at which he was at his sharpest and probably at his worst. If, however, they were aware of the other roles that their Indian associate played, it is possible that they might have held a different opinion.

Nevertheless, it is difficult to deny that in the markets of Surat, sharp practices were not unusual and that if the Indian traders indulged in them, the Europeans too were not exactly innocent. Possibly, this free-for-all is explained by the lack of social and business cohesiveness with its consequent lack of public ethos which, as compared to Ahmedabad, distinguished Surat. In Ahmedabad, a *Nagarsheth* could go bailee for his city and fellow traders; in Surat, his peer had no more than ritual functions, most of the merchants who mattered being beyond his pale—a law unto themselves. No one defended Surat and its markets when Shivaji raided; each merchant was for himself alone, including the officials responsible for the town.

These medieval merchants, large and small, it has to be stressed, were merchants operating in the world of exchange. I have not touched here on the role of financiers. Though smaller merchants and traders were multifunctional; some of the bigger ones like Shantidas Jhaveri functioned as bankers too, advancing loans to the Mughal princes, proceeding on highly hazardous enterprizes.

Nevertheless, the big bankers of the eighteenth and nineteenth century—the Travadis in Surat, the Mairalis and the Haribhaktis in Baroda—were generally not traders. At such levels, generally that of state level banking or the *potedar*, there is obviously no trading involved.

Traditional though they were, yet it has appeared to me that they did have the quality of entrepreneurship, if entrepreneurship is defined in terms of taking calculated risks, professedly legitimate and socially sanctioned, in search of profit and gain. The very fact that they operated in a setting which could be potentially explosive and in a market which was wholly open and competitive with high risks, the fact that Shantidas Jhaveri could advance a heavy loan to Murad banking on his success in war and Virji Vora to the English, both of which remained largely unpaid—facts like these do suggest an ability to take high level risks. Moreover, they ventured into far-off lands ranging from West Asia to the Philippines, a tradition which held since the age of the Solankis. After all, Islam was carried to Indonesia by Gujarati Merchants; and there is some evidence to suggest that they had agencies in Manila which dealt in silver from central and south America.

But traders and merchants they remained; they could not effect the great leap forward. Why they could not do so, is probably another large question which goes much beyond their social life or their business operations. After All, as Marx has noted, merchant capital, cannot by itself generate the capitalist breakthrough—if by the capitalist is meant industrial capitalism engaged in production not circulation.

SELECT BIBLIOGRAPHY

Commissariat, M.S., *Imperial Mughal Farmans in Gujarat* (reprinted from *Journal of the University of Bombay*, IX-I, July 1940).

Engineer, A.A., *The Bohras*, (New Delhi, 1980).

Desai, Mohanlal L. (ed.), *Jain Aitihasik Rasmala*, Vol. I, (Ahmedabad, 1912).

Das Gupta, Ashin, *Indian Merchants and the Decline of Surat*: c. 1700-1750, (Wiesbaden, 1979).

Gandhi, Lalchandra Bhagwan, *Sri Jinprabha Suri and Sultan Muhammad*, (Lohawat, 1939).

Husain, Abdul, *Gulzar-i-Daudi* : (Burhanpur n.d).

Jote, Ratnamanirao, *Amdavad*; *Gujarat-no Patnagar*, (Ahmedabad, 1929).

Khan, Ali Muhammad, *Mirat-i-Ahmadi*, Translation : (Baroda, 1965).

Khan, Ali Muhammad, *Supplement* to the Above, Translation : (Baroda, 1931).

Maulwi Muhammad Ali ibn Maulwi Jiwabhai, *Mausam-i-Bahar*. (Bombay, 1884), Vol. III.

Tripathi, Dwijendra, *The Dynamics of a Tradition*. (New Delhi, 1981).

Misra, S.C., "Some Aspects of the Self--Administering Institutions in Medieval Indian Towns", in J.S. Grewal and Indu Banga, (eds.), *Studies in Urban History*, (Amritsar, 1981).

Misra, S.C., *Muslim Communities in Gujarat*, (Bombay, 1964).

Triputi Maharaj, *Jain Parampara-no Itihas*, in 3 volumes; Vol. 2 consulted, (Ahmedabad, 1964).

5

Muslim Merchants of Medieval Gujarat

S.A.I. Tirmizi

The merchants of medieval Gujarat were either Hindus, Jains, or Muslims. The last could be divided broadly into three categories. Firstly, the itinerant merchants who visited Gujarat for purposes of trade but returned to their native countries after transacting their business. Secondly, the alien merchants who hailed from distant lands but settled down in Gujarat and, thirdly, the local converts from Hinduism to Islam. In order to appreciate the contribution made by these merchants in the development of mercantile capital to a degree unequalled by their co-religionists in other parts of India, we must start with a brief description of Gujarat.

The political map of Gujarat has been changing from time to time but our present purpose will be served if we define the boundaries of this state as it was known to and specified by the travellers who visited India during the medieval times. It is pertinent to point out in this connection that the Catalan map of 1375 A.D. does not mention the name Gujarat though it shows many towns situated in this State.[1] Marco Polo describes in detail the kingdom of Gujarat but he refers to the kingdom of Cambay as a separate entity.[2] Of greater assistance in this behalf are the Muslim geographers—Abul Fida and Rashiduddin—who specify that the boundaries of Gujarat reached the Gulf of Cutch in the north and Thana (near Bombay) in the south.[3] Varthema wrote in 1510 A.D. that he arrived from Combia (Cambay) at Cevul (Cheul) and that "the country between these two cities is called Guzerati (Gujarat)."[4] As to the inner frontiers we do not have at our disposal any particulars as to how far in the interior Gujarat extended.

This maritime state of Gujarat had direct routes of communication with the countries of the West as well as with the countries of the East. According to the European travellers there existed sea communication between the ports of Gujarat and those of the Gulf, Muscat and Ethiopia.[5] Gujarat also traded with the Mediterranean countries such as Sicily. In 1315 A.D. agents of the Genoese Bank of Vivaldi had trading stations in Gujarat.[6] Similarly there also existed communication route between Gujarat, Sumatra and Maldive Islands.[7]

More details have been furnished by the European travellers about the ships in which they travelled to and from Gujarat than the routes of communication. These ships were differently designated as *iasse*, *nase*, *vase*, *tava*. They were not nailed up but fastened with stitching of twine. They were frail and uncouth, made without iron, and had one sail and one mast. The sails were either of matting or of some cloth and the ropes of husk.[8] However, the ships used by Ibin Battuta were comparatively large for, seventy horses could be placed on them. They had a complement of rowers and fifty Abyssinian men-at-arms as guarantors of safety because of the pirates. These were the smaller ones. The second type which resembled a galley were those probably built in India. Ibin Battuta found place for seventy horses on his ship *Jagir* which took him from Qandhar to Gogha.[9] All the ships which traded along the Indian coast or between the West and Gujarat were usually small but those used for trips from Gujarat to the East and in particular to China, were much larger and called *junks*. According to Marco Polo they carried 200 or 300 sailors,[10] but according to Ibin Battuta they carried a complement of a thousand men, six hundred of whom were sailors and four hundred men-at-arms in order to protect the ship.[11]

As to the goods imported from, and exported to Gujarat, it is impossible to give detailed account for two reasons. Firstly, we do not find a description of such goods for Gujarat only; secondly, the European travellers of medieval times did not give a full account of such goods. We, however, know from Marco Polo and other European travellers that the chief goods exported from Gujarat were, indigo, hides, leather, precious stones, buckrams and cotton. Imports included metals like gold, silver, copper, horses and other things in demand.[12]

From the works of Arab geographers it is evident that there existed a highly developed trade between the ports of Gujarat and those of Hurmuz, Kis, Basra, Aden, Zanzibar, etc. Ibin Battuta mentions that many Indian merchants lived in Aden which was called 'the port of the Indians'.[13]

The Arab traders frequented the coastal towns of Gujarat as navigators and traders since remote antiquity. In the middle of the first century A.D. the Arab merchant ships were conducting regular commerce between Baryagaza (Broach) and the market towns of Muza, at or near modern Mokha.[14] In the Persian Gulf, Apologus on Eupharatus and Charaz Spasini (Muhammarah) on the Shatt-ul-Arab were the chief centres of trade. Large vessels were sent regularly to either place from Baryagaza loaded with copper, sandalwood and teakwood, logs of blackwood and ebony. Oman, on the southern coast of the Persian Gulf commanded a large ship-building industry, and all the three towns of the Gulf exported purple, clothing, wine, pearls, dates, gold and slaves to Baryagaza and Arabia.[15]

The local Hindu princes resisted, with all their strength, the Arab naval attacks on Hakam, and of Junayd and Abdul Malik on Thana, Broach and other parts in the seventh and eighth centuries A.D. but welcomed Muslim merchants to their territories. Since these merchants contributed greatly to the coffers of the local rulers, they were not only treated with consideration but were also allowed certain privileges. The itinerant merchants who visited Gujarat for trade were domiciled in such places as Alexandria, Damascus, Persia, Syria and Afghanistan.[16] These merchants carried much of the sea-borne trade across the Indian Ocean.

Of the itinerant merchants who subsequently settled down in the coastal towns of Gujarat, some came from far-off places like Egypt, Persia, Turkey and Arabia.[17] It is, therefore, not surprising if we find large communities of Arab merchants domiciled along the coastal regions of Gujarat. These settlers intermarried with local people and the children of such marriages came to be known among the Arabs as *bayasira*. The communities of these settlers had their own chiefs who administered the communal affairs. We are told by Masudi that when he visited Simur (Cheul) in 916 A.D. he found 10,000 *bayasira* there and met with Arab settlers from Oman, Siraf, Basra, Baghdad and other places. Among them were many merchants, and head of the Muslim community, the *al-hazmat*, at that time was Abu Said Maruf bin-Zakariya.[18] The Sicilian geographer, al Idrisi, describes Nahrwala (*Pattan*) as a very flourishing town and refers to its rulers as Balhara,[19] who may be identical with the Chalukya ruler Siddharaja. Muhammad Awfi records an incident to show how Siddharaja got the mosque of his Muslim subjects reconstructed which had been demolished by the Brahmans of that place.[20]

The epigraphical records which have come down to us go a long way to prove that the Arab and Persian merchants had settled down not only in the coastal parts of of Gujarat but had penetrated into the inland towns of Pattan and Junagadh where they were in such large numbers as to build their mosques. An Arabic inscription found at Junagadh records the construction of a mosque in 1286-87 A.D. by Afif-ud-Duniywad din Abul Qasim bin Ali al Iraji who has been described as "the Prince of the Ship-Masters and the prop of the pilgrims to the holy cities of Mecca and Madina.[21] Under the Khilji and Tughlaq Governors, Gujarat's commercial relations with the Western world received a fresh fillip. Ibin Battuta who visited Cambay in 1342 A.D. describes the city as one of the finest in regard to the excellence of its construction and the architecture of its mosques. This was due to the fact that the majority of its inhabitants were foreign merchants who always built fine mansions and magnificent mosques, vying with each other in doing so[22]

About half a century after Ibn Battuta's visit, the independent Muzaffarid dynasty was established in Gujarat. The rulers of this dynasty encouraged commercial intercourse with the outer world. Trade and commerce, therefore, became a very important element in the total economy of the Sultanate of Gujarat. Sikandar Lodi (1489-1517 A.D.) is reported to have remarked that the magnificence of the Sultanate of Delhi rested on wheat and barley, whilst that of Gujarat on coral and pearls as it had eighty-four ports under its control. The overseas and inland trade brought affluence to the state of Gujarat. Finding the tent of Bahadur Shah made of *makhmal* and *zarbaft* of high order, Humayun (1530-40 and 1555-56 A.D.) is reported to have remarked that the stuff was the result of the Gujarat's supremacy on the sea. We can have some idea of the magnitude of trade in the reign of Bahadur Shah (1526-37 A.D.) from the fact that a band of Khurasani merchants had to pay a custom duty of Rs. 60,000/- at the ports of Gujarat in a single trip. In 1537 A.D. the Portuguese writers were astonished at the wealth of Gujarati merchants, some of whom had capital worth Rs. 2,00,000/- at their disposal.[23]

The attempts of the Portuguese to control trade to the Red Sea and to make all ships take *cartazes* infuriated the Gujarati merchants who attacked the Portuguese ships. Such attacks, perhaps inspired if not aided by Malik Ayaz, virtually stopped in the 1530s and after that the Gujarati merchants accepted the Portuguese control.[24] When the Portuguese fortunes declined in the seventeenth century, the Gujarati merchants continued to take *cartazes* from the Dutch and the English.[25] Similarly the conquest of Gujarat by Akbar in 1573 A.D. made little difference to the merchants so long as they were allowed to ply their trade without any interruption. It was during the Mughal period that the *Sodagars* came from southern Arabia to Gujarat when it was a flourishing centre of cotton and textile manufactures. Their main business was to carry their precious and costly wares to West Asia. They maintained two establishments, one each in Pattan and Hijaz and spoke both Gujarati and Arabic.[26]

Among the local converts to Islam, the three sects most important commercially were the Khojahs, the Bohoras and the Memons. The first two represent the two branches of the Ismaili Shias. The Nizaris were the Khojahs and the Mutaqlis were the Bohoras. The Khojahs to-day recognise the Agha Khan as their chief. The Bohoras split into two groups in the early sixteenth century. The larger group constituted the Sunnis and most of them were peasants. Those belonging to the smaller group were Shias engaged in trade. In later times the Shia part split again by doctrinal disputes. Their *Dai* or *Imam* moved to Gujarat in the 1560s, residing first in Ahmedabad and then in Surat. The Khojahs as well as the Bohoras retained many Hindu characteristics in religious matters and inheritance practices. The most revered book of the Khojahs dealt with the nine incarnations of Vishnu who had been adopted by them as Adam with Ali as his tenth incarnation.[27]

The Memons were converts from the Lohanas of Thatta in Sind. Persecuted by the local people, one group migrated to Halar in Saurashtra and were known as Halai Memons. The second group went to Kutch and came to be designated as Kutchi Memons while the third group settled down at Surat and was known as Surati Memons. The Memons co-operated with the British traders and emerged as enterprising businessmen in the nineteenth century. They settled down in big cities of India and transacted business in all types of goods. By the end of the last century they were spread all over India and in other countries of Asia, and Africa. With the foundation of the Indian National Congress, the Memons participated in the freedom struggle and supported the movement financially. Umer Sobani associated himself with the Home Rule League. In 1918 when Mahatma Gandhi asked him to contribute to the Tilak Swarajya Fund he handed over a blank cheque to the Mahatma who wrote an amount of Rs. 1,00,000/- with his own hands. Subsequently he contributed an equal amount to the Khilafat Fund.[28]

The local convert Muslim merchants described above retained many Hindu inheritance practices and thereby avoided to a great extent division of property on death. Under the Muslim law, the property of a deceased was generally divided among nine specific relatives apart from the agnatic heirs entitled to fixed shares.[29] Thus, adherence to the Hindu succession practices helped these converts in accumulating merchant capital. Moreover these sects were not hindered by the Islamic prohibition of usury. This is not surprising. History tells us that attempts have not been lacking to regard the *urf* or customary law as one of the roots of *Fiqh* or Islamic jurisprudence, and thus to reconcile the rigidity of law with local requirements.[30]

The local traditional organisation was based on the agnatic patrilineal pattern which excluded women from inheritance. Delivering a judgment in 1922 Lord Dunedin of the Bombay High Court remarked, "There are, among the Mohomedans certain groups whose ancestors were Hindus and professed the Hindu religion and were then converted to Islam. Among these groups may be reckoned, as is shown by the decided cases, Khojahs, Sunni Bohras, Molesalam Girasias, Cutch-i-Memons, Nassanta Memons and lastly the Halai Memons to which group the deceased belonged. Now with regard to the Halai Memons, it has been held by a succession of cases beginning with a case decided by Sir E. Perry in 1847 that the converts had retained their Hindu law relating to the exclusion of females from succession and that law had been engrafted as a custom on the Mohammedan law although not in accordance with the Koran."[31] The Shariat Act of 1937 abrogated this custom to a very great extent. It, however, continued the power of testamentary succession enjoyed by certain communities like the Khojahs and the Memons.

Equally interesting is the fact that the Khojahs and the Shia Bohras, with independent religious heads, have developed a very sophisticated pattern of communal organisation which is a government by itself. Less elaborate but highly formalised are the *Jamats* or associations of widely spread and economically prosperous sects like the Sunni Bohoras and Kutchi Memons. They have registered constitutions and corporate organisations owning large properties, running schools, dispensaries and banks. The *Jamats* of the Kutchi Memons are found not only all over India but also in Pakistan, Mauritius and Tanzania. It was in 1973 that they organized themselves into an All India Kutchi Memon Federation.

By and large our enquiry has disclosed that the rich hinterland and easy access to it helped the people of Gujarat to develop trade and commerce to a degree unrivalled by other partsof India. Inland and overseas trade converted this maritime state into an emporium of commerce in medieval times. Commercial intercourse with the outer world brought in wealth, and the customary law of inheritance forbidding division of property led to the development of merchant capital to a considerable extent. What is more striking is the fact the Muslim merchants of Gujarat organised themselves into *Jamats* for the purpose of regulating their social and commercial activities, although the socio-political organisation of the time imposed certain limits on the transformation of their mercantile capital into industrial and financial capital.

NOTES

1. Ludwik Sternbach, Gujarat as Known to Medieval Europe, *Bharatiya Vidya*, XV, No. 2, 1955, Facing p. 65.
2. Marco Polo, *The Book of Ser Marco Polo II*, (London 1903) pp. 394-97.

3-4. Sternbach, n. 1, XV/1, p. 61.

5. *Ibid.*, pp. 71-72.
6. A.P. Newton, *Travel and Traveller in the Middle Ages*, (London, 1926) p. 140.

7-8. Sternbach, n. 1, pp. 72-73.

9. Ibn Battuta, *Travels in Asia and Africa II*, (London, 1952) pp. 229-30.
10. *Ibid.*, p 235.
11. Sternbach, n. 1, p. 82.
12. Marco Polo, n. 2, II, p. 398.
13. Ibn Battuta, n. 9, II, p. 110.
14. *The Periplus of the Erythrean Sea*, tr. W.H. Schoff, (London, 1912) Chs. 21 and 27, E.F. Hourani, *Arab Sea Faring in Indian Ocean*, (Princeton, 1951) pp. 32-33.
15. *Ibid.*, Ch. 37, Hadi Hasan, *A History of Persian Navigation*, (London, 1928) p. 50.
16. M N. Pearson, *Merchants and Rulers in Gujarat*, (New Delhi, 1976) p. 25.
17. Duarte Barbosa, *The Book of Duarte Barbosa*, I, (London, 1918) pp. 119-20.
18. Al-Masudi, *Murujuz Zahab Wa Maadinul Jauhar*, ed. & tr. Barbier de Meynard, II (Paris, 1861), p. 86.
19. Al-Idrisi, *Wasful Hindu wa Ma Yujawiruta minal Bilad*, ed. S. Maqbul Ahmad (Aligarh, 1954), p. 59.
20. Muhammad Awfi, *Jawamiul Hikayat* quoted in Elliot's *History of India as Told by its Own Historians*, II (Aligarh, 1952), pp. 162-63.
21. *Annual Report of Indian Epigraphy*, 1956-57, No. D-97.
22. Ibn Battuta, n. 9 II, p. 229.
23. Pearson, n. 16, pp. 27-28.
24. *Ibid.*, p. 93.

25. *Ibid.*, p. 94.
26. S.C. Misra, *Muslim Communities in Gujarat*, (Bombay, 1964) pp. 112-14.
27. Pearson, n. 16, p. 27.
28. *All India Cutchi Memon Directory* (Bombay, 1975).
29. N.J. Coulson, *A History of Islamic Law* (Edinburgh, 1964), pp. 16-17.
30. M.B. Ahmad, *Administration of Justice in Medieval India* (Aligarh, 1941), pp. 73-74.
31. Misra, n. 26, p. 162.

6

Jain Merchants in Eastern India under the Great Mughals

Surendra Gopal

At the dawn of the sixteenth century, the Jains were mainly concentrated in Rajasthan and Gujarat although in ancient times they were an important component of the population in the plains of north India. Under the Turko-Afghans, they had dwindled[1] considerably in the Gangetic plain; however, the Rajasthani and Gujarati Jains did not forget their association with the eastern region: several of their holy places such as those associated with the life and death of Tirthankars and other teachers were situated in Bihar and Uttar Pradesh.[2] This is evident from a number of inscriptions of the late fourteenth, fifteenth and sixteenth centuries discovered in these places.[3] However, we have no information regarding their professional activities in eastern India during this period though they were active in Delhi, where they enjoyed the respect and favour of the Delhi Sultans such as Ala-ud-din Khilji, Muhammad bin Tughluq and Firuz Tughluq.[4] This seems to have induced a stream of emigration to eastern Uttar Pradesh and Bihar, as a result of which the Jain presence in the local population must have been strengthened.[5] We find references to settlement of rich Jain traders in Uttar Pradesh between the river Yamuna and Ganga in the first quarter of the sixteenth century.[6] But their role in the economic life is not clear as no information is available. The turning point in the history of Jains comes in the time of Akbar the Great when we start meeting them again in ever increasing numbers.

Several factors contributed to this. From now onwards, the stream never dried up, though the volume occasionally fluctuated.

Akbar gave a new orientation to the Mughal state, by adopting a policy of religious toleration and friendship with the Rajputs which resulted in heavy induction of Rajput rulers and noblemen of Rajasthan in the Mughal army and bureaucracy. Many of the Rajput chieftains and noblemen who helped the Mughal rulers to conquer Bihar and Bengal were accompanied by their Jain compatriots in their entourage as advisers and assistants. This swelled the number of Jains in the Gangetic Valley. Thus Raja Man Singh[7] who conquered Bihar and Bengal on behalf of Akbar had in his entourage several Jains. Diwan Dhanna Rai appointed 500 Shrimali Jains in the Department of Revenue to collect land revenue in Bengal and Bihar.[8] Mahamatya Nanu was another important Jain who settled down in Raj Mahal, the newly established capital of Bihar and Bengal. He stayed there for fifteen years not only as the counsellor of the new Mughal governor but also as a businessman.[9] When Raja Gaj Singh of Marwar went to fight the battle of Hajipur in Bihar, he was accompanied by a Jain counsellor, Mehta Jaimal.[10] From now onwards the Jains moved to eastern Uttar Pradesh, Bihar and Bengal both for purposes of pilgrimage and trade. In 1591 Shah Than Singh of Jaipur organized a pilgrimage party to Pawapuri in Bihar.[11] He was followed by Hiranand Mukim of Agra in the early part of the next century.[12] Kharag Sen, a small trader from Jaunpur made repeated trips to Patna for purposes of trade and his example was followed by his son Banarsidas.[13] Other Jain traders such as Narottam also accompanied Banarsidas to Patna.[14] Thus by the turn of the 17th century the migration of Jains to Bihar and Bengal had become a fact of life and by the thirties, Jains were beginning to consider Patna as their homeland. Two inscriptions dated Samvat 1682 (1526 A.D.) and 1699 (1543 A.D.) refer to Patna as homeland of the donee Jains.[15]

As the diffusion of Jains was taking place in Bihar it is hardly surprising that their presence in the territory intervening between Agra and Patna also became pronounced. Undoubtedly, the richest and the most influencial Jain traders were concentrated in Agra. Probably the largest colony of

Jains in North India was also to be found in this city. Several factors account for this. All the important Rajput nobles at one time or the other stayed in Agra either as courtiers or as Mughal bureaucrats or again just to curry favour with the court or to keep it well disposed towards themselves so that they might secure some lucrative assignment which would add to their status. They brought the Jains from their homeland as counsellors or employed local Jains as agents. Akbar's policy of religious toleration also brought Jains to his court.[16] Among these, the most important was Karma Chand Bachchavat, who had served as Prime Minister of the State of Bikaner.[17] Some of the Jains attached to the Mughal court moved to Lahore when the emperor temporarily shifted his capital there. The Jain teacher Vijasena Suri was invited and the Jain devotees organized an important festival on the occasion.[18] But it seems that apart from migration on account of attachment to Rajput nobles, a more important motive was the lure of lucrative business which had witnessed a spurt on account of Akbar's policies.

Akbar announced that henceforth all land revenue would have to be paid in cash. The announcement had two implications. First, the landholder was uow forced to part with a part of his produce in the market and this contributed to the further monetization of the Indian economy[19] and thus widened trade opportunities which activated the Jains. Secondly, the State now opened more mints to fulfil the need for ready cash. Akbar's empire had 76 mint towns.[20] This resulted in the growth of more business for money-changers whose business was to exchange coins of different varieties and to give current coins in exchange for old coins. Hence we find that in Akbar's time the Jain traders discovered new areas for extending their activities and it is no surprise that we find them in all prominent urban centres extending from the river Indus to the Bay of Bengal.

The conquest of Gujarat in 1573 linked north India with the port towns of the province and, therefore, Western Uttar Pradesh and South-eastern Punjab now had unhindered access to the Sea; imported commodities from across the sea were transported to Delhi-Agra region. This also ensured overseas markets for the local farm produce as well manufactured goods. Agra became the chief mart in north India and the Jains did not fail to take advantage of this situation. Parimal, a contemporary Jain poet residing in Agra, described Akbar's reign as 'free from injustice' and 'unparalleled elsewhere'.[21] Another Jain scholar Samaysundar won the emperor's applause by narrating 10,000,000 meanings of a Sanskrit sentence.[22]

The Jain migration, begun in the reign of Akbar, received impetus in the reign of Akbar's successor on account of several new developments. First, Jahangir was able to establish peace with Mewar, the only state of Rajasthan which had declined to accept the hand of friendship offered by the Mughals. Thus, the Jains of Rajasthan had full opportunity to travel all over the Mughal empire.[23] Secondly, the activisation of Jains was furthered by the arrival of the English and the Dutch East India Companies in India. As distinguished from the Portuguese, the European newcomers entered the plains of northern India in search of commodities which they needed, at first, for export to Europe and then for other Afro-Asian countries. Thus internal trade was stimulated and Agra became a focal point for transhipment of north-Indian commodities, such as indigo, cotton textiles, sugar, saltpetre, etc., to Surat, the port in Gujarat, from where these were sent to their respective destinations in Europe, Africa or Asia.[24] Agra became the chief centre of activities for Jain traders, since it had emerged as the most important entrepot of trade in the region.

Thus, it is hardly surprising that throughout the seventeenth century, we have references to distinguished Jains of Agra, either traders or governmental functionaries. Jahangir's friendship with Hiranand Mukim is well known.[25] Jagjivan, a dewan of Jafar Khan, enjoyed a *mansab* of 5,000 under Shah Jahan. His contemporaries were Hemaraj, Ramchand, Sanghi, Mathuradas, Bhawaldas, Bhagwatidas, etc.[26] Other famous Jains of the period were Kunwar Pal, Salivahan, Parihanand and Sundardas. The latter was a famous poet; Shah Jahan bestowed upon him the titles of *Kavirai* and *Mahakavirai*.[27] The Jain saint Jinaraj Suri met the emperor at Agra shortly before his death.[28]

In the reign of Jahangir, the English and the Dutch successfully consolidated their position and became regular visitors to markets in north India. In Patna the English first arrived in 1620 and were followed by the Dutch in 1632.[29] Events in the reign of Shah Jahan, the successor of Jahangir, enabled European traders to consolidate their position in north Indian markets.

First, Mughal-Persian relations were in bad shape and so the overland trade with Persia was declining and opportunities for trade in this sector were dwindling. At the same time, Shah Jahan was engaged in a continuing conflict with the Deccan states with the result that the most attractive area for trade within the Mughal empire remained the territory stretching from the Indus to the Bay of Bengal. Hence, we find that the European traders started visiting this area in ever increasing numbers.[30] Rajasthani Jains were not slow to realise this and so they continued to emigrate to this region. It was during this period that Hiranand Shah arrived in Patna. He seems to have prospered and soon his successor became the most important and the richest trader in north India.[31] The movement of Jains to Bengal was but a continuation of the same process. This need not surprise us as Bengal and Bihar were intimately connected. In 1671, John Marshall found that people of Patna were moving to Dacca in search of a living on account of a severe famine.[32]

The stream of Jain migration seems to have continued unabated in the reign of Aurangzeb. Political-cum-economic factors again explain this phenomenon. During the first two decades of his reign, Aurangzeb's relations with Rajputs were cordial and so there was no problem for Rajasthani Jains in migrating to east India. The Rajput wars were a brief interlude as after their conclusion the emperor shifted his activities to south India and was not destined to return again to the north. In the meanwhile, the opportunities for trade in western India continued to shrink on account of Maratha attacks on Mughal territory, continuous Mughal war with the Deccan states, the decline of the Safavids and the Ottomans and the rise of piracy in the Arabian sea. As a result, the Europeans intensified their activities in eastern India and so the Gangetic Valley emerged as the most promising area in terms of business opportunity. The Rajasthani Jains did not fail to respond to the challenge and, thus, their numbers kept on increasing.[33] A Jain work *Digvijaya Mahakavya* written in Vikram Samvat

1627 describes Agra, Allahabad, Varanasi in glowing terms.[34] It goes on to shower praises on places associated with Jains in Bihar, such as the small town of Bihar Sharif, Rajgriha, Nawada and Sammet Sikhar, etc.[35] Thus, we find that throughout the 17th century, several factors were at work which promoted emigration of Rajasthani Jains all over the eastern India. It is, therefore, not surprising that Banarsidas mentions several places in Uttar Pradesh[36] where Jains lived in large numbers. Among places named by him are Agra,[37] Banaras, Jaunpur, Ayodhya, Allahabad, Kara, Manikpur, Fatehpur, Khairabad, Etawah, Meerut, etc. There are references to Jains in Lucknow as well.[38]

It would now be pertinent to discuss the amount of capital owned by the Jains and the commodities in which they traded.

Here we are faced with paucity of data. But the autobiography of Banarsidas written in the reign of Shah Jahan sheds a good deal of light on this area and gives some idea of the type of commodities in which they normally traded.

The Jain traders were not a homogeneous lot; there were several levels amongst them in terms of possession of capital. There were some who had at their command a large amount of capital; while others operated with very little.

Among the top echelons were Karmachand and Than Singh and Jeta Shah of Agra,[39] who in the reign of Akbar had organized a grand reception for Jain teacher Hirvijaya Suri when he arrived in Agra. He was received by a procession consisting of musicians, elephants, horses, camels and chariots. Gold and silver flowers were used for decoration. Geometrical patterns were made on the ground with the help of pearls.[40] Hiranand Mukim, a Jain trader of Allahabad, was so affluent that he led a congregation of lay Jains to Sammet Sikhar in Bihar in 1604. Jains were invited from different towns of Uttar Pradesh; the father of Banarsidas joined it from Jaunpur; they visited the various Jain places of pilgrimage in Uttar Pradesh and Bihar,[41] and returned after a year.[42] Hiranand shifted to Agra after Jahangir became the Emperor and invited him to a party at his house in 1610 and offered valuable presents.[43] Another Jain trader of Agra to win royal favour was Sabal Singh Mohita whose lavish life-style is vividly described by Banarsidas.[44] He was the chief of lay Jains of Agra. The story of the family of Hiranand Shah is well-known. He arrived in Patna in 1652 and his son Manik Chand migrated to Dacca and thence to Murshidabad where his successor Fateh Chand, secured the title of Jagatseth from the Mughal Emperor in 1722.[45] Not much is known about the affluence of Hiranand Shah, but his son Manik Chand prospered and the house became a significant factor in the economy and politics of eastern India[46] during the next six decades. All the foreign traders, the English, the Dutch, the French, the Armenians etc. and the local rulers maintained contacts with him.

But some Jains were at the bottom of the scale who were forced to borrow paltry sum to keep up their business. Banarsidas starved in Agra and then borrowed about two hundred rupees from his mother-in law to set himself up again in business.[47] He also mentions a host of other traders who were in similar circumstances.

In between these two extremes, there were levels of affluence. This is well illustrated by the history of the family of Banarsidas. He was a resident of Jaunpur which had been the capital of Sharqi Sultans a couple of centuries earlier. He was a jeweller and was in contact with the top administrators of the town. Banarsidas' father-in-law Kalyanmal was similarly a small trader of Khairabad.[48] When misfortune dogged Kharagsen in Jaunpur, he moved to Allahabad.[49] Banarsidas who was then around fourteen years of age sold *cowries* and earned a *paisa* or two.[50] It was not unusual for them to enter into business partnership to augment their small capital.[51] When Banarsidas dissolved the partnership after two years, he had earned a total profit of little more than two hundred rupees.[52] The poet described the situation as "discovering a shell after churning the ocean."[53]

It is difficult to enumerate with precision the exact number of commodities that were dealt with by the Jains; however, the range was fairly wide. Once again we turn to Banarsidas as an example.

When Kharagesn decided to set up Banarsidas in business, he started for Agra with twenty maunds of *ghee*, two barrels of oil, four packet of miscellaneous articles and some precious stones.[54] Cotton-textiles constituted another important commodity of trade.[55] But the small Jain trader virtually dealt in every commodity.[56] However, the affluence of Jains was the result of large-scale wholesale trade as was the case of with the Gujarati Jains, whose most well-known representative was Virji Vora of Surat during this period.[57] Their business extended to commodities such as indigo, saltpetre, sugar, etc. and imported commodities such as metals like quick-silver, lead, copper, etc. and precious and semi-precious stones. Thus, almost all items were included in the commodities they traded in, and the only exception seems to have been horse which they excluded on religious grounds.

In spite of dealing in a large variety of items, the general tendency was to concentrate on high-valued and easily transportable commodities, principally precious metals and stones. All the traders of Agra mentioned by Banarsidas such as Sanwal Singh, Ratan Chand, Bandidas traded in precious stones.[58] Banarsidas writes "The trade in precious stones is the best."[59] But the Jain trader did not give up commerce in low-valued commodities of everyday use, such as textiles, oil, *cowrie*, etc.[60]

The Jain trader, by virtue of his scale of trading operation was well-suited to act as representative and collaborator of foreign traders, who lacked local expertise and also monetary resources. The family of Hiranand Shah played this role. It could, therefore, be said that apart from being retail and wholesale traders, the Jains also acted as brokers and collaborators.

For the Jains the changeover to banking and money-changing was an easy job and both the functions were performed alongwith trading operations.[61] The history of the family of Hiranand Shah reflects this dimension of the activities of the Jains. In all the principal cities of north India such as Dacca, Hugli, Murshidabad, Patna, Banaras, Agra, Delhi, etc. the House of Jagatseth had its branches so that the transfer of money was no problem.[62] The Dutch record described Fateh Chand as the "greatest money-changer of Hindustan."[63] The Jains were able to play this role on account of their command over capital, existence of business ties all over north and western India and also presence of kinsmen and castemen in important trading centres.

At this point it is not difficult to appreciate the fact that the Jain traders commanding huge liquid monetary resources inevitably came in close contact with the various European trading companies, then becoming active in Eastern India, as well as with the ruling authorities. It is not surprising that some of the Jain traders became closely associated with the royal house. Hirachand Mukim was the personal jeweller of Emperor Jahangir.[64] They were appointed to important offices involving financial management. The examples of Dhanna Rai and Banarsidas' father have been cited above.[65] The family of Hiranand Shah established close ties with the ruling authorities in Bengal. Fateh Chand was put in charge of the mint at Murshidabad.[66] Frequently he advanced huge sums as loans to the Nawabs of Bengal.[67] He was responsible for transmitting the revenue of Bengal to Delhi.[68] His establishment functioned in Bengal as the state bank.[69]

The English East India Company had entered into business contacts with Manik Chand in 1706. Between 1718 and 1730 they borrowed at an average of one lakh rupees per annum. This was in addition to the sum borrowed from his other establishments in different towns all over north India.[70]

The Jains had, thus, entered into trade, banking, money-lending, transfer of land revenue to the imperial capital, financial management of the State etc.; thereby they acquired an influence over the local economy quite out of proportion to their numbers. The favourable politico-economic situation existing in the 17th century enabled the Jains to spread in eastern India and become a dominant force in the local economy. The success, thus, achieved spurred other Jains and Rajasthani Hindu traders to continue their movements towards the east in the 18th century because conditions in the north-west were becoming anarchic owing to the weakness of the Mughal empire, the invasion of Marathas and Nadir Shah; and were not conducive to the growth of trade. With the coming of the railways in the 19th century, this Rajasthani migration received further impetus.[71] Thus historical factor is partly responsible for the absence of the growth of indigenous entrepreneurship in the region in modern times, because the local economy never got out of the grips of outsiders. In the second half of the 18th century, the English became dominant following their victories in the battles of Plassey and Buxar. The region continues to be under the dominance of outsiders even today.

NOTES

1. Mahamahopadhyaya Vinaysagar, *Shasanprabhavak Acharya Jinprabh Aur Unka Sahitya* (Bikaner, 1975), p. 52. After Prithivi Raj Chauhan had been killed by Muhammad Ghori, his close associate Seth Ramdev wrote that the Turkish rule had been established and, therefore, the Jain images should be kept in hiding and his instructions were carried out.
2. The 24th and the last and the most well-known Jain Tirthankar Vardhman Mahavir was born in Vaishali and he died in Pawapuri, located in Bihar. Twenty Tirthankars, i.e excepting the first, twelfth, twenty-third and twenty-fourth, died on a hill top, Sammet Sikhar near Hazaribagh, again in Bihar.

   Angades and Champanagari, both in Bihar, were described by Mahakavi Brahma Raimall, who flourished in the reign of Akbar. Kasturchand Kasliwal, *Mahakavi Brahma Raimall Evam Bhattarak Tribhuvan Kirti* (Jaipur, 1978), p. 117.

   The city of Banaras is intimately associated with the seventh Tirthankar Suparsvanathji and the twenty-third Tirthankar Parsvanathji; Ayodhya in Uttar Pradesh is associated with the first Tirthankar Rishabhdev. See, P.C. Nahar, *Jain Inscriptions,* Part I, (Calcutta, 1918), pp. 84, 98; *Ibid.*, Part II, p. 145.

   A document of Vikram Samvat 1441 (1385 A.D.) refers to the travels of a Jain Saint in Ayodhya. Acharya Jinvijay Muni (ed), *Vigyaptilekhe Sangrah,* vol. I (Bombay, 1960), p. 2. Another Jain work of the fourteenth century refers to a number of Jain holy places in Uttar Pradesh and Bihar. Jain Parbah Suri, *Vividh Tirthakalp* (Santiniketan, 1934), pp. 11-28, 32, 65-70.
3. *Jain Inscriptions*, n. 2, I, Inscription nos. 151-157, 171-72, 175-181, 186-89, 211-223, 238-39, 256-58, 269, 274-295, etc.
4. *Shasanprabhavak*, n. 1, pp. 49-50, 54-59; Vidyadhar Zohrapurkar and Kasturchand Kasliwal, *Veer Shasan ke Prabhavak Acharya,* (New Delhi, 1975), pp. 116-121-27. It seems that in the fifteenth century there was a setback to the process because Bhattarak Shubhchandra had to transfer his seat to Chittor from Delhi as he

found the attitude of the local authorities hostile. *Ibid.*, p. 148. Nevertheless, even Sultan Sikandar Lodi treated Jain teacher Bhattarak Visalkirti with respect. V.P. Zohrapurkar, *Bhattarak Sampradaya* (Sholapur, 1958), p. 22.

5. See f.n. 3, *Infra*.
6. Kasturchand Kasliwal, *Kavivar Buchraj Evam Unke Samkalin Kavi* (Jaipur, 1979), pp. 179-81.
7. R.R. Diwakar (ed), *Bihar Through The Ages* (Delhi, 1959), pp. 490-91. Raja Man Singh became Governor in 1589. His son Jagat Singh held charge of the city of Patna.
8. Jyoti Prasad Jain, *Pramukh Aitihasika Jain Purus Aur Mahilayen* (New Delhi, 1975), p. 291.
9. *Ibid.*, pp. 287-88.
10. *Ibid.*, pp. 306-07.
11. *Ibid.*, p. 314.
12. *Ibid.*, p. 290.
13. Banarsidas, *Ardha Kathanak* (Bombay, 1970), VV, 35, 197, 240, 407.
14. *Ibid.*, V, 458, 461.
15. *Jain Inscriptions*, n. 2, Vol. I, nos. 332-333.
16. Krishnalal Varma (ed.) *Surishwar Aur Samrat* (Agra, 1922), p. 99. Some of the prominent Jains were Than Singh, Manukalyan and Amipal. Akbar's policy was continued by Jahangir, who had a number of Jain saints in his court and he once invited Vijaydev Suri, the Chief of Svetamber Jains, to his court. Meghavijay Upadhyay, *Devanand Mahakavya* (Ahmedabad, 1937), pp. 13-14.
17. *Pramukh . . .*, n. 8, p. 291.
18. *Surishwar . . .*, n. 16, pp. 155, 160-65.
19. Irfan Habib, *The Agrarian System of Mughal India* (Bombay, 1963), pp. 238-39. Prof. Habib remarks, "From the above information it may, perhaps, be safely concluded that apart from such isolated territories as Kashmir and Orissa, or the desolate portions of Rajputana, the cash nexus was firmly established in almost every part of the Empire. Its prevalence meant simply that the peasant was normally compelled to sell a very large—in not a few cases, the larger—portion of his produce in order to meet the revenue demand".
20. Sunita Budhwar, "Mines, and Their Administration in the Suba of Ajmer," Indian History Congress, *Proceedings*, Waltair, 1979, 321.
21. Kasturchand Kasliwal, *Bhattarak Ratnakirti Evam Kumudchandra, Vyaktitva Evam Krititva* (Jaipur, 1981), p. 31.
22. *Ibid.*, p. 36.
23. G.N. Sharma, *Mewar and the Mughal Emperors* (Agra, 1954), pp. 135-38.
24. Surendra Gopal, *Commerce and Crafts in Gujarat* (New Delhi, 1975), p. 127.
25. *Bhattarak Ratnakirti*, n. 21, pp. 40-41.

26. *Ibid.*, p. 27.
27. *Ibid.*, pp. 27-30.
28. *Ibid.*, p. 36.
29. Jagdish Narayan Sarkar, *Glimpses of Medieval Bihar Economy* (Calcutta, 1978), p. 48.
30. *Ibid.*, pp. 50-51.
31. For greater details, please see Surendra Gopal, "Jains in Bihar in the Seventeenth Century", *Jain Journal*, (September 1973), pp. 79-83.
32. Sarkar, n. 29, p. 113.
33. *Ibid.*, pp. 50-51.
34. Meghavijay, *Digvijaymahakavya* (Bombay, 1945), Sarg XI.
35. *Ibid.*, Sarg XII and XIII.
36. Ardha-Kathanak, n. 13, VV. 30, 33, 70, 109, 116, 132, 141, 144, 232, 240, 465, etc. Meerut was the home of maternal grandfather of Banarsidas. *Ibid.*, V. 584.
37. A Jain Saint Meghvijay wrote a work on grammar, *Chandraprabha* in Agra in Vikram Samvat 1700. *Devanand Mahakavya*, n. 16, p. 6.
38. Pushpa Prasad, "Jahangir and Jains," *Islamic Culture*, Vol. LVI, No. 1, (Jan. 1982), pp. 39-40.
39. *Surishwar . . .* , n. 16, pp. 222-23.
40. *Ibid.*, pp. 105-06.
41. *Ardha Kathanak*, n. 13, p. 30; Verses 224-228.
42. *Pramukh . . .* , n. 8, p. 290; *Ardhakathanak*, n. 13, V. 239.
43. *Ibid.*
44. *Ibid.*
45. J.H. Little, *House of Jagatseth* (Calcutta, 1967), pp. VI-VIII.
46. *Ibid.*
47. *Ardha Kathanak*, n. 13, pp. 42-43.
48. *Ibid.*, V. 101.
49. *Ibid.*, V. 134.
50. *Ibid.*, V. 135.
51. *Ibid.*, V. 352
52. *Ibid.*, V. 362
53. *Ibid.*, V. 365.
54. *Ardha Kathanak*, n. 13, VV. 283, 284. The list of precious stones is as follows : Manik-24, Mani-34, Neelam-9, Panna-20.
55. *Ibid.*, V. 399.
56. *Ibid.*, V. 119.
57. B.G., Gokhale, *Surat in the Seventeenth Century* (Bombay, 1979), pp. 137-46.
58. *Ardha Kathanak*, n. 13, V. 384, 393, 400, 445.
59. *Ibid.*, V. 393.
60. Little, n. 45, p. VII.
61. *Ibid.*
62. *Ibid.*
63. *Ibid*

64. *Pramukh*, n. 8, p. 290.
65. *Ibid.*, p. 291.
66. Little, n. 45, p. vii.
67. *Ibid.*, p. viii.
68. *Ibid.*, p. ix.
69. *Ibid.*
70. *Ibid.*, pp. ix-x.
71. Timberg, *The Marwaris* (New Delhi, 1978), Ch. III.

7

Business Elements and Business Class in Maharashtra: A Historical Analysis

V. D. Divekar

Before its colonization, Maharashtra was part of a great rocky forest inhabited by the black people called the Nāgas. Marathi language took shape some time between the 5th and the 10th century A.D. and a separate cultural region of Maharashtra was formed by about the 12th century A.D. Till the 17th century, with the doubtful exception of the Yadava times (13th century), this region was successively under the domination of the Andhra, Kannadiga and Muslim rulers.

During the times of the Kannada Rashtrakutas (760-973 A.D.) who ruled over Maharashtra with their capital at Malkhet in Karnataka, the 'home' country of the rulers had become a stronghold of Jainism with its many liberal features. Jainism which gave impetus to trading and literary activities in Karnataka[1] could not, however, prosper in Maharashtra. Under the later Chalukyas and Kalchuris (973-1190 A.D.) Jainism was replaced in Karnataka by the Lingayat sect which had a greater reformist outlook, and the sect became more popular among the Kannada trading population. In Maharashtra, however, though it was ruled by the Karnataka rulers, neither Jainism nor the Lingayat sect became popular. Possibly, due to the lack of suitable social conditions and the necessary minimum level of trading activities among the native populace, none of the two religions of the traders of Karnataka took roots in Maharashtra. Yadavas were the first Marathi rulers. However, the Marathi people even during the Yadava era were probably of a low social status and of a low trading culture. The prominent deities of Maharashtra at the time—Vithoba, Khandoba, Vyankoba, Renuka—were all Kannada in origin. The state ministers, army leaders, men of letters and learned pundits were Kannadigas.[2] The trading *shrenis* operating in Maharashtra during these times were also of Kannadigas,[3] and the denominations of the weights and measures and coins etc. in the Yadav Maharashtra were in Kannada language. The native Marathi people appear to have resided mostly in their nucleated villages with their local chiefs from the Maratha, and Koli and Naga hill communities.[4] Probably the hereditary administrative positions that were then held by the Marathas were mostly confined to the village level, like those of Patil, Chaugula, Kulkarni etc., and the Maratha Vanis like members of the village *baluta* system, operated mostly with their hereditary local occupational obligations and privileges. The large-scale and long-ranging trade was carried on internally by the Kannada Vaishyas or Lingayats, and on the coast by Gujaratis, Arabs and others.[5]

The Yadava rule in Maharashtra proved to be comparatively a short-lived one. In 1294, during the reign of their great and last king Ramdev when Marathi culture had really started acquiring its distinctive features,[6] the country was invaded suddenly by the Muslims. That must have changed the situation totally to the detriment of the Marathas. What little trading activities the Maratha Vanis might perhaps have commenced under the favourable atmosphere of the royal patronage of the Yadava rule must have come to an end, setting in a period of stagnation. The Muslim rule in Maharashtra continued for three and a half centuries (C. 1300-1650 A.D.) and it dominated the entire social, economic and political life of Maharashtra. Under the Deccani Bahamanis, such important trading centres in Maharashtra as Cheul, Dabhol, Junnar, Daulatabad and Paithan became the leading Muslim trading centres. Towards the close of the fifteenth century the Konkan sea-coast including Nagothane and Cheul went under the rule of the Gujarati Muslim King Mahmud Begda. And in 1509, the Portuguese took over Cheul and other coastal trading centres from Gujarat.

In the 16th century the Konkan ports were frequented by

different sets of traders: Arabs, Persians and Indian Muslims, Gujarati Hindus and the Portuguese. In the early 17th century they were joined by other Europeans, notably the English and the French. During all these great trading developments, the Marathas appear to have played, if at all, a very minor role of petty coastal traders. However, quite a large number of traditional fighting elements from among them were joining in the armies of the Bahamani rulers in great numbers, as were the peasants in search of a livelihood.

The Gujaratis and other traders were in a position to take adequate advantage of the penetration of European trading capital and activities on the coastal areas of western India. The Marathas, on the other hand, remained indifferent to these changes. In their own coastal region of Konkan, they did not in any way dominate the trade. Further inland also, their *Desh* that is, they had very little business dealings with the Europeans. Therefore it seems that they remained unresponsive to the great changes in the pattern of coastal trade brought about by European intervention. Because of historical reasons and the prevailing poor trading conditions, such changes, albeit on their own coast, fell short of stimulating the Marathas for taking effective interest in business activities. A more fundamental change was, therefore, needed to stir them up to develop interest in business activities. With no great rivers, with infertile lands and rocky mountainous tracts, the ecological variable could hardly be easily changed. However, an effective change in the socio-political variable was both opportune and possible. And any change to be successful had to be suitable and challenging to the genius of the dominant class of the society and the life style of their cultural region.

Such a fundamental change or 'breakthrough' did come about in Maharashtra in the second half of the 17th century in the form of the establishment, for the first time, of an independent sovereign political power of the Marathas. This political revolution was brought about by various socio-political forces, which were themselves generated mainly by alien rule: religious discrimination, general abject poverty of the masses, availability of a social infrastructure for raising the armies etc. Even a geographical factor of having a hilly region proved to be an important and useful variable in this regard. Having established political power at home it was necessary to bring in wealth from outside, and control the so far neglected areas of surplus agriculture and trade. This may also be viewed as part of a process of political decentralization that commenced in the late 17th century in different parts of India. It took the outward form of violent political protests against imperial centralization, but it had deeper economic implications as well. At that time the different cultural-economic regions of India were at various stages of economic development. It was imperative for any newly emerged cultural-economic region to do away in its own way the regional economic disparities that were protected and fostered by the imperial power.

It was under these conditions that Shivaji (1630-1680) founded the independent sovereign Maratha state, which also paved the way for the emergence of a new Maratha nation. With its establishment, and by earlier efforts towards that end, even the ordinary riff-raff of Maharashtra became galvanized and the centuries old situation in Maharashtra took an entirely novel turn.

By 1650 large parts of the Deccan had come under the control of the Marathas. By 1660s the entire Konkan coast was taken over. In 1664 Surat and later Hubli were attacked and the spoils of Gujarat and Karnataka were carried off. The capital of the new independent state was established at Raygad in Konkan (1674). A number of forts on the sea-coast were built and fleets were fitted out in imitation of foreign sea powers. This political revolution in its course, and also afterwards, opened up opportunities to the Marathi people to pursue different specialized callings, including that of business. It also proved to be a social movement which not only did away with the traditional monopolies of outside ruling and trading classes but threw open several opportunities to different sections of the society.

The warlike nature of the 'breakthrough' in the business history of Maharashtra also circumscribed the business activities of the indigenous business class. The *raison d'etre* of the new money-lending and business class that was to emerge was the great change in the political-military institutions within the region. With the extension of the Maratha power the scope for money-lending and business opportunities were to increase further. The politico-military elite would need the support of money-lenders and businessmen, and the latter in their turn would have to depend for their business on the ruling and military elements. Thus, there was going to be an umbilical relationship between the rulers-cum-war leaders and money-lenders-cum-businessmen.

Under this seething historical situation, which were the elements in the society which had the necessary potentialities for emerging as a specialized business class?

TRADITIONAL BUSINESS ELEMENTS

Rudimentary business elements certainly existed both in the villages and towns of Maharashtra. They were of two categories: one which operated within the framework of semi-legal hereditary occupational institutions, such as the *balutedari*, or village service; and the other pursued a calling under freer conditions. Poor as he was, the *balutedar* was not expected to follow any occupation other than the one assigned to him by the village in accordance with his caste. *Sonar* (goldsmith) was one of the twelve *balutedars*, but he was expected only to test the coin and prepare gold and silver ornaments. A poor artisan, he could not enter into any business transactions. Bhat (Brahman priest), Mulla (Muslim priest) and Gurav (temple ministrant) were non-artisan members of the village *balutedari* system but received as village servants the smallest share of crop from the village cultivators. Thus, neither the village goldsmith who worked with coins, gold and silver, nor the village priest, who had a good social status, but no economic standing was in any position to pursue a business calling.

The village trader or trader-cum-moneylender worked outside the village *balutedari* system. But he worked under many constraints. For example, the village community as a whole, and the village panchayat in particular, which was dominated by the agriculturist Kunbi population, would not allow the shopkeeper or moneylender to attach the defaulting peasant's property. Except in a few fertile areas, most of the

Kunbi peasantry in Maharashtra was poor. There were no specialized exportable commercial crops in the region, like poppy, indigo, tobacco, etc. And because of several institutional constraints, as the one mentioned above, the village traders or moneylenders were not in a position to appropriate in any significant way any agricultural surplus of the village, and, therefore, not in a position to ever emerge as a significant business class.

In towns too, everywhere in Maharashtra, a number of artisans and businessmen worked as *vatan* holders with their occupational duties and privileges, often hereditary in nature, laid down in specific terms. But in towns there were also artisans who worked on daily wages or contract wages, as well as traders and moneylenders who worked under lesser constraints.

V.K. Rajwade is of the view that during the times of the Yadavas there did exist indigenous business elements like *sheths* and *mahajans* in Maharashtra. However, according to him, their trading activities were later taken over by the Vanis from Gujarat and Marwar. According to him, Gujarati and Marwari businessmen migrated to Maharashtra during the Muslim rule, and, as a result, the Marathi *sheths* and *mahajans* fell back upon agriculture for their livelihood.[7] Rajwade has not substantiated his views with historical evidence. The available records in the Pune Archives which throw light on the immigrations of Gujarat and Marwar Vanis into Maharashtra suggest that it was—at least in its sizable form—a phenomenon of not earlier than the 18th century. Secondly, the institution of *sheths* and *mahajans* working as trade functionaries is known to have existed in Maharashtra, from the available inscriptional and archival records, even during the intervening centuries, i.e., from the 13th to the 17th centuries. In Marathi inscriptional records, for example, dating from the 12th century onwards, enough references are found relating to traders such as Sethis, Mahajans, Mhataras, Sovanis, Kotharis, Vanis, etc.[8] Such inscriptional records in Marathi language are found to the east up to Chandrapur and Yeotmal, to the north up to Khandesh and Thane, and to the south up to Goa and Belgaum. This geographical area includes the regions of Pune, Ahmednagar, Satara, Sholapur, Nasik, Osmanabad, etc. What appears to have happened, therefore, is that the institution of *sheths* and *mahajans* did continue in Maharashtra throughout the centuries, but due to the low trading activities in the area and the built-in limitations of that institution, it was incapable of developing itself into a specialized business class.

In the 17th century, when Shivaji founded the Maratha state, the *sheths* and *mahajans* were already considered as old members of principal *Deshaks*, i.e., the leading local functionaries in towns and villages, and recognised as such by the state. They were also included among the *mirasdars* of the towns or villages along with Deshmukhs, Deshkulkarnis, Patils, Khots, Vartaks etc. But their operations were fixed by the government *vatan* deeds to establishing market wards and superintending weights and measures and such other activities. There were also *vatan* holding traders who enjoyed a monopoly right of trading in a particular commodity and in a particular region as stipulated in the *vatan* deed. A *vatandar* trader was also obliged to supply freely stipulated quantities of his commodity, or service, to some other *vatandars* of the region. For example, a *vatandar* dealer in betel leaves would be required to confine his trading activities to, say his village, pay a fixed amount per year to the government, and supply freely, say 50 betel leaves daily to the Patil, 30 to the Kulkarni of the village and so on. Thus, as the *balutedars*' activities were fixed by the villages the *vatandar* traders' occupational rights and obligations were fixed by a government deed. This served the trading activities up to a limit but also provided a built-in obstacle which made them stagnate thereafter. For the emergence of a specialized business class, therefore, neither the *balutedari* elements as goldsmiths and priests, nor the *vatandari* elements as *sheths*, *mahajan* and *vatan*-holding traders were properly qualified. Freer elements in the society were necessary for this purpose.

Maratha Vanis, who were somewhat free, were also obliged, especially in small towns, to provide, free of cost, stipulated quantities of commodities to different *vatandars* on certain days in the year. This was done according to the rules of the town called *gāonki*. But otherwise they were more free than the *vatan*-holding traders. However, they did not hold at any time a high status in the Maratha society. In Konkan and in some areas in the Deccan, there were Vaishya Vanis, but unlike Gujarati and Marwari Vanis, they ate fish and flesh and consumed liquor, which was one of the indications of their lower status in the society.

In Konkan there were also regional Vani communities, like Kudāli (coming from Kudal in Savantwadi), Sangameshwari (from Sangameshwar in Ratnagiri) and Patne (from Patan in Satara). They were poor and their social position was low. Patne Vanis from the Deccan, for example, had migrated to Deccan not in pursuance of any trade. They had simply fled there from their homes in Patan to save their lives at the time of the great Durga Devi famine of 1396-1408.

Another type of Vanis, who were basically husbandmen, were Kunbi Vanis, or Kunam Vanis. They ranked as Shudras or lower class Hindus. They lived mostly in the Deccan region. The case of the great Marathi saint-poet Tukaram (1607-1649) may be cited here. He was a Kunbi Vani and a hereditary *mahajan* but economically poor. During a famine, his distress was extreme, as his wife died of starvation, and he lost his cattle as well as his other possessions.

Many Marathi Vanis also engaged in cart driving, pack-animal transport, pedlary and other laborious work.

Here it would be pertinent to observe two facets of the trading occupation in historical times. First, although general trading was undertaken by Maratha Vanis, much trading activity was also carried on directly by various artisans themselves. In fact, this was characteristic of the prevailing economy. For example, the *Shimpis* sold cloths and clothes, *Kasars* sold metal vessels, *Sangars* sold blankets, *Telis* sold oil and so on. Thus, the producer or the artisan also engaged in trading activities. The general economy being in an undeveloped stage, the division of production and distribution activities among different sets of people was not only unnecessary, but was not possible or profitable in the case of most of the trades. Second, general business, including the grocery, was not confined only to Vanis. Others, like Brahmans, also pursued that calling to some extent.[9] In fact, much of the generalization regarding immobility in occupations in pre-British India appears to have been influenced by what is stated in works like *Manusmriti*. The actual situation needs to be further examined historically in details, especially relating to urban areas, both regionwise and occupationwise. It would be beyond the scope of this paper to examine this question even in the case of Maharashtra.

Among the different castes in Maharashtra, it appears that Brahmans enjoyed a wider choice of occupations. According to religious codes also (which were generally framed and interpreted by Brahmans themselves) Brahmans were free to pursue a number of callings. Being at the top of the caste hierarchy they enjoyed a privilege for greater occupational mobility than members of other castes. The earlier writers on the *Dharmashastras* had permitted the Brahmans to pursue the callings of trade, banking, agriculture, army, etc. as *appaddharmas*—to be followed in times of extreme difficulties. But the writers of the later *Smritis* (of the period 750-1000 A.D.) made these and similar other avocations as 'normal' for Brahmans. *Kusida* (banking) was recommended as an ideal profession for the Brahmans.[10] One important feature which may be noted here is that although Brahmans in Maharashtra followed different occupations, they did not divide themselves into so many different castes based on their occupations. There was probably more occupational variety and mobility among the Brahmans—from one generation to the next, or even in one's own lifetime or among the members of the same family.

Some Brahmans worked as *balutedars* in rural areas but many of them owned their land and cattle. Because of their training in correspondence and accounts, a number of Brahmans were better equipped to pursue a variety of callings: clerks, accountants, diplomats, businessmen, bankers, etc. Politically too, except a few communities like Marathas, Kayasthas etc., they held a superior position in the society. It may be noted here that in Maharashtra there was a long tradition, from the times of the Satavahanas (250 B.C.-250 A.D.), of the Brahmans occupying high positions in state polity and warfare.

Sheths, mahajans, Vatandar traders, Vanis, artisan-cum-traders, Brahmans—these were then the different elements from which the new business class was to emerge in Maharashtra, when, as a result of a great breakthrough in their history in the 17th century, the Marathas established their independent sovereign state, and further expanded the areas under their control in the eighteenth century. In order to know the elements which were better suited to emerge into a business class, it is also necessary to understand the nature of Maratha public economy that came to prevail as a result of the establishment and expansion of Maratha power.

Maratha State Economy

The public economy of the Maratha state was sustained by two main sources: the collection of revenues and the system of war finance. A large number of *kamavisdars* or revenue commissioners were appointed for different regions. The *kamavisdars* were required to remit the anticipated revenue of their region to the state treasury—before its actual collection. Such remittances were sometimes made for years in advance. These remittances were, therefore, in the form of loans advanced to the state. Over and above such advance remittances of revenue, the *kamavisdars* were often required to lend money to the government for war and other administrative purposes. Revenue and other governmental dues were collected in cash as also in commodities such as grains, salt, oil, ghee, etc. Government used part of the collected commodities to pay the wages of its employees, especially of those who served on forts etc. Part of the collected commodities were sold through the government shops. On the other hand, the rulers and the war leaders entered the market either directly or through their agents for making large quantities of purchases necessary for routine administration, and for feeding, clothing and equipping the armies.

Military expeditions were undertaken by raising large amounts of loans from different sources. Along with the *kamavisdars* and similar other revenue agencies, the war leaders depended for their finance more on private moneylenders and bankers.

Wars and military expeditions were not always lucrative enterprises and at times involved huge losses. The expenses on the army had to be incurred whether the war was won or lost. Marathas were also not efficient collectors of revenue from outside regions and the tributes from the enemy agreed upon at the time of the treaties, were not always, or regularly, and fully received. To recover them the armies had to be sent again. Marathas never looted huge amounts of wealth as much as, say, Nadirshah did. In fact, they were not at all adept and thorough in the methods of plunder.[11]

As repayment of loans at stipulated times was not always possible through government treasuries, it was quite often effected through various other means—by raising fresh loans to pay off earlier debts in arrears, by granting a *kamavisi*, that is, commissionership of a revenue region, as a *quid pro quo* to the moneylender to enable him to recover his amount with interest,[12] to launch new expeditions to realize unpaid tributes from big and small potentates, which, in turn, involved raising of fresh loans.[13]

The interest paid on loans was generally at the rate of 15 per cent per annum. In some cases it was as high as 36 per cent. Moneylending in one form or another became, therefore, a risky but lucrative business. It was risky because, till the Maratha government was in power, it borrowed money from outside regions from one quarter or another and tried to repay the public debts incurred earlier. But in the event of a total and final defeat of that government in war, the successor government would not have honoured the army debts of the earlier government. This must have, however, appeared a distant possibility, or rather improbable, to the Maratha moneylenders in the heyday of Maratha power.[14]

There was, thus, a new and in some ways a striking development in the 18th century in the public economy of Maharashtra. It needed a specialized indigenous business and moneylending class to provide the necessary financial infrastructure from within the region. It was also in the immediate interest of the newly emerged class to perpetuate the system as long as possible.

Varied but allied functions were needed to be handled, such as those of revenue commissioner-cum-moneylender to the government, banker to the government-cum-private trader, agent for securing to the war leader loans-cum-state official, private trader-cum-moneylender, market official, etc. Many of the functions were interdependent and together formed the Maratha political economy. Naturally, therefore, those who were nearer the wielders of political and military power had better chances of operating financial and business system.

EMERGENCE OF THE BUSINESS CLASS

The work of collection of revenue and accounts-keeping at village level in Maharashtra and especially in the Deccan had been with the Deshastha Brahmans even during the Muslim times. Under the Maratha rule many of them started acquiring the *kamavisis* of revenue and octroi provinces. Some of them also took to money-lending and trading and established themselves as businessmen in urban centres. The lists of such businessmen prepared on different occasions are available in archival records.

In 1725 the *jagir* of Pune was conferred on Peshwa Bajirao, and Pune became the *de facto* capital of the expanding Maratha state. In the Pune Archives is available a list of persons to whom the Peshwa distributed *til-gul* (*halwa*) on Makar Sankranti day, 14th January 1739.[15] The list includes the names of the following *savakars*: (1) Bapubhat Moghe, (2) Baji Naik Kambaras, (3) Raghoba Naik, (4) Bavaji Naik Kadu, (5) Ramji Gham, (6) Pandurang Naik Dasputre, (7) Ramji Naik Bhide, (8) Bhagwant Naik Kanade, (9) Govind Naik Anagal, (10) Moroba Naik Tambavekar, (11) Dadabhai, (12) Sheshadri Shashtri, (13) Konda Joshi, (14) Govindbhat Barve.

A good number of the above names can be identified as of Deshastha Brahmans. It is estimated that by about 1740 there were more than 150 big and petty *savakars* in Pune who had, at different times, advanced loans to the government,[16] either directly or through the agency, *gujarat*, or some major *savakar*. The more important *savakar* families included: Anagal, Bhave, Bhide, Bhokare, Bivalkar, Chiplonkar, Damle, Datar, Dikshit-Patwardhan, Gadgil, Gadre, Gosavi, Gujar, Gune, Joshi, Karje, Lele, Madhave, Moghe, Oak, Omkar, Pathak, Patwardhan, Raste, Sane, Shrotri, Tambavekar, Thatte, Tulsi-bagwale, Vaidya, etc. The Peshwa was a Chitpavan Brahman of the Bhat family. And many of the Pune *savakars* were Chitpavan Brahmans. Deshastha Brahmans were also there as *savakars* in good number as well as some Karhada Brahmans, Shimpis, Sonars, Marathas, Shenvis among the important traders and bankers. Among the Pune *savakars,* the dominance of the Chitpavans grew with time because of their close relations, including in many cases the ties of kinship, with the Peshwas and other sardars.

Although divided into many castes and communities, the Marathas of the 18th century belonged to the same regional culture. The coming of independence and the expansion of political power provided opportunities for many people to move up the ladder of power and riches. Thus, the Holkars, who were originally shepherds, became one of the important and powerful sardars and the chief of a large state in the Maratha confederacy. Similarly, a boy servant of a *savakar* became the Chief Judge of the Maratha Court (Ramashastri Prabhune), a domestic family priest became the chief of a state (of Sangli), a petty local trader of Satara became one of the leading moneylenders to the Peshwa government (Morshet Karje), a petty contractor undertaking odd jobs became a well-known army leader (Trimbakji Dengla) and so on.

A number of professional Brahman priests, by saving the *dakshinā*, the priestly charges, received by them became middling, or even rich *savakars*, and some, by virtue of their diplomatic, military or even clerical skill became army generals. Culturally and by caste there was no difference between a humble Brahman and a rich Brahman *savakar* or an army general of the same caste. Matrimonial relations, therefore, were possible and did take place between them without an air of unusualness. This also must have helped considerably to increase the occupational variety and mobility among the Brahmans. In fact, occupational mobility among the Brahmans was probably the highest as compared to that prevailing among other castes and communities. Also probably, relatively a greater number of Brahmans were town dwellers. In the business class, although the important members were Brahmans, there was no separate 'business community' among them. Similarly, there was no separate 'army community' in Maharashtra, although many of the leading army leaders and their soldiers were Brahmans and Marathas by caste.

Except the traditional calling of priesthood followed by a small section among them, the generality of the Brahmans in Maharashtra were secular in outlook, and religiously and morally neutral to pursue any of the large variety of callings: agriculturist, cook, messenger, banker, clerk, army general, soldier, doctor, trader and so on. Even a religious leader like Brahmendraswami Dhavadshikar (1649-1745), a Deshastha Rigvedi Brahman, in course of time, by saving the alms received by him, became a great moneylender to the Peshwa and his other sardars. The loans given by him ran into lakhs of rupees and he came to wield considerable influence in the political affairs of the day.[17]

The entry of outside traders and moneylenders, especially the Gujaratis, in the markets of Pune and other Marathi places, and their importance there, may form an interesting subject for historical research and the student can refer to contemporary lists, account papers, relevant memorials to the government, correspondence, etc. For example, a representative list of important moneylenders of Pune who entered into business transactions with one particular banking firm of the city in the year 1755-56 is available.[18] It includes 75 names of moneylenders out of which 12 appear to be those of Gujaratis, like Kandas Purushottam, Dayaram Atmaram, Dulabhadas Govindji, Bhukanji Kasidas, Veniram Dave, etc. A decade later, in a list pertaining to the year 1768-69,[19] names of nine bankers appear from whom the Peshwa government had received loans to the tune of Rs. 13,39,773. Out of this loan, the two important Marathi bankers, Paranjape and Kabaras had supplied about Rs. 7½ lakhs, that is more than half the amount. Out of the nine names in the list only one non-Marathi, Gujarati name appears, and it is that of Vaghaji Bagadia who had advanced a small loan of Rs. 5303 to the government.

The situation at Satara, the seat of the constitutional head of the Maratha state, appears to be rather different. When a tribute was levied, the amount could not always be collected in cash on the spot. In such cases it was sometimes realized by *hundis* drawn through the agency of bankers. In 1753-54, a tribute of Rs. 10,00,900 was levied on Shrirangapatan. The bills for the amount were taken in the names of twelve bankers of Satara.[20] They were: 1. Bhukanji Haridatta, 2. Bhagwandas Gowardhandas, 3 Balkrishnadas Jeevandas, 4. Shridharji Daji, 5. Jagannathdas Dwarkadas, 6. Giridhardas,

7. Vrindavandas Raghudas, 8. Vishwanathdas Kashidas, 9. Vallabha Sundardas, 10. Annaji Govind, 11. Venkoji Lingeji, and 12. Sadashiv Venkoji.

This and similar available lists relating to Satara are important in this regard. It may be noticed that except perhaps the last three names, the other bankers mentioned in the list are Gujaratis. Even among the last three, the last two appear to be Kannada Lingayats. For similar transactions in Pune one would generally come across mostly the names of Marathi bankers. It is likely that due to the paucity of Marathi Brahman *savakars* at Satara, the seat of the Maratha King, the Gujarati bankers were relatively in greater number there and assumed importance. Also, the Peshwas turned their attention to the south and started sending their army on regular expeditions to Karnataka, with a view to levying tributes and collecting revenues, generally after their defeat in the north at Panipat in 1761. Therefore, the Marathi *savakars* appear to have developed their business transactions in bills with Karnataka more from about the 1760s. Up to the end of the 1770s there are only a few names of Gujarati moneylenders in Pune in the archival records. After that period, however, Gujaratis slowly started gaining importance in the Pune money market and other centres of trade in Maharashtra. Thus, for example, in 1795, the Maratha Vanis of Jejuri, a small town near Pune, memorialized the Peshwa government requesting that a Gujarati Vani, newcomer to the town, should be disallowed to open his shop in the town.[21] The Maratha Vanis feared that they would not withstand the Gujarati Vani competition!

The wars were probably becoming costly affairs to the Peshwa and other Maratha war leaders for two important reasons. Prices in Pune markets were rising continuously from about 1740.[22] Secondly, Marathas, as they expanded outside Maharashtra, had to abandon their old technique of guerilla warfare and were required to adopt the technique which involved heavy infantry and cavalry. This meant a heavy and constant demand on horses. Increased war expenses led to increasing dependence on money-lenders. As Pune was the metropolis of the Maratha confederacy, not only the Peshwa who had his capital there, but the chiefs of various other Maratha states also had to maintain close financial relations with the moneylenders and traders of that city. The other Maratha states had to, or were expected to, share some stipulated amount of revenue and other incomes with Pune.[23] For this and similar other reasons, a considerable volume of financial transactions passed on between Pune and other places. As a result, the city of Pune became, in the second half of the 18th century, an important centre of *hundi* transactions in India. For example, a banking firm of Dikshit-Patwardhans at Pune had *hundi* transactions with centres like Varanasi, Burhanpur, Jalnapur, Aurangabad, Nasik, Thalner, Paithan, Bombay, Narayan Peth, Siva Pattan, etc. Another firm, that of Tulsibagwale, received *hundis*, in one single month in the year 1769, worth Rs. 1,42,502 from different places in the country. Out of them, *hundis* worth Rs. 50,000 were issued by the firm of Nagar Lakshmidas of Surat.[24] Since money business in Pune and other Marathi centres was transacted in both small and large quantities, such developments as mentioned above probably greatly added to the number of moneylenders, their agents and other like functionaries constituting together the banking business class.

The middlemen or agents who organised loans, provisions, equipage etc. on credit on behalf of the army leaders belonged to different castes and communities, like Brahmans, Marathas, Prabhus etc. The middleman's job was a responsible and delicate one, and could be handled efficiently only by those who enjoyed the confidence of different concerned parties: the government. the army leader, the bankers and the traders.[25]

Although the rulers and war leaders received large amounts of money from bankers, some of whom happened to be their blood relations also, there are many instances where moneylenders by virtue of their money power meddled in politics or claimed high political positions. Brahmendraswami Dhavadshikar's case has already been alluded to. The case of Babuji Naik is rather more striking in this regard and forms an interesting chapter in the early history of the Peshwaship. He was a relative of the Peshwa Bajirao, a successful businessman and moneylender, and also an army leader. After the death of Bajirao I (April 1740) Babuji Naik made a strong claim to the Peshwaship on the basis of the loans he had advanced to the late Peshwa. He was supported by Raghuji Bhonsale.

Though Babuji Naik was not successful in his efforts his case, however, shows the extent of political intervention possible by moneylenders in the Maratha polity.

Apart from money loans, the government required a number of commodities for a variety of purposes—administrative, military, diplomatic, ceremonial and others. The government received commodities as part of revenue, octroi collection etc., and also bought them on credit and on cash terms. Cloth happened to be the major item in government purchases. This will be clear from the *Ainjinsi* (commodity accounts) for the following five alternate years taken from the Peshwa government accounts.[26]

COMMODITIES PURCHASED ON CREDIT BY THE PESHWA GOVERNMENT

Year	Cloth (in Rs.)	Other valuable commodities (in Rs.)
1763-64	3,16,402	16,004
1765-66	1,50,712	28,742
1767-68	3,32,512	17,200
1769-70	2,17,600	9,848
1771-72	5,13,437	12,392

These purchases on credit were made from different regions including Karnatak, Konkan etc. The Pune-Junnar region appears, however, to be a major supplier in this regard.

Government purchases were also made on cash terms. Also, some part of the commodities received by the government as revenue through confiscation etc. were sold and the money realized was utilised towards the purchase of commodities needed. Thus, in a single year 1763-64, the Peshwa government made cloth purchases worth more than 25 lakh rupees.[27] The number of cloth merchants could, therefore, be considerable, as many purchases were made in small quantities from different traders.

Many of the moneylenders were also cloth merchants. They belonged to different castes and communities. A list of thirty cloth merchants of Pune from whom the Peshwa government received cloths on credit during the year 1768-69[28] includes the names of 12 Chitpavan Brahmans, 9 Deshastha Brahmans, and other including Marathas, Shimpis etc. The list, however, does not include a single non-Marathi or Gujarati name. The total value of the cloth purchased from the thirty cloth merchants came to Rs. 2 82,519. According to the list, Ramachandra Naik Paranjape was the biggest supplier who supplied cloth worth Rs. 54.732. Figures for other major merchants like Kabaras, Bhide, Pargaonkar, Tatake, Vanavale etc. varied between about Rs. 10,000 to Rs. 30,000. But there were some traders like Tambekar (Rs. 862), Dinanath Mahajan (Rs. 675) and Gopal Kanade (Rs. 573) from whom the government received on credit cloth worth even less than one thousand rupees.

Another list of 71 traders containing the names of merchants in the Pune cloth market is available for the year 1773.[29] Out of the 71 names only two, those of Chhabildas Burhanpur and Madhavdas Godidas, appear to be non-Marathi, that is, Gujarati names.

From this and similar other lists it would therefore be safe to presume that during the second half of the 18th century Marathi businessmen were numerically strong and were also the leading members of the newly emerged business class in Maharashtra. The outsiders like Gujaratis were few, though not unimportant. Among the Marathi businessmen, the Chitpavan Brahmans, and next to them the Deshastha Brahmans, were the more important traders.

One important feature that appears in different lists, prepared at different times, needs to be noticed. No Marathi businessman of the 18th century is on record to have lent as much as even five lakhs of rupees at a time. Even the major advances at a time made by a banker were generally in the order of Rs. 20,000 to 50,000, and not more. And the little sums which the Peshwa government received as loans from the moneylenders were sometimes as small as three digit figures.

With all their possible limitations, the available lists of moneylenders and traders are very useful in that they help the historian to understand the major trends in business developments during the times, and the principal actors.

We have mentioned in the above paragraphs the activities of mostly those who had business dealings with the Peshwa government. But there were also other Marathi businessmen who had business relations not so much with the Pune rulers but with state and army leaders outside. Their names, therefore, do not appear in such lists. Secondly, there appears to have emerged a large number of petty traders and moneylenders whose operations were mostly limited to private individuals, who advanced loans purely for private purposes and sold goods for domestic consumption.

The new economic change generated in Pune probably did also have its multiplying effect in other regions of Maharashtra. As the change was based mainly on the transfer of money incomes with little of industrial content, the multiplier effect of the change was somewhat slow and limited in extent. Nevertheless, its presence was evident. Petty traders, not always of Brahman caste, having some business connection with Pune and other market centres were, it appears, growing in number along with their increasing trading activities. Some traditional Maratha Vanis appear to have started transporting goods on pack bullocks or in boats, and were engaged in relatively long distance trading activities. Still their scale of operation was limited in geographical extent and also small in value as compared to that of traditional pack animal carriers like the Vanjaris or traders like the Gujaratis. In many of their available memoirs and petitions made to the government, as also in the government orders relating to them, the petty traders are mentioned as *Garib Sahukars.*[30]

The government encouraged the trading activities of petty traders by issuing orders exempting them for certain periods from the payment of excise duties etc. In such orders one usually comes across phrases, such as, "... so that the trade in these goods may prosper ..." or "... so that this market may develop ..."[31] Monopoly trading rights were issued periodically for such commodities as tobacco, salt, coconut, ghee, etc. in different parts of Maharashtra, and petty traders of different castes and communities, including the Muslims, got them by paying the necessary licence fees.[32]

In 1763-64 the two *kamavisdars* of the excise district of Pune and Junnar approached the Peshwa government and requested it to issue a general policy statement relating to the rates of excise duties and the collections to be made from the Vanis and Udamis, "as their number in Pune is growing. . . ." The government thereupon issued a detailed notification laying down different excise rates for different cases.[33] Some petty traders opted for running of government shops, for which they received advance investment loan from the government at the rate of interest like 12 per cent per annum.[34]

As a large number of Vanis and other traders and artisans started migrating to Pune and other towns in Maharashtra, the demand for the work of *sheths* and *mahajans*, such as establishing of new market wards and superintending the market operations, also increased. More and more businessmen in addition to the hereditary *sheths* and *mahajans*, appear to have taken up this work by entering into necessary financial and other agreements with the government. Thus, from five market wards at the beginning of the 18th century the number of wards in the city of Pune increased to eighteen by the end of that century, involving an increasing participation by businessmen, money-lenders, artisan suppliers, settlement officials, building contractors, *sheths*, *mahajans* and others.

It appears that immigration of traders and artisans to other urban centres was always encouraged by the Peshwa government as a matter of state policy. This was done by extending to the prospective businessmen-settlers such incentives as granting of exemption in excise duties, conferring robes of honour, titles to palanquine, presenting a free house to live and/or a land for constructing a warehouse etc. The two businessmen, Shenvi by caste, Vithoji Krishna Kamat and Pundlik Krishna Kamat were thus encouraged (1743-44) to settle in Vasai in Thane district and to open their business there. In the case of Pundlik Krishna, an order was also issued that revenue right of a village be granted to him after he finally settled in Vasai.[35] If we take up the case of Vasai alone, similar concessions and privileges, for attracting the traders from outside, granted in later years may be noticed.[36]

The state activity gave rise to demands for all sorts of works which were got executed through the agency of contractors. A large number of Peshwa records abound with references, orders, and accounts relating to big and small works of various descriptions given out by government in contract. Such works required the services of contractors with different work experiences and qualifications: construction of buildings and channels; daily arrangements for meals, water, lighting, flowers, and other necessities for palaces; postal service; mining; building of ferries, vessels, manufacture and supply of cannon balls, rockets, paper, ink and other requirements. The government also required directly, or for their different *karkhanas*, that is departments, the services of such artisans as goldsmiths, blacksmiths, coppersmiths, carpenters, weavers, tailors, etc. Their services were also required privately by members of the public. The artisans themselves were often given work on contract basis by supplying them the required material, as they were also employed on wages for particular works—the wage rates differing from one type of work to another. Thus, a new and quite a sizeable class of contractors appears to have come into existence. And their services were needed both by the government and the public.

A class of businessmen with various descriptions—traders, bankers, moneylenders, market functionaries, contractors etc.,—had thus, emerged in Maharashtra in the 18th century. This class was the child of the great political revolution which was still continuing. It was a very hectic period full of changes and expectations. War had become a permanent feature of life. Not only the enemy from outside but sometimes military adventurers even from within harassed the businessmen for money. Towns and villages were plundered. Pune itself was plundered by the enemies thrice—in 1763, 1797 and 1802. Yet, the central part of Maharashtra appears to have enjoyed a sense of security for about half a century or so. When the British conquered the territories of Maharashtra in 1818, it was certainly not a stagnant society that they occupied. In fact, with the replacement of a responsive government of the local people by a foreign government with alien interests, the prospects of business and agriculture in Maharashtra came to be seriously injured. The one important indication of this was that the commodity prices and areas under cultivation started falling everywhere in Maharashtra after the advent of the British.[37] However, this facet of the business history of Maharashtra is beyond the scope of the present paper and, therefore, we may not pursue the subject further.

As discussed in the above paragraphs the government in Maharashtra in the 18th century played a major role in the emergence of an indigenous Marathi business class—a totally unprecedented and strikingly new phenomenon. As D.R. Gadgil has pointed out, there was indeed no emergence of a specialized business caste or community in Maharashtra.[38] But then the business class of the 18th century Maharashtra consisted of many castes and communities, and the Brahmans were in the forefront. Among the Brahmans who took to business there was no separate caste formation due to great variety and mobility in occupations followed by members of the same family among them. This was also true in the case of members of other castes.

The business class that emerged in Maharashtra in the 18th century was mainly dependent on governmental and war-like activities. The members of that class had close relations of kith and kin with the rulers and army leaders. If an army expedition for which money was advanced failed, the Marathi money-lender could wait and recover his loans later on, or get a *kamavisi* right for a revenue or octroi region, or a monopoly trading licence for some commodity. The entire political-economic picture of Maharashtra in the 18th century was an integrated whole of which the business activities of the indigenous business class formed an organic part. Foreign trading elements would not have liked to take risks of a political nature in such a situation. During their rule the Marathas had neither enough means nor organisational capacity (which often comes by cultural tradition, which they lacked) to introduce innovations like trade guilds, to launch business enterprises of permanent character or to successfully introduce commercial crops in the region. Probably due to ecological and historical reasons, commerce was not a part of the genius of the Marathi people. Therefore, the Marathi business class which emerged as a sizeable entity with all apparent vigour in the 18th century proved to be only a transient phenomenon. It suddenly lost its vigour and became insipid at the beginning of the 19th century when the principal supporting political base was removed by the introduction of the British rule. A large number of the moneylenders even became insolvents after the British took over, mainly because they were not in a position to recover their loans advanced to earlier army leaders.[39]

The Marathi businessmen and bankers of the 18th century remained throughout as traders and usurers and never became entrepreneurs nor investors of capital. During the whole of the 19th century under the British rule, when nearby Bombay was emerging as the commercial and industrial capital of India, the old banking families and merchants of Pune were nowhere near the scene; nor was there evidence of any significant Marathi business leadership in the city of Bombay.[40] Some rich people, no doubt, had deserted Pune after the coming of the British.[41] However, many had continued to reside there. But they did not come forward to enter into the modern business and industry. An editorial comment in the *Jnyāna Prakāsh* of Pune, dated 31 January 1859, poignantly put this issue before its readers and suggested that rich people of Pune like Sardar Natu should emulate the example of Bombay businessmen and start investing in capital enterprises. But this did not come about.

Outside trading elements like Gujaratis and Marwaris had already started penetrating into Maharashtra at the fag end of the Peshwa rule. During the 19th century, they spread throughout the region and became its principal traders and moneylenders both in the urban and rural areas.

It is only in the twentieth century, and especially after the opportunities created by the Second World War, that a totally new Marathi business class has emerged again on the scene. Its members belong to different castes and communities. It is relatively small with a few prominent business houses like those of Kirloskars, Garwares, Chaugules, Dahanukars, Dempos, Gogates and some others. They have entered into a variety of industries like machines, electricals, nylons, shipping, mining, etc. It may be observed that the names of the modern prominent business families are different from the family names that appear in the lists of the 18th century Marathi businessmen mentioned above. Again, unlike the case of the 18th century businessmen, their present-day counterparts have hardly any family relations with the ruling elite. These and similar other features indicate a complete break and a century-long discontinuity in the business history of the Marathi people. Such features also support the view that the basis on which business and moneylending was flourishing in the 18th century Maharashtra was an unstable, unsound and transitory phenomenon.

In the rural districts of Maharashtra, a number of co-operative sugar factories have sprung up since the Second Five Year Plan which laid down the policy of encouraging agricultural and industrial cooperatives. These factories in rural areas have provided political basis and politico-economic infrastructure useful for the activities of the leadership of the ruling party. The cooperative sugar factories, with their huge finances, are controlled by the Maratha rural elite. Hardly any of them, however, has moved outside the safe field of cooperative sugar factories, and ventured independently into other branches of modern industry. The newly-rich rural business elite depending for their strength on cooperative sugar politics and not coming out of that shell may remind one of the 18th century Marathi businessmen who depended for their business on state finances, and who never ventured to invest in new industries.

NOTES

1. There were a number of Kannada Jain *Shrenis* or 'trade guilds', and there also came into prominence, in the tenth century, many Kannada men of letters who were Jains—the great 'Adi Kavi' Pampa being the foremost among them. A.S. Altekar, *Rashtrakutas and their times* (Pune, 1934) pp. 105, 411-3
2. The names of prominent Kannadigas of Yadava times were Nagaras, Sovideva, Shivaraj, Kholeshwar, Hemadri, Lakshmideva and others. The name of the illustrious Jnyaneshwar (1275-1295), the great Marathi philosopher and litterateur may be cited as an exception. Another important religious leader of the Yadava times was Chakradhara (1194-1274), but he was from Gujarat.
3. S.G. Tulpule, *Pracheen Marathi Koreev Lekh* (Pune, 1963); A. Appadorai, *Economic Conditions in Southern India*, 2 Vols (Madras, 1936), p. 391; M.G. Panase, *Yadava-kaleen Maharashtra 1000 to 1350* A D. (Bombay, 1963) pp. 65, 215-7.
4. In 1340 A.D. when Muhammad Tughlak marched against Kondana, a hill fort near Pune, the chief of the fort whom he defeated was one Nag Naik, a Koli chieftain.

5. Panase, n. 3, p. 217.
6. The great Marathi literary work of *Jnyaneshwari* was written during the reign of Ramdev. The Marathi cultural region had its centre in the 13th century in the Paithan area.
7. V.K. Rajwade, *Lekha-sangraha*, 3 Vols (Pune, 1928-1935); Vol 1. *Aitihasik Prastavana*, p. 352.
8. Tulpule, n. 3, pp. 92-3, 275, inscriptional record nos. 12, 17, 34, 53-5.
9. From early times *sheths* and *mahajans* in Maharashtra belonged to different castes. *cf.* evidence given in Altekar, n. 1, pp. 201-4.
10. Brihaspati, as quoted in *Smriti Chandrika Acharkanda*; *Kurma Purana*; *Apastambha Smriti*, etc.
11. G.H. Khare, *Maratha History Seminar, May 28-31, 1970 Papers* (Kolhapur, 1971).
12. In 1733-34, a Maratha moneylender, Khandoji Gogawale was thus promised that his loan taken for Rajapur campaign would be repaid with interest, at the rate of 3 per cent per month, after the successful completion of the campaign; failing which an appropriate revenue region in *kamavisi* was promised to be granted to him. G.C. Vad (ed.), *Selections from the Satara Raja's and the Peshwa's Diaries* (Henceforth referred to as SSRPD), 9 Vols (Pune, 1906-1911); Vol. 1, No. 364.
13. For example, from the annual *tarjumas*, i.e., consolidated state accounts of the Peshwa government, available in the Pune Archives, one finds that in year 1763-64, the government cleared off the earlier loans by raising fresh loans to the tune of Rs. 24 lakhs during the year. Similarly in 1764-65 a fresh loan of Rs. 36 lakhs was raised for clearing off the earlier loans.
14. Such a calamity did befall the Marathi moneylenders as the British government later refused to honour the army debts. *cf.* ruling given by John Warden, Deputy Agent, Deccan on 2-6-1832, N.G. Chapekar, *Peshawayichya Savaleet* (Pune, 1937), p. 268.
15. The list is printed in D.R. Gadgil, *Pune Shaharatil Mahajan va Nagarsheth* (Pune, 1962), p. 20.
16. V.K. Bhave, *Peshweakaleen Maharashtra* (Pune, 1935; reprinted, New Delhi, 1976), p. 252.
17. P.L. Saswadkar, *Brahmendraswami: His Life and Role in Maratha History* (Unpublished thesis, Univ. of Poona, 1964).
18. N.G. Chapekar, "Toda" Bharata Itihasa Samsodhaka Mandala *Traimasik*, Vol. 22, no. 3-4. (Jan-Apr 1942), pp. 89-93.
19. SSRPD, Vol. 7, pp. 309-11.
20. SSRPD. Vol. 3, p. 145.
21. R V. Oturkar (ed.), *Peshwekaleen Samajik va Arthik Patravyavahar, 1722-1854* (Pune, 1950), pp 83-4. Memorial dated 22 August 1975.
22. For commodity prices at Pune in the 18th century, see H. Green, *The Deccan Ryots and Their Land Tenure* (Bombay, 1852), Appendix II.
23. *cf.* Pune Finance Minister Nana Phadnis' letter to Naro Shivdev

relating to Holkar's dues (1783 A.D.), V.S. Bendre, *Junya Masik-traimasikat Prasiddha Jhalelee Maharashtretihasachi Sadhane*, 3 Vols. (Bombay, 1966), Vol, 3. p. 247.

24. Chapekar, *Peshwayichya Savaleet*, n. 14, p. 121.
25. For how efficiently Raoji Apaji of the Prabhu caste organised (in 1770) the collection of money and supply of provisions for an army expedition, see his personal account in *Chandraseniya Kayasthya Prabhunchya Itihasachi Sadhane*, Vol. 1, no. 6 (Jan 1882), pp. 1-11.
26. Pune Archives, Ghadni Daftar, No. 748.
27. *Ibid.*
28. SSRPD, Vol. 7, pp. 309-11.
29. *Selections from the Peshwa Dafter*, 46 Vols, ed. by G.S. Sardesai (Bombay, 1934), Vol. 22, pp. 131-3.
30. Thus, for example, in 1774-75, two Pune Vanis, namely, Mahadshet Gondhale and Khandu Nagarkar, calling themselves as *Garib Sahukari*, memorialized the government regarding what they had brought from Bombay, dates, alum, etc. of a load of 100 pack-bullocks, worth Rs. 1200.
31. *cf.* SSRPD, Vol. 7, p. 69.
32. *cf.* SSRPD, Vol. 3, pp. 322-8. record nos. 464, 467.
33. SSRPD, Vol. 7, p. 68.
34. *Ibid.*, pp. 288-9.
35. SSRPD, Vol. 2, p. 139.
36. A Government order of 1751-52, for example in respect of certain three Vanis, says that concessions be given to them to open their shops in Vasai and Sashti: a house each to live, a piece of land, and 50 per cent exemption in excise duties. SSRPD, Vol. 2, p. 140.
37. Eor Pune market prices between 1775 and 1852, see Green, *op. cit.*, appendix II; for fall in area under cultivation in Maharashtra after 1818, see Great Britain, House of Commons, Select Committee on the Affairs of the East India Co., *Minutes of Evidence* (London, 1832), Vol. 3, p. 160, evidence given by William Henery Sykes, Statistical Reporter to the Bombay Government.
38. Gadgil, n. 15, pp. 12-7; also his *Origins of the Modern Indian Business Class: an Interim Report* (New York, 1959).
39. Chapekar, n. 14, pp. 124-5, 256.
40. A very few exceptions were like: Jagannath Shankarshet (1803-1865), or Javaji Dadaji Chaudhary (1831-1892).
41. Ballhatchet, K.A., *Social Policy and Social Change in Western India, 1817-1830* (London, 1957).

8

More about the Parsi Sheths: Their Roots, Entrepreneurship, and Comprador Role, 1650-1918

*Amalendu Guha**

Popularized by D.R. Gadgil as a socio-economic category and also used in this paper, the term "business community" needs some clarification. Until recently, all successful businessmen in India used to hail almost exclusively from certain castes and narrow sects only. Not all members of such castes and sects were, however, necessarily connected with business. These businessmen, even when in the same field, tended to form clusters on the basis of their narrow caste or sect ties. As a result, class formation by way of interpenetration and fusion of their capital and diverse business practices at the local, linguistic-regional and pan-Indian levels remained somewhat difficult. That is why, it appears, Gadgil found "business community" more useful as a category than "class" *per se*, in his search for the origins of Indian capitalism.

In the specific historical context under review, the Parsis in business will be categorized as a business community throughout this paper. However, to us the category is not a static one; it reflects a fluent historical situation. Different business communities are seen frequently crossing their narrow ethnic boundaries in the matter of forming partnerships, associations and, from the 1830s, even joint-stock trading, banking, and

*I am grateful to Ramkrishna Chatterjee and Amiya Kumar Bagchi of my Centre, and also to David Hardiman, for their comments on an earlier draft which helped me finalize this paper.

manufacturing corporations. The market increasingly brought them together on the same platform, both for organization and agitation during the latter part of our period. Business communities and classes are not, therefore, mutually exclusive categories in our analysis. Community and class consciousnesses overlapped. During our period communities were bounded social groups from which classes were emerging—a process that was still immature and weak.

Whatever new business personnel and leadership emerged in British India in that processs on a stable basis were, by and large, from the same traditional business communities of the pre-British times. They increasingly seized the available economic opportunities—both old and forthcoming. What was new was the distorting colonial circumstances and the fact that the Parsis had the best of it. For a long time, caste—rather than nationality—remained a major determining factor in the businessmen's group consciousness and habit of organization. This did not, however, prevent them from simultaneously coalescing at the local level and, in due course from merging into a larger class at the appropriate national level through interpenetration of their capital and acumen across the caste frontiers. For the period under review, the Gujarati-speaking Parsi business community is, therefore, viewed as a contingent of the still unconsolidated Indian bourgeoisie. It would have been worthwhile to examine exhaustively how, at the first instance, consolidation was taking place at the regional-linguistic level (Gujarat); and, secondly, also at the Pan-Indian level. But this is beyond the scope of this paper.

Urbanization

For an understanding of the business practices of the Parsis, some demographic features of this non-proselytizing, endogamous community need to be noted. Their number in India was 85,397 in 1881; 89,887 in 1891; 93,952 in 1901; 100,096 in 1911; and 100,772 in 1961. In the light of these figures as well as of the likely demographic effects of the Gujarat famines of 1596, 1631, 1684, 1698, 1790 and 1813, it could be assumed that their total number had ranged between half-a-lakh and one lakh during our period. The all-India urbanization rate was as high as 94 per cent for the Parsis in 1961 as against 54 per cent for the Jains, and 16 to 27 per cent for India's several other religious communities. In the same year, 71 per cent of the Indian Parsis lived in metropolitan cities (70 per cent in Bombay alone), 23 per cent in other cities and towns and only 6 per cent in the rural areas. The urbanization rate for the Parsis in Maharashtra where 77 per cent of them are today concentrated, was found still higher. There, 90 per cent of them lived in the metropolitan city of Bombay, 9 per cent in other cities and towns and only 1 per cent in the rural areas. In Gujarat, which accounted for almost the entire Parsi population till the close of the 18th century and where 17 per cent of them still live, the rate of urbanization was 73 per cent in 1961.

The above figures and available historical data for our period indicate not only a continuing rural-to-urban migration movement among the Parsis since the early 17th century, but also an urban-to-urban movement—the latter particularly in favour of Bombay since about the 1790s. In fact, already by 1850 more than half the Parsi community had become urbanized, long in advance of their westernization in other respects; by 1881 it was 70 per cent urban.[2] The urbanization process involved not only place mobility, but also mobility from manual to non-manual occupations, from primary to secondary and tertiary economic sectors and, in particular, from agriculture and artisan crafts to trade and industries. In other words, what happened was an intra-community structural change, an enbourgeoiment—however immature—of more or less the entire Parsi community. During 1650-1750, it was still in its pre-bourgeois phase, but it carried within it seeds that were sown by the Mughal monetization process and its commercializing impact. This process of change continued with some adjustment during 1750 to 1850, a period that coincided with the British industrial revolution and the early phase of British rule in India. Finally, this process gathered momentum in its third phase, 1850-1918, when the Parsi bourgeois led whatever limited and lopsided industrialization took place at private initiative within the colonial constraints. The first phase saw the slow growth of trading capital at various points of the Parsi society. The second phase saw its centralization in Bombay as well as spread and diversification of its investments. During the third phase, this trading capital was transformed largely into industrial capital and was increasingly deepened. Thereafter, signs of exhaustion and from the 1930s also a relative decline were visible in the role of the Parsi bourgeois.

Though latecomers in trade and finance as compared to the Chettiars, Bohras and Gujarati-Marwari Banias, the Parsis were the earliest to enter modern industries, and they were able to maintain their lead in this field until well after World War I. How did this happen and why? Their religious work ethic, their special minority position, their lack of caste prejudices, their production-oriented peasant-artisan background and, above all, their acceptability to British patrons as stable collaborators—one or several such factors have been highlighted by sociologists and economic historians of diverse schools in their attempts at explaining the Parsi success. Likewise, in the two published articles, "Parsi Seths as Entrepreneurs: 1750-1850" and "The Comprador Role of Parsi Seths: 1750-1850", an attempt was made in 1970 to come to grips with these issues within a specific chronological frame.[3] Our present survey extends over a much longer period as the title of this paper suggests. The Parsi case will be exmined here more thoroughly in its wider national context, with a reference to the aforesaid three distinct phases of the community's development. The objective is to understand it more in terms of the productive forces and relations inherent in the situation, both intra-societal and extra-societal, rather than of ethnic qualities, value systems or other factors that are purely external.

I

Unlike the Muslim Bohra and the Jain-Hindu Bania castes, the Parsis constituted overwhelmingly an agricultural community before 1650. They remained so till the end of the 18th century, despite their increasing migration in trickles to the urban areas. They had their settlements along the marshy, irregular Gujarat coast, over a tract stretching for some twenty miles inland between the two ports of Daman and Broach and dotted with small commercial centres like Navsari, Gandevi, Bulsar, Rander,

Ankleswar and the great port of Surat. Nucleating around Navsari, their religious nerve centre since about 1516, they constituted an important minority in this region. Quite understandably, their villages were at a reasonable distance from the coast-line, "often broken by estuaries of the rivers and dotted with tidal flats which were submerged in high tide".[4]

EARLY COMMERCIALIZATION

The Surat-Burhanpur caravan route passed through Vyara in Navsari district where the Parsi settlements were mostly concentrated. In their black-soil region, interspersed with sandy, light red soil, they too, like others, raised a variety of cash and non-cash crops. The date-palm, in particular, grew abundantly in plantations, mostly tended by Parsi toddy-tappers in and around Navsari. Besides, the region was endowed with a powerful breed of cattle-stock believed by John Fryer to have been first raised by the Parsis.[5] Vicinity to terminal points of the sea and caravan routes, an easy access to timber resources of the neighbouring forests and a varied cropping pattern with scope of further micro-regional specialization—all these factors combined to expose *inter alia* the Parsis to the 17th century commercialization process of Mughal India. This process was expedited by a progressive substitution of cash rents for rent in kind and by increasing bullion imports by the European companies into India to back up their demand for export goods.[6]

This process had an impact on all communities of Gujarat, but in different ways. In non-Parsi Gujarati society, this impact was largely absorbed along the caste lines. Many of the trading and artisan castes underwent stabilization and consolidation; even some new castes presumably came into existence by way of fission, as in Bengal, to accommodate further narrow specialization in occupation.[7] But the Parsi society's response to this impact was of a different nature. In terms of strict rules of endogamy and commensality, it continued to constitute a single multifunctional caste as before in relation to the society at large. But internally, it also continued to maintain freedom of choice of occupation for all. Increased division of labour did not take the form of creating hereditary castes and sub-castes though tendencies towards such formations were not altogether absent. The hereditary clerical (*Mobed*) clan did tend to crystallize into a caste by setting up marriage barriers between themselves and the laity (*Behdin*) during the 18th century, but failed to emerge as such. The corpse-bearers (*Nasasalar*), working at the Towers of Silence, continued to be treated almost as untouchables in the matter of religious and social intercourse.[8] Besides, the pre-1750 orthodox Parsi society was neither permissive of long-distance seafaring, nor of occupations like smithery that involved a defilement of the 'sacred' fire, though cases of non-conformist practice were also there.[9] Within such restrictions, all Parsis including members of the *Mobed* and *Nasasalar* clans could opt for any occupation.

Certain other aspects of the Parsi social structure may also be noted here before we come back to the theme of the Mughal impact on division of labour in Parsi society. In the absence of smiths of any kind and other hereditary occupational castes amongst themselves, the Parsis could hardly fit into the Indian village community system. Even if they could in combination with non-Parsi artisans, their intra-village jajmani production relations would have remained tenuous and unstable in such cases. Perhaps this explains why the Parsi peasantry could always bring to the expanding market a larger surplus than what their communized counterparts in Gujarati caste-society could, in response to Mughal India's commercialization process.

Undoubtedly commodity production and division of labour were more pronounced among the Parsis than among other communities. In Parsi villages spinning, weaving, carpentry, dairying, brewing, sugar-making and other such crafts began quite early to be increasingly separated from crop cultivation. Parsi artisans and petty traders left their villages not only for the city of Surat, but also for the smaller ports and market centres like Cambay, Broach, Daman, Diu, Navsari, Gandevi and Bulsar. European travellers of the times took note of their conspicuous connection with a superior cattle breed, the newly introduced tobacco cultivation, the textiles manufactures, ship-building, liquor brewing and transportation by boats and ox-drawn carts to waiting ships.[10]

The famous perfumed oil of Navsari, associated with Parsi

enterprise, found a mention in the *Ain-i-Akbari*.[11] George Roques who visited Broach sometime during 1676-86 wrote that the Parsi weavers of the town "devote themselves greatly to this (i.e. cloth) manufacture, and excel therein over all other workers. Their *baftas* are much sought after and have a great market in the country for the use of Indians." According to him, they made both fine and coarse varieties of *bafta* and also *allegas*, a mixed fabric of silk and cotton.[12] "In all their callings", J. Ovington observed in 1689, "they are very industrious and diligent and careful to train up their children to arts and labour. They are principal men at the loom in the country, and most of the silks and stuffs at Surat are made by their hands."[13] Ship-carpenters (generally, Konkani Muslims or Parsis by ethnicity) of Surat were highly praised by him for their workmanship, and it is known that a Parsi master-builder named Cursetji was engaged by the English at Surat in 1672. Another Parsi master-builder of Surat, Lowji Nasservanji Wadia (d. 1774) was invited to Bombay to build ships for the English East India Company from the 1730s onwards.[14] Fryer in the 1670s was not, however, impressed by the sight of Parsi petty traders who used to carry wood and water to the ships and bring supplies to the port of Surat in their ox-drawn carts. "These are rather husbandmen than *merchants*, not caring to stir abroad", he contemptuously said of them. Yet he was particular to include them along with the Banias in his abusive category of money-suckers—a species of "Vermin . . . that hang like horse-leeches."[15]

Throughout the second half of the 17th century then, the Parsis—drawn though to the commodity circulation process—were not yet generally connected with big trade. Parsi trader were still, in gerneral, operating on a small scale in fields immediately related to their respective production bases—cotton-processing, wood-processing, toddy-tapping and short-distance transportation. We know of one Cawasji Cawsi in the service of the famous Bania brokers, Bhimji Parekh (d. 1686) and his brother Vitthal. The nature of assistance he provided to these merchants is not known. Jamsetji and Byramji and Edulji worked as brokers for the English Company; the former at Broach in 1680, the latter and Bairamji Cowsi at Cambay in the 1730s. They must have been respectable though not necessarily big merchants. But there were also several ship-owning traders among the Parsis. Rustomji Manok Dalal (d. 1719), a broker since the 1670s, and Dhanji Bairamji of Surat were two such traders. One ship of Rustomji and one ship of Dhanji were mentioned in contemporary Dutch shipping lists; the latter made her voyage from Surat to Hughli in 1702-03. A ship jointly owned by a Parsi and a Portuguese was mentioned to have been engaged in coastal trade in 1674.[16] Tradition has it that Banaji Limji (d. circa 1734) and his son Bairamji Banaji (1681-1753) carried on from Bombay in the early 18th century a lucrative trade with Pegu in timber, silk and opium in their own ships. The first Parsi to start a Calcutta-based business was Dadabhoy Bairamji Banaji who came there in 1767. Like the Banajis, Dorabji Nanabhai Patel (d. 1689), his son Rustomji Patel (1667-1763) and also the founders of the Dadyseth and Cama families started trading houses in Bombay. Rustomji Manok's three sons, including the famous Nowroji Rustomji (died c. 1740), settled down as traders in Bombay permanently in 1728, with nearly Rs. 6 lakhs realized as their arrear dues from the English. Nowroji had meanwhile spent more than a year with his family in England in 1723-25 for settling the claim against the company before coming back with a kit of equipments for liquor distillation.[17] In 1756 Jivanji Readymoney visited China in an Armenian vessel for exploring trading opportunities.

Thus by the 1750s one could no more complain that the Parsi traders cared not "to stir abroad'. Superstitious prejudices had begun to retreat by then before the power of wealth. Parsi artisans were daily defiling the sacred fire in Bombay dockyards and gun-powder works; and traders were crossing the seas. According to the estimate of a knowledgeable contemporary Dutchman (see Table 1), the Parsis in 1746 accounted for nearly 10 per cent of Surat's total estimated trading capital—a share that was much above their percentage ratio to the population of the region. However, while only 6 per cent of the Surat-based Muslim and 38 per cent of the surat-based Hindu/Jain trading capital had become dependent on European protection by then, such dependence in the case of their Parsi counterpart was 100 per cent. In their case 42 per cent of their capital was under Dutch and 58 per cent under English protection. Thus, under the rapidly changing political circumstances, the Parsi traders had already decided to seek foreign patronage. By 1750 they knew whom to look forward to, for such patronage. With the eclipse of the Dutch and rise of the English as a major territorial power in India in the 1750s, it became obvious to the Parsis that they had much to gain as traders from an undivided loyalty to the English. On tactical considerations they opted for collaboration.

TABLE 1

A. SURAT-BASED NON-EUROPEAN TRADING CAPITAL: 1746 (ESTIMATED IN RUPEES THOUSAND)

	Under European Protection	Independent	Total
Total	2786 (31.86)	5956 (68.14)	8742 (100)
Jew	100 (1.14)	—(0.00)	100 (1.14)
Armenian	—(0.00)	515 (5.90)	515 (5.90)
Parsi	869 (9.84)	—(0.00)	869 (9.94)
Hindu	1642 (18.78)	2670 (30.54)	4312 (49.32)
Muslim	175 (2.00)	2771 (31.70)	2946 (33.70)

B. BREAKDOWN OF SURAT-BASED TRADING CAPITAL UNDER EUROPEAN PROTECTION: 1746

Protected Under	Rupees Thousand
Dutch	1760 (63.2)
English	886 (31.8)
French	130 (4.6)
Portuguese	10 (0.4)
Total	2786 (100)

Source: Processed from Schreuder's estimate cited in Holden Furber, *Bombay Presidency in the Mid-Eighteenth Century* (Bombay, 1965), pp. 64-65.

II

The 1750-1850 phase of the evolution of the Parsi business community was dealt with in some details in my aforesaid 1970 articles. We had argued then that, *inter alia,* the growth of their ship-building skill, mercantile capital and manufactories were an indication of their ripeness for capitalist industrial transformation. They saw that their immediate economic ends could be best advanced only through close cooperation with the then politically dominant British traders, in the absence of any other alternative in sight. The latter needed willing collaborators at different levels of their business. Those who picked up a smattering of English as well as the new style of business and were willing to work as brokers and agents for the foreigners were sure to succeed in money-making provided their ambitions were limited to what colonialism permitted. The case of the Parsis exemplified this. They committed themselves to and achieved the task of an all-round transformation of their community—social, economic and cultural—to get fitted into the situation.

In this section of our paper, we shall take up only some select issues for a further scrutiny, rather than presenting once more a chronologically structured narrative of the Parsi success story over the period in all its details. Their association with ship-building by itself or their comprador role as such would have hardly led them to whatever success they had, unless other circumstances also conjuncturally favoured them at decisive moments. We shall argue that their artisan background, however important, was less so than their trade both in the matter of capital formation and setting up of manufactories. The other point to be underlined here is that the Parsi businessmen were "comprador" only in a limited sense; more or less, to the same extent as other Indian business communities were. They were all "comprador" so far as they were directly employed by British firms, worked for them as junior partners or they themselves set up firms to sell imported British manufactures and procure raw materials for the British shippers. This was done more or less by all business communities of India, though the Paris had taken the lead in this matter. However, all these business groups had, by and large, also independent lines of business and ships of their own, often in competition with the British traders. Thus, unlike their counterparts in China of the same period, the Indian comprador of the coastal ports was not merely a collaborator; he was also a competitor of the foreign merchant. Both collaboration and conflict were reflected in his vacillating political stand and economic position.

ROOTS OF ENTREPRENEURSHIP

According to the 1864 Census of Bombay Island the Parsis, though only 6 per cent of its population, accounted for 17 per cent of those enumerated in the occupational sector of wholesale trade, brokerage, banking and money-changing.[18] This appears to have been more or less the pattern even early in the century. Bombay attracted not only the Parsi, but also other business communities of Gujarat in large numbers. The fact, nevertheless, remains that the former could make the best of the situation, while others initially lagged behind. As traders, both the Konkani Muslims and the Bohoras had a background of production-orientation; the former in ship-building and the latter in saltpetre production.[19] Again, as can be seen from Table 1 above, dependent Bania capital (under European protection) in 1746 was twice as big as dependent Parsi capital in Surat; and Bhimji Parekh, a headman of the Banias, had been in the good books of the East India Company as a broker, long before Rustomji Manok the Parsi. An artisan background and early linkage with the British alone do not, therefore, explain the Parsi success. What is significant in this context is to be sought elsewhere. When they responded to the challenge, they were not yet tied to a deep-rooted trading network of their own, even within their own region, as the Banias or the Bohoras were. They, the Parsis, had neither any long-standing vested interest in the Gulf trade oriented to Surat, nor any stake worth mentioning in the local governments of the region they lived in. Nor were they involved in overland trade with the interior. Hence, they could extricate themselves from their local commitments more quickly than the Banias or the Bohoras could, in the matter of opting for Bombay as their new haven and for new avenues of business. However, the Banias, Bohoras, Khojas and Bhatias did not lag behind the Parsis even in this respect. They followed the Parsis close on the heels to Bombay.

A majority of the migrant Parsis in Bombay worked initially as weavers, carpenters and artisans of other sorts, and a much lesser number as traders and contractors, catering to the needs of the various departments of the Company's Government. The relative importance of artisan crafts and trade as sources of capital accumulation in the hands of the Parsis is, therefore, worth examining. Weaving, liquor-brewing (from *toddy* and *mowrah*) and carpentry being their major crafts, let us first look into the potentialities in this respect during the pre-1850 period.

Parsi weavers' pecuniary condition was no better in Bombay than it had been in Gujarat. Tied to advances and poorly paid, they neither had a capacity to save nor had any initiative left for innovations. It is, therefore, no surprise that, later during the first half of the 19th century, they gradually left the craft for other occupations. No Parsi was found practising weaving as a handicraft, while only 366 of Bombay's 49,201 Parsis were recorded as belonging to the occupational category of textile workers in the Bombay Census of 1864.[20] There is no evidence either of any cotton weaving manufactory being set up by a Parsi master weaver. Sir Jamshedji Jijibhai (1783-1859) is said to have been born in Surat in a poor weaver's family of priestly lineage. But he started his career, while still in his teens, as a China trader's employee and, later, enriched himself by trading with China on his own account.

Toddy-tappers, in contrast, had better luck in the liquor distillation business. Some of them established distilleries in due course, but it was the retailing of foreign and country liquor that attracted most of them. Occupational category-wise, Bombay's 2,421 Parsi liquor-dealers accounted in 1864 for 21 per cent of all alcohol dealers in the Island. In the Bombay Presidency as a whole, this business was dominated by the Parsis. Carpenters other than those who built ships had gradually withdrawn from manual labour already by 1850, while many of them emerged as small-scale businessmen in the field of wood-processing. There were 5906 Parsis in the wood-processing, occupational group, and they together accounted for 18 per cent thereof in 1864. They were mostly middlemen, not toiling artisans as such. For as early as in 1848, the *Bombay Times* had lamented: "Our shopkeepers are nearly all Parsis—so are our furniture-makers also—but the workmen employed in the manufacture of Bombay furniture of so exquisite design . . . are nearly all men from Cutchh and Gujarat." Their skill in carpentry helped several Parsis to set up manufactories for making coaches and bullock-carts.[21] But all such activities, though a breeding ground of small capitalists and a capitalist outlook, accounted for only a small fraction of the community's wealth that had accumulated by 1850.

Even for the master ship-builders, the scope of growing into full-fledged industrial entrepreneurs in their own line was more limited than what is generally believed. First, the docks where the Wadia master builders built ships for their customers were the East India Company's properties. Secondly, even the bulk of the working capital respresenting material inputs was not theirs. The terms of their contract with the Company are not fully known. Nevertheless, it is clear that they did not participate in risk-taking and that they worked for remuneration, a part of it being paid since 1789 as commission on the marine bills. Occasionally, they also received land grants as rewards.[22]

The ship carpenters who worked under the Wadias apparently received wages paid through the latter and were organized on the basis of an elaborate division of labour. The Royal ships had the privilege of being repaired in the Bombay dockyards against the payment of regular monthly rent to the Company. Some of the Royal ships were also built there, but not before 1804. Ships were in general constructed on the basis of orders from customers. A rental for the use of the dock facilities was charged at the rate of Rs. 10 per ton of tonnage capacity when ships were built on slips; and at a higher rate when built in docks. This is what we learn from John F. Mitchel. who gave evidence before a parliamentary committee in 1814. The Company, supplied according to him, not only the dockyard facilities, but generally also the main input—

timber, and for this it charged 20 per cent upon the cost of the timber. When the customer was allowed to use his own timber, he had still to pay an extra 10 per cent to the Company upon the cost for this privilege. But this privilege of using one's own timber was withdrawn after 1813.[23]

As the principle of costing is not very clear from this evidence, we cannot say definitely what was the basis and mode of payment to ship-carpenters in general or as to who advanced most material inputs other than timber, such as cordage, sails, articles of copper, anchors, guns, resins pitch and tar etc. All major material inputs excepting timber, light cordage and light sails, as Mitchell tells us, were imported items supplied from the Company's own stores. In any case, the actual manufacturing of the hull and its fitting-out were left to the master-builders and the over-all control and ownership of the ship manufactory to the Company. There was a separate Parsi contractor to supply timber to the Company and a Parsi inspector to inspect the deliveries. Under the circumstances, even if the master builder's skills were of a high order, V.I. Pavlov's surmise that the working capital for ship-building was mainly supplied by them does not appear to hold good. His view that the "sphere of application of private Indian initiative was sufficiently extensive" in the Bombay Dockyard as such is questionable.[24] For the building of the Royal or Company's own ships, the plans generally came from U.K. No special commission seems to have been paid to the master-builders of such ships over and above their usual remuneration, except for rewards from time to time. But, for all private work on the Company's dockyards, they used to receive according to R.A. Wadia, a 2 per cent commission on the marine bill, following a London Court of Directors' decision of 1789.[25]

Under the circumstances, profits of the Bombay dockyards went mainly to the Company and only partly to a number of contractors including the master-builders in charge of the labour force. There is no evidence of substantial accumulation of wealth in the Wadia family before several of its members had turned to trade in the 1780s and later also to landed properties. Although their initial trading capital had originated in artisan production, it was their participation in the China trade in raw cotton and opium that enabled them in their third generation to become substantial shipowners and real estates owners by 1809. Nasservanji Manokji (1754-1814), Pestonji Bomanji (1758-1816) and Hormusji Bomanji (1766-1826), who were the first Wadias to enter into trade, must have found their artisan background useful for getting their ships constructed or repaired in the best possible manner.[26] Not production, but trade, nevertheless, remained their chief concern.

What we want to highlight is that the Wadias failed to grow into owners of ship manufactories or other manufactories ancillary to these, or even of a shipping navigation company on modern lines. It was not a Wadia shipwright, but a Banaji trader, Rustomji Cowasji (1792-1852), at whose initiative was established a ship manufactory in Calcutta in 1836. The famous shipwright of Bombay, Dhanjibhai Rustomji Wadia (1799-1854) first joined this concern as an employee. In 1843, he left it to join the Mazagaon Mughal Dock of Bombay, which was established in 1835 under the ownership of Aga Muhammad Rahim Siraji, a Konkani Muslim merchant. Finally, along with his services the Mughal Dock was sold out to the P. & O. Co. in 1846. The Calcutta concern where Dhanjibhai had earlier worked also did not survive long after that. Sir Jamshedji Jijibhai owned a big ship-building dock and, on the average, reportedly employed about 3000 hands. But he, too, was a trader. His investments in ship-building yards, newspapers and banks came from fortunes he made in China trade, and he belonged to a priestly clan. Incidentally, the Konkani Muslims also had several private docks at Mazagaon for building smaller crafts (*dhows*).[27] But like the Parsis they too failed to grow into entrepreneurs on their own productive base.

Jamsetji Bomanji (d. 1821) and his son Nowroji Jamsetji (1774-1860) built a number of UK-designed sailing ships for active service in the British Royal Navy. They were able to do so even without a foreign training. Later, Nowroji, Jamsetji, Jahanghir Naoroji (1821-66), Ardesir Cursetji (1808-77), Hirjibhai Merwanji (1817-83) and Rustomji Ardesir (1828-?)—the latter four had training in U.K. as engineers—also successfully assembled and launched a few steamers, during the years 1830-64. But the service-orientation of these Wadias did not take them far. Nowroji remained where he was, as a master-builder in the decadent Bombay Dockyard. Hirjibhai joined his elder brother's trading firm which later had the credit of introducing imported kerosene oil and sewing machines in the Indian market. Ardesir Cursetji, Fellow of the Royal Society, ended up his career as a salaried engineer in British concerns. An apprentice, draughtsman, pattern-maker, fitter and builder in turn in the Bombay Dockyard during 1844-64, Rustomji Ardesir, too, did not develop into a technician-industrialist.[28]

Thus, though the Wadias were equal to the task of transferring new technology through adaptation, they failed to establish a modern ship-building corporation or, for that matter, even a coastal shipping line. It was not because of a dearth of skill or capital that they failed. By then the Wadias and several other Parsi families had accumulated enough trading capital which could be drawn upon. Indeed they did not fail but were failed by the non-permissive colonial policy. By 1850 they knew that they would have to try their luck elsewhere than in the ship-building industry, which needed active state patronage. Others like Rustomji Cowasji Banaji tried a breakthrough and had their fingers burnt for their foolhardiness.

CHINA TRADE

In fact, what brought a sharp turn to the fortunes of the Parsis—this was more or less true also of other Gujarati trading communities—was not artisan production or ordinary trade as such, but the circumstances of a suddenly expanding China trade in the wake of the industrial revolution in Britain. In the 1780s U.K. could afford to drink more tea than before. Hence, and also on considerations of re-export prospects, there were drastic cuts on her duties on tea imports from China in 1784. This, in turn, led to big induced changes in the colonial trading pattern. Now the balances of payments in the triangular trade of U.K., India and China could be multilaterally settled with minimal use of bullion and with maximum advantage to the U.K. Since there was yet no large-scale demand for British manufactures in China, a systematic promotion of opium and raw cotton exports from India to China became henceforth the cornerstone of the British Indian imperial policy and remained so throughout the 19th century. India's favourable trade balance arising out of raw cotton and opium exports to China could be utilized, on the one hand, to pay for China's tea exports to U.K. and also, on the other, India's remittance problem in one and the same stroke.

China's opium imports from India were hardly 200 chests a year and the annual raw cotton imports not even two million lbs before 1767. As a result of the shift in U.K.'s Imperial trading priorities, India's exports of opium increased to 2,000 chests and of raw cotton to 31 million lbs by 1800. It was in 1773 that the East India Company had taken over the Patna opium monopoly. It also adopted the policy of marketing the drug abroad on a large scale on its own account. However, in the face of an increasing opposition from the Chinese authorities, the marketing of the Company-controlled drug abroad was finally left to private traders with effect from 1786. India's country ship tonnage increased from 44,865 tons in 1783 to 175,407 tons by 1791, and the number of the ships from 128 to 575. Having been in the China trade since 1722, the Armenian private traders gained most from this policy change. They almost monopolised this trade in opium until replaced by the Parsis in their role by 1809. There were 29 large ships trading from Bombay by 1812-13, 19 of them above 600 tons each. Of these large ships, apparently 12 belonged to Parsi and 17 to British country traders, Besides, several of the ships trading from Calcutta were also Parsi-owned. Opium far surpassed raw cotton in importance in the China trade by 1823. The Company at first tried to restrict and suppress the Malwa opium exports. But this proved impossible. So, from 1830 onwards the Company introduced a new pass system which allowed Malwa opium to pass through Bombay to China on payment of a heavy excise duty. The Parsis, together with the English private traders (Beale and Magniac Co./Jardine, Mathesan and Co.), maintained their dominance in the opium trade throughout 1810-42. Their share began to decline thereafter because of the entry of the Jews and other Gujarati trading communities.[29]

The nature of the trade in raw cotton, however, was quite different. There was a legitimate demand for raw cotton in China following repeated cotton crop failures there since the

1770s. With the progressive destruction of the local handloom industry during 1780-1880, large quantities of raw cotton became increasingly available in India for export. Until 1800 China remained practically the sole market for export of this surplus raw cotton, particularly from the ports of Bombay and Surat. After 1800, and particularly after 1813, U.K. emerged as another important market for Indian raw cotton, by then exported also from Calcutta and Madras. The average quantum of raw cotton exports from western India to China and U.K. increased roughly six times between 1800 and 1850, when total exports from India increased in general. For an understanding of the origin and direction of India's raw cotton exports, let us take the 13-year period from 1833-34 to 1845-46, for which processed data are available. The annual average for the period was 153.2 million lbs, of which 76.5 per cent was shipped from the Bombay port, nearly 13 per cent from Calcutta and the rest from Madras and Tuticorin. Of the total export, 61.6 per cent went to China and 40.2 per cent went to UK. In the case of the relevant exports from Bombay, these percentage shares were 53 and 47 per cent, respectively.[30] By 1850 the structural change in India's trading pattern was more or less complete in so far as cotton and silk manufactures were replaced by raw materials like opium and raw cotton as major export items alongside of indigo.

Trade in opium and raw cotton was then the mainstay of the Parsi Seths. To China, they sent their goods mostly in their own ships. But to U.K., they had to send their consignments in British ships because of the prohibitive operation of the Navigation Acts (1646-1849) that penalized the Asian ships if they ventured to go beyond the Cape of Good Hope. There is evidence that the Parsi export firms often outnumbered British firms in Bombay over the period from 1780 to the Opium War (1839-42) and that they had a larger share in the raw cotton and opium consignments sent from Bombay. They had also a larger share in the ownership of shipping tonnage, registered in Bombay. Even so, a lion's share of the total gains from opium and cotton trade apparently went to the British private traders. Not because they almost equalled—or at times even surpassed—the Parsis in the matter of owning country ships,[31] but because they were in control of the entire trading network.

The British private traders were disproportionately dominant in the fields of marine insurance and cotton-pressing. The bulk of shipping was insured by the Bombay Insurance Society, which was overwhelmingly dominated by European shareholders even though by the early 1850s a majority of its shares were reportedly held by Indians. Raw cotton used to reach Bombay in loose or half-pressed bales from the interior and needed to be fully pressed in the port before shipping. The gigantic cotton screws, each worked by 240 men at a time for this purpose, were mostly owned by the British traders. Of the total cotton pressing at the port during the 13 years from 1833-34 to 1845-46, the Apollo Press Company alone accounted for 63 per cent, Forbes and Co. for 15 per cent, the Colaba Press Company for 5 per cent, two Parsi firms for 11 per cent and Khimchand Motichand, a Gujarati Bania, for 5 per cent. With the sole exception of one Parsi-owned cotton screw at Khamgaon and a few in Gujarat ports, there were no full-pressing facilities anywhere in western India outside the port of Bombay before 1850. The role of the Parsis in the cotton-pressing industry appears to have remained somewhat less significant than that of the British traders even if we take note of the fact that by 1848 a majority of the Apollo shares, and probably also, of the Colaba shares were Indian-owned. In any case, the domination of the British shareholders did not depend on the number of shares they held, but the colonial connections they could tap, if vested with control.[32]

Whatever fortunes the Parsis built in the raw cotton and opium trade under the circumstances were mostly derived from the exports to China. Other sources of their earnings were the sale of imported British manufactures in the home market and brokerage commissions. Even while acting as agents, brokers or partners of the British firms, they often maintained their independent existence, they formed partnerships with other Indian firms, as and when needed; and they found themselves constantly in conflict with British interests. They too were discriminated against like other Indians. Take, for example, the case of Jamsedji Jijibhai, a loyal admirer of the Raj and collaborator of the Jardine, Matheson and Co. in the opium smuggling trade. Once having sent a 1400-ton ship to U.K., he was obliged under the discriminatory Navigation laws to recruit 70 English sailors on the top of his usual crew to qualify for a return journey to India. After this bitter experience, he decided not to send any more ships to U.K. on such humiliating and ruinous terms.[33] His unpublished correspondence now preserved in the Bombay University Library shows his concern for Indian traders' interests in the face of the then British competition and domination.

DIVERSIFICATION OF INVESTMENTS

We may now turn to some opulent Parsi Sheths to have an idea about the magnitude and the use of their capital and its use before 1850. The wealth accumulated by the Banajis could be gauged from the number of ships they owned—more than 30 around 1840—and the investments they made in such diverse fields as newspapers (*Times of India*), banks, coastal shipping lines, paper and silk manufactories, cotton screws, horticultural farms, salt pans, ship-building, docks and the insurance business—all these in Bombay and Calcutta. The docks were purchased from European owners at the cost of Rupees five and a half lakhs by Rustomji in the 1830s for the Calcutta Docking Company, a joint-stock venture of which he was the secretary. His 15 ships requisitioned by the Government during the Opium War fetched him an annual rental of Rs. 115,000. The Banajis incurred heavy losses in China—more than Rs. 2 million by Dadabhai Rustomji alone—during the Opium War and their remaining family fortunes were virtually wiped out by the economic crisis of 1847-48.[34]

Of the three Wadias who first entered trade, Nasservanji Manokji, owner of four ships, failed in 1810 for Rs. 12 lakhs. The other two Wadias, Pestonji Bomanji and his brother Hormusji, Bomanji, both ship-owning China traders, invested considerably in real estates so that in 1809 they were reported having an annual rent income of £ 15,000 each, besides their profits from trade. Pestonji's fortunes were inherited and expanded by Dadabhai Pestonji Wadia (1802-85), his adopted son. Continuing to trade with U.K. and China and broking for European firms, he had also investments in cotton screws, ships, banks, land and salt pans. He was reported to have purchased landed property worth about Rs. 5 million, yielding a rent income of

Rs. 124,000 a year; he owned about a quarter of the Bombay Island and, at one time, also three-eighth of the share-capital of the Bank of Western India. His firm, too, could not withstand the 1847-48 economic crisis and failed in 1850 with a liability of Rs. 33 lakhs.[35] His loss of Rupees one million due to the failure of a European firm, his over-investment in illiquid assets and the shifting of the head office of the aforesaid bank from Bombay to London—all these contributed towards the firm's failure. Hormusji's two sons—Bomanji Hormusji (1808-62) and Ardesir Hormusji (1812-82)—and several other Wadias apparently survived the economic crisis and continued as traders even after 1860. The latter built a cotton textiles mill in Bombay.

Amongst the oldest and continuing trading firms, the Readymoneys were the first Parsi family to start trading with China in their own ships since 1775 or a little earlier. The family's fortunes were mostly inherited by Kawasji Jahanghir Readymoney (1812-78) and his brother Hirji Jahanghir Readymoney (1808-1901). Both remained basically traders and financiers. Sir Jamsedji Jijibhai, also a child of the China trade as mentioned earlier, put some of his money in newspapers, ships, ship-building docks and shares of joint-stock banks. After 1850, the family's trading with U.K. continued, while its interests in ships, ship-building and China trade lapsed. Kharshedji Fardunji Parekh (1812-96), a relation and once a partner in the business of Jamshedji, also made his fortune in China trade. His purchase of properties was estimated at Rs. 35 lakhs, inclusive of a famous diamond valued Rs. 6 lakhs. Jijibhai Dadabhai (1786-1849), son of a master tailor made fortunes as a contractor supplying clothes to the East India Company and served as a guarantee-broker for nine European firms. His capital was employed in China trade and to finance coffee, rubber and coconut plantations in the Malabar coast, Ceylon and Java. He also purchased shares of joint-stock banks and the Bombay Steam Navigation Company. His firm was not affected by the economic crisis,though it was dissolved after his death in 1854.[36]

The above cases and other relevant data of the pre-1850 period suggest that the Parsi Sheths put a sizable part of their trading profits not only in some proprietary manufactories with processing equipments, but also in several new joint-stock ventures in non-manufacturing lines. The Bombay steam Navigation Co., established in 1845, with a proposed share-capital of Rs. 10 lakhs divided into 200 shares, had 3 Indians (including Dadabhai Rustomji Banaji and Jijibhai Dadabhai) on its 8-member directors' board. In 1847 it had five steamers with regular services connecting Bombay with Karachi, Colombo and Surat. By 1854, of its five directors only one was European and one Parsi (Jijibhai Dadabhai). The venture, by then almost wholly under Indian control, staggered for many years and survived into the 20th century.[37]

Several joint-stock banks were founded on the basis of Indo-British collaboration in Bombay between 1840 and 1850. The Bank of Bombay, established in 1840, had Dadabhai Pestonji Wadia as one of its promoters; Framji Cowasji Banaji and Jamshedji Jijibhai were also associated with it as its directors and/or promoters. The Parsis played an important role, next only to that of the Europeans, in promoting this bank with Government participation, as can be seen from Table 2.

TABLE 2

THE BANK OF BOMBAY: STRUCTURE OF SHARE CAPITAL

	1840		1848	
	No. of share-holders(%)	Share-capital Rs. 1000(%)	No. of share-holders(%)	Share-capital Rs. 1000(%)
Resident Europeans	173 (52.0)	3261 (62.4)	91 (29.0)	1473 (28.2)
Non-Resident Europeans	—	—	95 (30.3)	2365 (45.2)
Parsis	109 (33.0)	1233 (24.1)	88 (28.1)	877 (16.8)
Other Indians	50 (15.0)	431 (8.2)	39 (12.6)	210 (4.5)
Bombay Government	1 (–)	300 (5.3)	1 (–)	300 (5.3)
Total	333 (100)	5225 (100)	314 (100)	5225 (100)

Note: The domicile of shareholding increasingly shifted to U.K., as European shareholders, on retirement from service in India, returned home. The general decline in Indian shareholding was largely due to the 1847-48 economic crisis, causing the failure of several big Parsi firms.

Source: C.N. Cooke, *The Rise, Progress and Present Conditions of Banking in India* (Calcutta, 1863), pp. 165-6.

The Parsi Sheths also played an important role, together with European traders, in promoting two other joint-stock banks—the aforementioned Bank of Western India, established in 1842 and renamed the Oriental Bank Corporation in 1845; and the Commercial Bank of India, established in the latter year. Dadabhai Rustomji Banaji, Jijibhai Dadabhai and Dadabhai Pestonji Wadia were among the promoters/directors of the first bank; and, as we have already noted, the last-mentioned held at one time three-eighth of its share-capital. In 1845, its headquarters and control were shifted to London to facilitate its chartering as a limited company for lack of similar facilities then in India. Its Bombay directors tried their best to halt the decision; they even tried to stop the London Board from functioning in 1846, but infructuously. The dissatisfied Indian shareholders subsequently lost their interest in the bank. In contrast, the Commercial Bank of India, an Anglo-Parsi venture with a paid-up capital of Rs. 5 million, remained much more Indian. Bomanji Hormusji Wadia, Jijibhai Dadabhai, Cursetji Cowasji Banaji, Cowasji Nanabhai Davar (1815-1873) and Manokji Limji were five of its ten promoters, the other five being Europeans. Among the bank's 348 shareholders, the Parsis perhaps had an edge over the Europeans. For, of its 10,000 authorized shares, 8772 "were taken up almost in a day, by a large body of residents". However, the chairman and the majority of the directors were Europeans at the time Cooke wrote his book. The bank was incorporated in 1857 under Indian legislation and was granted a royal charter in 1864 with business jurisdiction spreading over from London to Shanghai and San Francisco. It crashed in 1866 due to over-speculation. That the Bombay Sheths were looking forward to modern joint-stock banks as yet another field for their operations can be shown by another instance when Robert Montgomari Martin made an infructuous attempt in 1841 to float the Bank of Asia in London with shares subscribed in U.K. and abroad.

> "In Bombay alone the amount of shares applied for was about 4,000, although the number of shares allotted to Bombay was only 1,000. The shares were principally taken by native gentlemen, and they were *at a premium of twelve per cent* on the scrip being issued."[38]

In fact, there was considerable interlocking and fusion of finance and merchant capital in the world of India's private trade, to which practice the Parsi Sheths were no exception. We have already taken note of Jijibhai Bairamji's financing of plantations. British country traders brought with them neither capital nor novel business methods until 1850 They had however a politically commanding position and, given this advantage, they could largely trade with borrowed capital. Parsi partners and brokers provided, in many cases, the bulk of this borrowed capital in Bombay. There were also Parsi bankers who financed princes of native states. Take, for example, the banking business carried on jointly by the two brothers—Vicaji Maherji (1781-1853) and Pestonji Meherji (1799-1854). We shall give here some more details about this firm than what had been given in our August 1970 article.

THE LAND NEXUS

The Meherji family had for centuries followed "the employment of husbandmen" (in the words of John Pyne, a British officer), before they moved to trade and banking. The two brothers were in charge of the revenue management of the Konkan districts under the Peshwas. Their services were retained even after the British take-over of the northern Konkan in 1817. They were then entrusted for several years with the farming of land and sea customs over a large tract of the erstwhile Peshwa territories of the Bombay Presidency, until the farming system was abolished by 1836. Simultaneously functioning as traders, bankers and revenue farmers, they undertook a number of rural development works to facilitate transit of cotton by land from the interior to the port of Bombay. For example, they cleared jungles in the collectorate of Khandesh and provided for bridges, wells, tanks, *dharamasalas* etc. along some stretches of roads in the Presidency. In 1825-26, they consequently succeeded in making the first-ever importation of Berar cotton to Bombay in 500 bullock loads (120.000 lbs or so) worth Rs. 25,000. By 1836, the annual arrival of Berar cotton to Bombay reached the figure of two lakhs of bullock loads (40 millions lbs or so). The Meherjis, Jamsedji Jijibhai and several Bania traders were pioneers of this diversion of Berar's surplus cotton to a heretofore unused route to Bombay. This new route was difficult, but shorter by 1000 miles than the 1500 mile circuitous land-cum-river route to Calcutta via Mirzapur.[39]

The Meherjis also made several stretches of roads cartable and brought from Bombay upwards a hundred newly designed bullock-carts for distribution amongst the traders in Berar. Berar's lone cotton screw, set up at Khamgaon in 1836, also belonged to them. In 1834-35, they purchased salt from the East India Company for sale in the Nizam's territory and, from 1836 onwards, undertook as bankers to provide advances towards the monthly pay of the Hyderabad Contingent. As a part of the deal, their firm was in turn put in charge of collecting revenue from Berar, the city of Aurangabad and certain districts of Ballaghat "not by way of farm", but on a commission basis. By an adjustment in 1841, they surrendered some districts, together yielding a gross annual revenue of Rs. 10 lakhs. But they still retained on mortgage the remaining districts, yielding an annual gross revenue of Rs. 13 lakhs against the outstanding debt. But these districts too were forcibly taken away from them in 1845. On the whole, during the years from 1836 to 1845, the total of the debit side of the Nizam's dealings with the firm amounted to Rs. 108 lakhs gross, including the principal sum of Rs. 83 lakhs. The earlier customary practice in Hyderabad used to be to make up the accounts every two or three months and allow a quarterly rate of interest on the balance; this, when compounded, was seldom below 30 per cent per annum. The Meherjis, however, used to charge at first an 18 per cent rate of interest per annum and later only 12 per cent. The mode of advances was drawing bills on branches from time to time. They also set up a mint at Aurangabad for issuing legal tender coins on behalf of the Nizam. After the hitch of 1845, when the firm pressed for their outstanding net claim of Rs. 41 lakhs, the Nizam's Government procrastinated and. finally, on 7 January 1848 admitted a debt of Rs. 31 lakhs only, exclusive of the advances to other parties on their security. To fulfil their commitments to the Nizam, the firm had earlier raised sums from bankers and other constituents in Bombay, Poona, Surat and other places. Now they all pressed for repayment. The aggregate amount of the firm's own debt to creditors was not more than one half of what the Nizam owed them in 1848. Yet, the year 1847-48 being one of an acute economic crisis, the firm was forced to close its doors in February 1848 in Bombay, Poona, Calcutta, Singapore, Canton and other places. The case of the Meherjis shows how the feudal milieu in a native state could initially help the growth of a firm's trading and usury capital under its patronage and, then, cause its collapse by a sudden withdrawal of that patronage.[40]

There is a general belief that, since they were not associated as dominant landholders with the Mughal administration in Gujarat, the Parsi owners of capital did not develop any special aptitude for acquiring land. This is, however, not borne out by facts. The *Baroda Gazetteer* (1923) mentions that Parsis held *desaigiri* of Navsari and Panchol Parganas of south Gujarat as early as the 15th century and continued to hold it under the Mughals and the Marathas. They were also found as revenue farmers in the states of Vansda and Dharampur in south Gujrat in pre-colonial times, according to the *Bombay Gazetteer* (1880). Ancestors of Dadabhai Naoroji, Naoroji Fardunji (1817-1885) and Pestonji Jahanghir (b. 1831) were known to have received rent-free lands or small *jagirs* in Gujarat during the Mughal times. Kharsedji Jamsetji Mody (1755-1815) served Peshwa Bajirao II for a few years as the Sarsuba of Carnatic. Describing opulent Parsis as "merchants, shipowners and landholders" in 1820, Hamilton observed that there was no bar for a Parsi in Gujarat to become a *Gerasia* by way of purchases of claims, money-lending or farming-in of land revenue collection rights. Framji Cowasji Banaji and his brother Cursetji Cowasji (1790-1847) in 1830 and three Wadias in 1849 were granted by the British extensive *inam* lands in the island of Salsettee. The Meherjis were granted not only land revenue collection rights, as we have seen, but also *inam* villages. It was therefore not without a reason that the Parsi newspaper, *Rast Gaftar* was bitterly opposed to the work of the Inam Commission and Naoroji Fardunji himself was active before the Commission on behalf of the landed proprietors of Surat in the 1850s.[41]

If there had taken place large-scale migration of the Parsis from their traditional villages to towns during the 17th-18th centuries, it only follows that as a matter of consequence landholding became increasingly concentrated in fewer hands and the peasantry differentiated within those villages. We could also reasonably assume that Parsi villagers who migrated to Bombay during famines had sufficient resources to arrive there relatively unscathed, as compared to other migrant peasants from Gujarat. The push and pull factors did not operate in the same way for both. As for the Parsi migrants, a sizeable number of them must have been viable peasant proprietors and small landlords while in Gujarat, who could get settled on their own. Besides, some opulent Parsi merchants were already then in Bombay to extend relief and hospitality to their less fortunate caste-men.

There is evidence that the Parsis of Bombay were quite keen on acquiring landed properties from an early date. In 1787 Dr Hove, a Polish traveller, noted that the houses in the Malabar Hills were mostly owned by the Parsis and were rented out to Europeans. When retiring European officers sold their houses, the purchasers were generally the Parsis. Maria Graham also noted in 1812 that almost all European-occupied houses were Parsi property.[42] That the craze for urban landholding and real estates persisted even thereafter is evident from the few examples, as given above, of Parsi Sheths having extensive investments in land and real estates. A few more are given below.

Framji Cowasji, an active member of the Agri-Horticultural Society of Bombay, tried to grow silk and a number of other cash crops in his extensive Powai estate that yielded a net revenue of Rs. 20,000 per year. His brother, Cursetji Cowasji, owner of six sailing ships, received 7 villages from the Government at a rental of Rs. 2,708 per year in 1830. He finally purchased this estate in 1843 at Rs 30,000. He also constructed at Colaba the 'Grant Buildings' which later became the property of Kharsetji Fardunji Parekh. Another Banaji and ship-owner, Bairamji Cowasji (1775-1828), took to cultivation and leased a village for which he paid to the Government of Bombay an annual rent of Rs 800. This kind of land nexus for the Parsis was not totally missing even in a later period. Ratanji Framaji Daboo (1846-1908)—at first a railway employee and postmaster in turn and then a forest and liquor distillation contractor in the Baroda State—took up for development 35,000 *bighas* of Government wastelands in Baroda, against an annual assessment of

Rs 50,000. Nasservanji Ratanji Tata (1822-86) left behind considerable landed property for his heirs at Navsari. It is true that the "landlordism of the great shetias did not extend far beyond the island" and that the interest some Parsis showed in agriculture during the 19th century was more an exception than the rule.[43] Yet the fact remains that, contrary to general belief, Parsi capital was considerably involved in land and real estates, sometimes even to the extent of wild speculation and wasteful expenditure on country houses and mansions. In 1864, one-fifth of all those enumerated as house and real estate owners in Bombay Island were Parsis.

III

By 1850, the Parsis had already lost their lead in the opium trade following the entry of the Khoja and Jewish traders into the field; and by the 1880s the Baghdadi Jews took over almost the entire trade. In 1901 Indian opium exports to China amounted to 51,000 chests; however, because of China's stiff resistance, these virtually came to an end by 1912.[44] Even in the raw cotton export trade, the Parsis were exposed to an increasingly stiff competition. The first two decades following 1850 saw rapid changes in transport and communications that led almost to a revolution in the field of commerce. A big increase in the volume apart, there was now speed in the movement of commercial intelligence and commodities, both within and outside the country. For Bombay-based European firms, it was now more convenient to procure raw materials directly from the interior through their own agents, rather than through relatively independent Indian traders. To minimize railways transport cost, they began to establish a network of steam-driven cotton presses in the interior market centres, so that raw cotton could travel in fully pressed form. They also increased their scales of operation since, with the advantages of their intimate contacts with the U.K. commodity and credit markets, they could mobilize the necessary resources to cope with the changing situation.[45]

But in all such vital matters, the Indian firms lagged behind. The European traders continued to enjoy an extra advantage, that of state patronage, since the administration and the public utilities in India were controlled at every level by officers of their own blood. For instance, 86 per cent of India's salaried civil service officers, drawing Rs 500 and above per month, in 1887 and 74 per cent in 1913 were Europeans.[46]

FROM TRADE TO INDUSTRIES

Thus the foreign trade in opium and raw cotton after 1870 no longer remained the most important fields for money-making for the Parsi traders in general. A recent study has shown how the Indian consignors' share of the total quantum of raw cotton exports from Bombay to Liverpool, the major receiver port for Bombay cotton, sharply came down to 27.8 per cent by 1875 from 55.6 per cent in 1851 and 67.2 per cent in 1861. A number of Indian cotton exporters—Kharshetji Fardunji Parekh, B.H. Cama and S.N. Nanabhai included—crashed in the financial crisis of 1865-66. Some of those who survived such as Dinshaw Manekji Petit (1823-1901), Merwanji Framji Panday and N.R. Tata and his illustrious son Jamsetji Nasservanji (1839-1904)—they all clung to the rising textile industry.[47]

Even as foreign trade in opium and raw cotton was slipping out of Indian hands throughout the late 19th century, the Parsis, along with other western Indian traders, made a bid to spread out into other fields of economic activities. After the Davars had shown the path, the Petits, the Wadias, the Pandays and the Tatas invested in the textile industry in a big way. As joint-stock companies could now be floated with limited liability under the new legislation, the base of shareholding expanded. Bankers, liquor-sellers, hoteliers, contractors, brokers and commission agents, owners of manufactories, ginneries, cotton presses and shops, even salaried and professional people—they all contributed towards the capital formation in the textile industry. Hence, profits from the China trade alone did not account for all the investments. Take, for example, the case of the Tatas. They were almost ruined by the crisis of 1865-66, but they somehow managed to survive by selling away the real estates. It was the fabulous profits they earned as contractors for military supplies during the Abyssinian War of 1867-68 that enabled them to enter the textile industry and revive their trade with China and Japan by 1872.[48]

The years 1850 to 1918 saw not only a general expansion of trade and modern industries, but also a process of concentration of capital and control and a simultaneous growth of corporations and managing agency houses. In all these, the Parsis played a significant role together with members of other trading communities. The survey of this period has been made in a number of studies and, hence, we need not go into all those details. We shall touch upon only a few Parsi ventures, that too selectively, to the extent these are relevant to some of the debated general issues.

If their artisan background is to be associated with the entrepreneurial success and qualities of the Parsis, one has to look into its impact on the Parsi social outlook in general, rather than search for the artisan roots of successful entrepreneurs. The Wadias, we noted, failed despite their roots in ship-carpentry to grow into owners of a modern ship-building industry, or even a shipping line. Instead, they became great traders. They enriched themselves in that process and, then, stepped into the textile industry. In Indian conditions, both pre-colonial and colonial, even master craftsmen remained handicapped for shortage of capital which could be amassed only in trade. What was striking in the Parsi society was its density and the co-existence in constant social intercourse therein of numerous artisans and traders. They interacted and, through that interaction, an entrepreneurial climate emerged. The role of the Bombay Dockyard is significant in this respect. Employing nearly 2000 workmen in 1850, it had created over the preceding decades a skill base that could be drawn upon by the textile and other industries after 1850. Bomanji Warden (1828-85), for example, was an ex-fitter of the Bombay Dockyard who later became a much sought-after mechanical engineer in the textile industry. In the absence of proper skilled personnel even wood carpenters were welcome since their skills as draughtsmen, fitters, pattern-makers, designers and painters, could be adapted to servicing metal appliances with a little effort.

There were also instances of manufactories growing into modern factories. Pestonji B. Press (1854-1930) was born into a coach-builder's family. His Fort Coach Factory, established in 1879, began to build motor car bodies after the advent of automobiles in Bombay early in the 20th century. The coach manufactory that was established in 1808 by P.B. Palkhiwalla, on the other hand, closed down for lack of such adaptiveness. The case of Cowasji Nowroji Chhoi (1853-1929), a silk trader and manufacturer of Surat, was "a unique instance of a handloom cloth manufacturer who . . . rose to the position of an owner of four mills" in the silk textile industry. But the transformation in this case took place not directly and uninterruptedly from the artisan base as such, but via trade. In the face of stiff competition from machine-made products, Chhoi had to close down his silk manufactory around 1873 and begin selling the products of the Sassoon Silk Mill to his Arabian market. Only by 1892 was he able to found his own concern, the Chhoi Silk Mills Ltd., in Bombay and start also a managing agency firm of his own.[49]

Many stepped out of carpentry works to become entrepreneurs elsewhere. Dorabji Naegaumwalla (1804-82) did not provide the only instance of a carpenter being turned a big entrepreneur. Another Bombay carpenter, Pestonji Nasservanji Godiwalla (1834-1909), made his fortunes as a contractor, owned a dry dock at Mazagaon for several years and later became a director of the Bombay-Persia Steam Navigation Co. Ltd. Nowroji Nasservanji Wadia (1849-89) provided the example of a foreign-trained mechanical engineer who later turned into a successful industrialist, controlling three cotton textile mills. Shorabji Shapurji, a foreman of the East India Company's gun and ammunitions factory, established a small iron foundry in the 1850s, with machinery imported from U.K. He also established a cotton gin and a flour mill in Bombay. His foundry, however, just maintained a precarious existence and by 1919 his heirs had become primarily importers of mechinery from U.K.[50]

The career of A.B. Godrej (1867-1936) was interesting in another way. He first joined a European-owned solicitors' firm after his graduation and, then, started a repair shop for surgical instruments. As the concern did not thrive well, he began manufacturing cupboards, drawer-locks and safes and, still later, vegetable toilet soaps, printing ink and boot polish. He also developed large soyabean plantations near Nasik.[51] All these instances show the wide range of Parsi entrepreneurship (short of machine-making) and its diverse roots. J.N. Tata perhaps best symbolized the entrepreneurial spirit of the Parsis of the age, with his interest in all round national development. He did not rise from an artisan base, nor did he belong to an aritsan lineage.

We shall now resume, for a summing up, the discussion on the causes of the Parsi success up to 1918. It was a combination of factors and a conjunction of favourable circumstances that had led to this success. Together with other Gujarati trading communities, the Parsis shared the advantages of belonging to the economically most advanced region of India. In contrast to another advanced region, Bengal, they also shared in common the advantages arising from the fact that the belated British imperial expansion in western India allowed for large-scale survivals of pre-British administrative structures. As a result, the numerically less imposing presence of Europeans in the Bombay Presidency was a boon for them. Two stray figures may be cited here as evidence. According to an official return ordered to be printed on 25 February 1830, the Company's European civil servants—military and medical officers as well as covenanted assistants—all of them together numbered only 237 in the Bombay Presidency, as against 731 and 338, respectively, in the Bengal and Madras Presidencies in 1827. In 1828, there were altogether only 286 private Europeans in Bombay as against 1595 in Bengal and 116 in Madras; the corresponding figures for 1815 were 240, 1100 and 115. Surely, because of these reasons colonial capitalism was forced to leave more room to its partners in empire in western India than in eastern India.[52]

That colonial intervention faced a bigger challenge from the traditional business communities in western than in eastern India is largely to be explained also with reference to the difference in their respective cash-cropping patterns. Western India's major cash crop, cotton, had a developed all-India market since the medieval times. Its further expansion in modern times could not have been achieved otherwise than on the basis of accommodating the old market links under the compelling circumstances. But in eastern India, old cash crops like silk and sugarcane declined early not only because of the competition of foreign products, but also because of interventions in production by the East India Company and privileged European private traders. Indigo since the late 18th century and tea as well as low-land jutes since 1850 were the new cash crops growing there under the shadow of British capital. These had extremely limited linkage effects as compared to the cotton of western India. This was because of the nature of those crops, their market channels and the absence of a pre-existing traditional trade network for them. When Bengal's sugarcane cultivation got a new shot on its wings after 1784, its earlier traditional trade network had already been knocked off.

If the Parsis had an edge over other trading communities of western India, or if they had adjusted themselves to the situation, the reasons are to be sought in the exigencies of circumstances rather than in their intrinsic qualities and religious value-system. For example, had the religious value-system or caste considerations been the crucial determinant, how is it that a Parsi was associated with an iron foundry as early as 1852 and that the establishment of India's biggest iron and steel industry awaited another Parsi who had his roots in a priestly lineage? One could still argue that such cases were exceptions to the general rule. But that there was an early and total transformation in the attitude of the Parsis to 'the defilement of fire' and sea voyages could not at all be explained by this kind of vulgar sociology.

Compradors or Nationalists

If there was any difference between the business behaviour patterns of the Parsis and the non-Parsis, this was one of degree and not of kind. Neither the community feeling nor the collaborative attitude to colonialism was an exclusive monopoly of the Parsis. In business and politics, community and class feelings coexisted with one another—not always parallely, but often, also interlaced and dovetailed—among the rising capitalists of all Indian communities. Similarly, even while collaborating with foreign capital and the *Raj*, both the Parsi and non-Parsi capitalists played an oppositional role as well. Dobbin's "Shetias" and "intelligentsia" were but two sections of the same Bombay-based contingent of the composite Indian bourgeoisie. Their conflicting attitudes were not only a reflection of their diverse sectional interests, but also of their opinions regarding what long term policy the class should stand for. Even Dobbin does not fail to conclude that irrespective of ethnicity, the Bombay "Shetias" and the intelligentsia were coming increasingly closer, as the educational gap between the two began to narrow down and a new interest in the cotton industry developed.[53]

Colonial discrimination made no exception of the Parsis. The restrictive Navigation laws had been relaxed for a brief period during the Napoleanic Wars to enable Indian ships to carry goods to Europe. Within that brief period, the Indian shipping and ship-building industry made a big advance, with orders from the Royal Navy and private traders at home and abroad. Had this climate continued and state patronage extended, a breakthrough in this industry could have been possible. After 1850, U.K.'s navigation laws and protective tariff were no longer there. Her mature economy and new imperialism no more needed them. In the age of the railways and steam ships, the Indian Marine Service and its Bombay Dockyard were abolished and no state patronage was provided to make a transition to the manufacture of steam ships with iron bottoms possible. In fact, all old-type dockyards, manufactories, and even a modern concern like Heathe's iron works (in South India), were allowed to perish when the railway construction drive could have actually brought them under its protective wings. Understandably, colonialism was not permissive of this kind of induced development.

If the Parsis were the beneficiaries of the British rule, they were also the victims of its policies, since British monopoly capitalism would not tolerate rivals in the same market. Take the bitter experience of the Tatas, for example, in the field of shipping. The new shipping line they established with Japanese collaboration in 1894 to carry goods between India and the Far East had finally to succumb to a fierce war of rates launched by the P & O Company. The latter went so far as to offer even free carriage of cotton to Japan. Indeed, Tata's fate was no different from that of Chidambaram Pillai whose fledgling shipping ventures in Indian waters were crushed about the same time and in the same way by British monopoly capital. In fact most of India's 102 navigation companies, registered between 1860 and 1925, had to go into liquidation under similar pressures.[54]

In such a setting, the Parsi capitalists were perhaps as much or as little nationalists as their counterparts in other trading communities until 1918. Both were under the spell of moderate politics, until peasant nationalism began to make dents on bourgeois politics since about the time. The moderates' policy of tactical collaboration was not totally devoid of an oppositional role. It only revealed that this role was played with all the vacillations of a weak and yet unconsolidated bourgeois. In any case, as Dobbin noted, there was a transcending of local and communal concerns. Parsi and non-Parsi bourgeoisie were together involved not only in partnerships, joint-stock companies and chambers of commerce, but also in the Bombay Association, (1852-79), the Bombay Milowners' Association (estd. 1875) and in the Indian National Congress (estd. 1885) at least in its moderate phase. Dadabhai Naoroji, D.E. Wacha (1844-1936) and Ferozeshah Mehta (1845-1915) gave leadership to the Congress, S.S. Bengali (1831-93), Nowroji Fardunji and B.M. Malabari (1853-1912) devoted their attention to social reforms movements of an all-India dimension. The Parsi contribution to the modern Gujarati literature, too, deserves a special mention. The cotton duty controversy reflected an economic nationalism that was shared by all sections of the bourgeoisie. Dadabhai's exposure of the colonial drain was intellectual food even for the extremists.

Let us see, in this context, what role the Tatas played. If Dadabhai Naoroji was a pioneer of the ideology of economic nationalism in India, Jamsetji Tata and his sons gave it a tangible form. This they did through the founding of an iron and steal industry against all odds and through their promotion of the cause of electrification, technical education and science. Politically, Jamsetji had a dual role. "Through their peculiar position", he publicly declared, the Parsis had "benefited more than any other class by English rule, and . . . their gratitude to that rule is, as it ought to be, in due proportion to the advantage derived from it. . . ."[55] Yet he was also a nationalist who remained close to the Congress through his contacts with Dadabhai and D.E. Wacha. That one of the textile mills of the Tatas was named after the Empress and another was named 'Swadeshi' signifies how tactical considerations dominated his nationalism and politics. Jamsetji's heirs too maintained close links of finance and friendship with the Congress and profited from the Swadeshi movement.[56] They stood for a smooth transfer of power through a compromise with British imperialism and thus reflected their own class character. Leading Marwari houses like the Birlas, too, exhibited more or less the same attitude.

Many more Parsi capitalists maintained their links with the national movement, however tenuous and transitory those might have been. S.R. Bomanji, B.P. Wadia and J.B. Petit—all of them rich—were active in the Home Rule movement, and Petit was amongst the financiers of the Swarajists in 1924. A.B. Godrej, whose entrepreneurial zeal owed much to Gandhian influence, was a big donor to the Tilak Swaraj Fund. Sir Ness Wadia, the textile magnate, too, was known to have funded the Swarajists in return for their support on the fiscal question. When, despite a boycott call, the wealthy Parsis voted the Prince of Wales an address of welcome in 1921, as many as 1500 Parsis signed a protest document. Men like K.F. Nariman, S.D. Saklatwalla and Madame R.K. Cama contributed consistently even to left nationalism. It is true that only a minority of the Parsis came out in support of the national cause and that support was often ambivalent, hesitant and conservative.[57] But was the political behaviour pattern different in the case of other Indian business communities like the Khojas, the Bohoras and the Marwari Banias? Surely there was a difference but it was one of degree not of kind. And such a difference was increasingly perceptible only after 1918. Parsi enterprise declined in significance after the crisis of 1929. Economic problems apart, the Parsis were by then increasingly facing many social problems of their own creation. These resulted from such things as their easy access to the Parsi Panchayat controlled institutional charity, their inbreeding, their self-imposed checks on population growth and their high degree of Anglicization.

Today the community is seized seemingly with a sense of rootlessness, despite its basic Gujarati-linguistic indentity. The Parsis took more than their due part in India's nation-building activities once. Nonetheless, they failed to integrate their community fully with the emergent nation at large. Their disproportionately large presence on all-India platforms of the Congress movement until about 1906 could have been envied by the

Khojas, the Bohoras or even the Marwari Banias. They migrated to the west from time to time in considerable numbers, yet significant numbers remained to conserve a distinct Parsi community in India. In this respect they have been quite unlike the Indian Jews and Armenians.

NOTES

1. D.R. Gadgil, *Origins of the Modern Indian Business Class: An Interim Report* (New York, 1959), pp. i-iii and 16. Gadgil notes that the Indian business communities form an integrated economic pattern and that the activities of any of them could not be studied in isolation from the rest. Yet, he confirms his earlier 1951 finding that historically, the members of the different communities did not "show a similarity of behaviour patterns or a degree of social cohesion which would justify their being called members of one business class".
2. We have dated estimates—whatever their worth—of the number of Parsis in various towns before and after 1850. For example, the number of the Parsis in Bombay was estimated at 29,000 in 1844. It was censused at 49,201 in 1864 and 44,091 in 1872. For Surat, this number was above 13,200 in 1807, 10,000 in May 1816 and 6,500 in 1872; for Broach, 3,101 in 1807 and about 2,000 in 1872. Amongst other sources, W. Hamilton, *A Geographical, Statistical and Historical Description of Hindostan and Adjacent Countries* (London, 1820), Vol. I, pp. 616 and 722.
3. *Economic and Political Weekly*, (EPW), Vol. 5, 29 August 1970 and *ibid.*, 28 November 1970, respectively. We raised some of the relevant issues also earlier in another paper entitled "Why Industrial Revolution Did N t Take Place in India?—A Note for Discussion", form'ng a part of the unpublished *Proceedings of the Seminar on Problems of Social and Economic History* (Aligarh Muslim University, 16-20 December 1968). I make a mention of this working paper, even though unpublished, since it has been widely commented upon by V.I. Pavlov in his *Historical Premises for India's Transition to Capitalism: Late 18th to Mid-19th Century* (Moscow, 1979), pp. 27-31, 232-3, 243, 290 and 332-51.
4. Quote from A. Das Gupta, *Indian Merchants and the Decline of Surat c. 1700-1750* (Wiesbaden, 1979), p. 2.
5. *Imperial Gazetteer* (New Edn.), Vol. 18, pp. 423-5; Hamilton, n. 2, p. 615; John Fryer, *A New Account of the East India and Persia, Being Nine Years' Travels, 1672-81*, Vol. 1 (London, 1909), p. 295.

   The strain of cattle, mentioned by Fryer appears to be what, according to *Imperial Gazetteer*, was known as 'hedia' in Navsari

Prant. It can be identified with the famous Kankrej breed, also known *inter-alia*, as 'Wadhiar'. This breed originated in the south-east of the Rann of Kutch amongst professional semi-nomadic cattle-breeders. Later it spread across Gujarat and was highly prized for draught and milk purposes, particularly, in the neighbourhood of Surat and Baroda. See B.L. Kaura, *Indian Breeds of Livestock* (Lucknow, 1952), p. 16. That Fryer note a special association of the Parsis with this cattle breed is significant, while his belief about its origins may be overlooked. I am indebted to H. Guha, Director of Animal Husbandry Government of West Bengal, for drawing my attention to the last-mentioned source.

6. The mechanism of converting the surplus output, extracted from agriculture as rent into commodity was varied and complex. Even in cases where the peasants paid their taxes in kind the quantities of agricultural produce so extracted went largely into market circulation, rather than directly into consumption. In fact, in the later part of Aurangzeb's rule and under the Marathas, the peasants were asked to pay their dues in kind in Gujarat.
7. For example, the Tili caste in Bengal was split into two castes—one specializing in the procesing of oilseeds and the other specializing in the trade of oil and general trade. Similarly, the weaving caste of Bengal was also split into one of yarn and cloth traders (*basak*) and another of weavers (*tanti*).
8. E. Kulke, *The Parsees in India* (Delhi, 1974), pp. 48-49; Hamilton, Vol. I, n. 2, p. 614.
9. Manucci's observation, "these people have made a vow never to go upon the sea", quoted in B.G. Gokhale, *Surat in the Seventeenth Century: A Study in Urban History of Pre-Modern India* (Bombay, 1979), p. 38. Taboos regarding cooked food made long-distance sea voyages difficult for the Parsis, as in the case of the Hindus. For the other point, Hamilton, n. 2, p. 615; also, Kulke, n. 8, pp. 55, 79n and 106n.
10. J. Davies, trans., *The Voyage and Travels of J. Alber de Mandelslo* (London, 1669), p 59; Gokhale, n. 9, pp. 37-38 and 81; Alexander Hamilton, *A New Account of the East Indies* in V.J. Pinkerron, ed. *Voyages and Travels in All Parts of the World*, Vol. 8 (London, 1811), p. 320.
11. Abul Fazal, *Ain-i-Akbari*, Vol II (trans. from Persian. Calcutta, 1949). p. 262. The Parsi association with the oil can be inferred from the Parsi character of the town mentioned, and the fact that an ancestor of Dadabhai Naoroji from the same town won special favours from Nur Jahan in 1618 for his skill as a perfumer.
12. Indrani Ray, *Of Trade and Traders in Seventeenth Century India: An Unpublished French Memoir by George Roques* (Mimeographed Occasional Paper No. 26. CSSSC, Calcutta), p. 48
13. J. Ovington, *A Voyage to Surat in the Year 1689* (H.G. Rawlinson, ed., London, 1929), pp. 216-22. Another European traveller during the 16th

century also noted the persence of an "inclination for hard work" amongst the Parsis, see Kulke, n. 8, 30n.

14. Ovington, n. 13, p. 166; Gokhale, n. 9, pp. 90-91 and Surendra Gopal, *Commerce and Crafts in Gujarat 16th and 17th Centuries* (New Delhi, 1975), pp. 214 and 215n.
15. Quotes from Fryer in Gokhale, n. 9, pp. 38-39.
16. *Ibid.*, p. 122; Gopal, n. 14, pp. 103, 184 and 206 and Das Gupta, n. 4, pp. 38, 278n and 81n; Om Prakash, *The Dutch East India Company and the Economy of Bengal 1650-1717* (Unpublished Ph.D. thesis, Delhi School of Economics, 1967), p. 471 and Appendix F (Tables 1 and 2) containing an analysis of the Hughli and Balasore shipping lists. Of the 215 non-European ship-owners' names entered for 1681-1718 in the Hughli lists, only two could be identified by him as Parsis, as against 33 as Hindus and 180 as Muslims. There was no Parsi name amongst the one hundred entries in the Balasore shipping lists for the same period.
17. W.H. Coates, *The Old Country Trade of the East Indies* (London, 1911), p. 56; K.N. Banaji, *Memoirs of the Late Framji Cowasji Banaji by His Great Grandson* (Bombay, 1892), pp. 6-8; D.F. Karaka, *History of the Parsis.* Vol. II (London, 1884), pp. 54-55; Holden Furber, *Bombay Presidency in the Mid-Eighteenth Century* (Bombay, 1965), p. 4 for information on Naoroji Rustomji's purchase of 12 pewter distilling worms and 3 small stills. In 1737 Naoroji was once more back in Surat as the English Company's broker.
18. As analyzed and tabulated by Kulke, n. 8, pp. 51-54.
19. W. Foster, (ed.), *English Factories in India* (1646-50), pp. 157 and 255 and *ibid.* (1650-60), pp. 76 and 162 cited by Gopal, n. 14, p. 225. The Bohoras were originally a peasant community.
20. See n. 18. For evidence on the low remuneration and oppression of weavers see Pavlov, n. 3, pp. 234-37. The weavers were completely dependent on their *muquaddams*, through whom they received advances.
21. Quote by Pavlov, n. 3, p. 334; also the source mentioned below in n. 49, Pallonji Bomanji Palkhiwalla's carriage manufactory, established in 1808 with an initial capital of Rs. 500, was a going concern till the end of the 19th century; some of its European-type coaches used to have a foreign market. The first manufactory to produce a new type of bullock-carts, designed by a British revenue survey officer (Lt. Gaisford), was set up with the help of a Parsi at Timbhurni in Sholapur district.
22. W. Hamilton, *East India Gazetteer*, Vol. I (London, 1828), p. 261; Hamilton. II (1820), n. 2, p. 156; R.A Wadia, *The Bombay Dockyard and the Wadia Master Builders* (2nd edn., Bombay, 1957), p. 170: evidence of John F. Mitchel in *Minutes of the Evidence Taken before the Select Committee of the House of Commons on Petitions Related to East India Built Shipping*, *P.P.* No. 115, London), pp. 527-41.
23. Sources mentioned in n. 22. In Surat during 1720-50, a master ship-

carpenter's daily wage was one silver rupee, usually equivalent to 64 copper pice, as against 40 pice for other ship-carpentry and 28 pice for ordinary carpenters. Das Gupta, n. 4, p. 44.

24. Pavlov, n. 3, p. 331.
25. Wadia, n. 22, p. 170.
26. *Ibid.*, p. 69; Maria Graham, *Journal of Residence in India* (Edinburgh, 1812), pp. 44-45; for bio-data of the Wadias, H.D. Darukhanawalla, *Parsi Lustre on Indian Soil*, Vol. I (Bombay, 1939), pp. 84-85 and R.A. Wadia, *Scions of Lawji Family* (Bombay, 1964).
27. Wadia, n. 26, pp 48-52; Banaji, n. 17, pp. 18-19; B.B. Kling, *Partner in Empire: Dwarkanath Tagore and the Age of Enterprise in Eastern India* (University of California Press, 1976), pp. 63 and 90-91; Mrs. Postans, *Western India in 1838*, Vol. I. (London, 1839) p. 122; Christine Dobbin, *Urban Leadership in Western India: Politics and Communities in Bombay City 1840-1885* (Oxford, 1972), pp. 14, 18, 22-23 and 54.
28. For the bio-data, Wadia, n. 26, pp. 42-65; Darukhanawalla, n. 26, pp. 316-17; C.R. Low, *History of the Indian Navy 1613-1863*, Vol. I (London, 1877), pp. 278 and 298.
29. Amalendu Guha, "Raw Cotton of Western India: Output, Transportation and Marketing 1750-1850" in *Indian Economic and Social History Review*, Vol. 9, No. 1, pp. 2-4 and 33-34 (appended statistics); Compilation Group, *The Opium War* (Peaking, 1976), pp. 8-9 and 37; for the data on ships, C.N. Parkinson, *Trade in the Eastern Seas 1793-1813* (London, 1937), p. 336; Karaka, n. 17, Vol. I, pp. xx-xxi; on opium, *Imperial Gazetteer*, Vol. 3, n. 5, p. 244.
30. Bombay Cotton Committee, 1847, cited in Guha, n. 29, pp. 9-12, 28 and also, pp. 33-34. For the 1833-34 to 1845-46 period, we have overlooked the quantitatively insignificant raw cotton exports from the port of Cochin.
31. *EPW*, 29 August 1970, n. 3. During the period, it was difficult to determine the ownership of a ship from the declared owner's name. Since ships were often jointly owned by European and Parsi firms and these frequently changed hands. The declared owner was not always the sole or even the real owner. So was the case with the consignments. Yet, the limited data that are available, suggest that the Parsi firms had an edge over their European rivals until the Opium War.
32. Guha, n. 29, p. 19. The information that majority shares were held by Indians in the Bombay Insurance Society in 1852-55 and in the Apollo Press Company in 1848 is supplied by A.K. Bagchi. His source is *Sir Jamsetji Jijeebhoy Papers*, Vol. 44 (Bombay University Library).
33. Evidence of W. Prideux in *Report from the Select Committee on the Growth of Cotton in India together with the Minutes of Evidence, Appendix and Index* (*P.P.* No. 511, London, 1848), p. 47.
34. Darukhanawalla, n. 26, pp. 10-12 and 437; Banaji, n. 17, pp.

15-19 and 40-43; Pavlov, n. 3, pp. 329-30; Dobbin, n. 27, pp. 13-18 and 22; J.C. Bagal, "Rustomjee Cowasji", *Modern Review*, Vol. 54, No. 1, July 1933.

35. Wadia, n. 26, pp. 67-69 and 92-116; Darukhanawalla, n. 26, pp. 84-87, *Times of India*, 21 July 1885.
36. Karaka, II, n. 17, pp. 132-33 and 140-41; G.A. Natesan (comp.), *Famous Parsis* (Madras, 1930), pp. 1-19 and 45-56; Darukhanawalla, n. 26, pp. 93 and 340-41; Dobbin, n. 27, pp. 14, 18 and 54.
37. Coates, n. 17, pp. 159-60 and 203; R.S. Rungta, *Rise of Business Corporations in India 1851-1900* (Cambridge, 1970), pp. 43n and 92. *Gazetteer of Bombay City and Island*, (Bombay, 1969), Vol. 1, p. 393 and Bagchi, n. 46 below, pp. 263 and 350-1.
38. For quotes and the information, C.N. Cooke, *The Rise, Progress and Present Conditions of Banking in India* (Calcutta, 1863), pp. 141-42, 329-36 and 342; Wadia, n. 26, p. 113; Darukhanawalla, n. 26, pp. 340-41; Rungta, n. 37, pp. 19n and 38n; Dobbin, n. 27, p. 18.
39. *Viscajee Merjee and Pestonji Merjee* : *Copies of All Papers Relating to the Case of Viscajee Merjee and Pestonji Merjee, British Subjects and Parsi Inhabitants of Bombay and Hyderabad* (P.P. No. 996, House of Commons, London, 20 August 1853), pp. 6-10, 31-38, 50, 86-92 and 104-13; Guha, n. 29, pp. 8-9.
40. The same as n. 39. The Meherjis were also involved in the China trade and had ships. Two members of the family paid a short visit to U.K. in 1851 in connection with their dispute with the Nizam.
41. Dobbin, n 27, pp. 96-97; Pavlov, n. 3, pp. 226 and 331; Darukhanawalla, n. 26, 101-102; Hamilton, I, n. 2, pp. 607 and 615. My attention to *Baroda Gazetteer*, (Bombay, 1923), Vol. 2, p. 698 and *Bombay Gazetteer*, (Bombay, 1880), Vol. 6, p. 247 on the relevant points was drawn by David Hardiman who was also kind enough to check these for me.
42. For Dr. Hove's comments, *Selections from the Records of the Bombay Government*, No. 16, New Series (Bombay, 1855), p. 8; Graham, n. 26 pp. 44-45.
43. Banaji, n. 17, pp. 16-18; Karaka, II, n. 17, pp. 113-14; Darukhanawalla, n. 26, pp. 101-02 and 120; Dobbin, n. 27, pp. 12-13; S.K. Sen, *The House of Tatas 1839-1939* (Calcutta, 1975), pp. 22-3.
44. Karaka, I, n. 17, p. 259; D.E. Owen, *British Opium Policy in China and India* (New Haven, 1934), pp. 334-44.
45. Marika Vicziany, "Bombay Merchants and Structural Changes in the Export Community, 1850 to 1880" in K.N. Chaudhari and C.J. Dewey (ed.), *Economy and Society: Essays in Indian Economic and Social History* (Oxford, 1979), pp. 163-96.
46. Bagchi, A.K., *Private Investment in India 1900-1939* (Cambridge, 1972), pp. 168-9 and particularly Table 6.2.
47. Vicziany, n. 45, pp. 163-96.
48. Harris, F.R. *Jamsetji Nusserwanji Tata: A Chronicle of Life* (Oxford) 1925), pp. 5-15.

49. *The Gazetteer of Bombay City and Islands*, I, pp. 475-76; for quote and information Darukhanawalla, n. 26, pp. 382-3 and 416-7.
50. *Ibid.*, pp. 198, 201, 423-4 and 435.
51. *Ibid.*, pp. 450-51.
52. For the 1827 data cited by Rammohan Roy see S.C. Sarkar, (ed.), *Rammohun Roy on Indian Economy* (Calcutta, 1965), p. 22; for the remaining data, *First Appendix to the Third Report of the Select Committee of the House of Commons and Minutes of Evidence of the Affairs of the East India Company, 17th February to 6 October 1831* (P.P. No. 320 A). p. 328.
53. Dobbin, n. 27, pp. 259-60.
54. Harris, n. 48, pp. 98-105 and N.G. Jog, *Saga of Scindia: Struggle for the Revival of Indian Shipping and Shipbuilding* (Bombay, 1969), pp. 13-16.
55. Tata's statement in the *Times of India*, 12 April 1894.
56. A.D.D. Gordon, *Businessmen and Politics: Rising Nationalism and a Modernising Economy in Bombay 1918-1933* (Delhi/Canberra, 1978), pp. 66.
57. For information, *ibid.*, pp. 49, 66, 157-62 and 185; Kulke, n. 8, pp. 190-203.

9

Class Character of the Gujarati Business Community

Dwijendra Tripathi & M.J. Mehta

About three decades ago, D.R. Gadgil observed that India developed a number of business communities rather than a business class.[1] Though he did not state explicitly, he perhaps implied that this development in India differed markedly from the development in Europe and other countries where capitalistic enterprises flourished. The observation was made in a research proposal aimed at investigating into some aspects of business leadership in India. Gadgil never completed his research on the subject and, in fairness, his hypothesis should not be taken to represent finality in his thinking. One could have, thus, ignored his remarks but for the fact that he was expressing a widely held belief. Besides, a number of scholars claiming a much greater rigour in their analyses have followed his line of thinking and discussed the evolution of the Indian business with reference to the role of the so-called business communities.[2]

None of the scholars in this genre has explained adequately the precise meaning of the term "community" or what distinguishes a community from a class. Nor do their listsof so-called business communities give us any meaningful clue to the criteria of their classification. Ethnicity, mother tongue, religion and regional affiliation are the basic characteristics which seem to have been used to divide businessmen into various categories. For a group to deserve the status of community, it is not necessary to possess all these characteristics;

in some cases the presence of only one of these criteria has been considered sufficient for a group to be treated as a separate category. In the opinion of these analysts, it appears, the term "business community" denotes a group of businessmen who, in addition to their common occupational affiliation, share certain socio-cultural features inherited from birth. It has been assumed by these analysts that the members of these business communities belonged either to Hindu castes for whom business had been the traditional occupation under the scriptural sanction, or such non-Hindu groups who had remained in business for a long time past. An indispensable common feature of these communities, their separate distinguishing characteristics notwithstanding, is that their members belong to the traditional trading castes or groups. In fact, at least one analyst has used the term community as a synonym of caste.[3]

Whether its proponents intended it or not, the community approach has an element of cultural determinism popularised by Max Weber and his followers.[4] It subsumes that the families belonging to certain specified castes which embraced business as a profession failed to transcend their narrow social limits in their occupational sphere, that the economic and infrastructural changes over a period of time made little dent on the caste basis of business profession, and that the members of the so-called non-business castes remained aloof from business. The composite effect of all this, the approach implies, was that a number of different socio-cultural pluralities, though wedded to a common occupation, failed to evolve into a composite collectivity held together by a community of economic interests.

The objective of this paper is to test the community approach of analysis with reference to Gujarat. The vastness and the complexity of the country precludes a national focus in a study of this kind and regional variations affecting economic and business activities justifies concentration on a particular region. Gujarat has been chosen because of several considerations. During the pre-industrial times, the region was the scene of thriving commercial and trading activities, thanks to its location, its long coastal lines and its ports, reckoned to be the finest in India. A rich hinterland fed the economy of the region, major trade routes that passed through Gujarat facilitated its interaction with other parts of India, and the resultant business opportunities contributed to the growth of vigorous urban centres and attracted to it enterprising merchants and traders who enriched the commercial sphere. Gujarat's trade with other countries and with other parts of India led to the accumulation of sizable capital with the consequence that the region was among the earliest to witness the rise of factory based modern industries.[5] Presenting a spectacle of changing economic environment and business opportunities over a relatively long period of time, Gujarat, thus, provides an excellent reference point to analyse the impact of these changes on the changing structure of business leadership.

Perhaps it requires no special insights into the social history of India to assert that for several centuries the business profession in Gujarat, as in the rest of the country, must have been controlled overwhelmingly, almost exclusively, by the Vaishya castes. In a society where social divisions originated in and coincided, in a broad sense, with occupational affiliation, prescriptive sanction must have had a decisive influence on economic choices. Strong economic stimuli beaconing to higher rewards outside the traditional occupational mould could have challenged the stranglehold of prescription, but such counter-forces remained too feeble or almost inoperative on the Indian scene for a long time. The dominance of the Vaishya castes on business activities during these periods must be seen in this perspective.

It is by no means easy to determine when the equilibrium between the social division on the one hand and the occupational division on the other began to be disturbed, but there is evidence to suggest that certain degree of occupational mobility had already taken place in the major urban centres of Gujarat when the trading operations of the major European companies with India began. Prospects of material gain generated by flourishing opportunities for inland as well as foreign commerce had created what one may call a business culture. Folk tales were woven around "*shah sodagars*" or great businessmen, and merchants and traders occupied a place of honour in popular imagination. In many parts of India business and businessmen were looked down upon,[6] but not so in Gujarat. A modern writer has rightly observed: "Its [Gujarat's] traders and financiers, not its royal officials, nor its landholders and chieftains, nor even its Brahmins, set the tone of society in Gujarat long before modern times and made business valued more than normally respected for all."[7] In fact, rarely was the business activity considered inferior to the priestly or martial profession associated with the Brahman and Kshatriya castes. Referring to this aspect of Gujarati life, Abbe Dubois, a French scholar and traveller, wrote in the early years of the 19th century that trade was never a taboo in Gujarat, and in fact Gujarati Brahmans were "excellent men of business."[8]

The Abbe's references is to the manner in which most of the Gujarati Brahmans were carrying on their ordained priestly occupation as well as their mercantile activities which had lured at least some Brahmans much before the French clergyman's visit to India. Numerous references to Brahman businessmen are contained in a group of documents known as *Khatpatras*. A large number of these quasi-legal documents pertaining to transactions in real estate are preserved in the library of the Gujarat Vidya Sabha at Ahmedabad. One of these mentions that in 1642 one Trikamlal Bhatt, a Brahman, sold his shop at Mangalore in Surat district to a utensil manufacturer. Another Brahman businessman has been mentioned in a *Khatpatra* of 1656 which records that Kalyan Joshi of the Shrimali Brahman caste sold his shop in the Manek Chowk area of Ahmedabad to a Jain businessman.[9] Manek Chowk, it must be added, has been the principal commercial centre in the city ever since the birth of Ahmedabad.

Ahmedabad was not the only urban centre where members of the so-called non-business castes transcended the barriers of scriptural injunctions to partake of gainful opportunities. In the records of the English East India Company, we come across some instances of Brahmans and Khastriyas having taken to trading and money-lending in Surat in the 17th century. Somji Chitta and Chhotadas Thakur, who served the English as brokers, came from the Rajput stock, whereas Venidas and Dayaram, belonging to the same profession, were Nagar Brahmans.[10] The Nagars of Gujarat had achieved great heights in educational and administrative fields previously but business had seldom been an area of their interests. It is possible that the need for native intermediaries to facilitate the foreign traders' interaction with the Indian merchants lured the Nagars into the lucrative business of brokers.

The same factor helped the banking business of a Nagar family. Arjunji Nathji Travadi (c. 1680-1760) originally belonged to Banaras where he was operating as banker. What connections he had with Surat is not known, but it seems that sometime around the turn of the 18th century, he migrated to the famous port city in Gujarat. In the Surat factory records beginning with 1719 the Travadis have been referred to as "our principal shroff". On more than one occasion, the English interceded with the Mughal authorities on behalf of the Nagar bankers who operated on a large scale and maintained cordial relations with the English company. According to a newspaper report of the 19th century, the Travadis were the first bankers of the East India Company.[11]

These, admittedly, are stray examples but they are illustrative of a trend. Also, simply because all brokers with whom the Europeans had dealings have been referred to as "*Banias*" in the factory records, it should not be assumed, as is commonly done, that all of them belonged to the Vaishya groups.[12] The fact is that the Europeans used the word "Bania" in a generic sense referring to businessmen in general rather than in a specific sense to signify their caste affiliation; for the Hindu population in general the word used was "Gentoo". Thus it is not easy to determine the caste affiliation of a large number of brokers, shroffs and merchants whose names are not always mentioned with their caste names in the European records. But our examples are sufficient indication that the number of persons who deviated from the preordained occupational pattern to take advantage of the burgeoning economic opportunities was much larger than we perhaps know. There is no denying the fact, however, that a large majority of businessmen in the 17th and the 18th century Gujarat belonged to the Vaishya stock. This was so because the cake of custom, to borrow a phrase from Edwin F. Gay,[13] could be broken only gradually.

Three groups were important among those who could be identified with the Vaishya subdivision of the Hindu *Varnashrama* scheme: the Vaishnava Banias, the Jains, and the Bhatias. Of these, perhaps only the Vaishnava Banias could claim a direct lineage from the original Vaishya stock. The Jains technically did not belong to any caste or even to the Hindu fold. A large majority of the Gujarati Jains were Oswals who claimed a Kshatriya origin. The forefathers of some of the most prominent among them had migrated from the Marwar region of Rajasthan in olden days, but the later generations adopted Gujarati as the mother tongue and assimilated various traits of the Gujarati culture.[14] The Bhatias, like the Jains, were migrants from the Lahore-Multan region and like the Jains, claimed to belong to the Kshatriya sub-division. Having settled down in the Kutch-Kathiawar region of Gujarat in the 14th century, they embraced Vaishnavism two centuries later and adopted many of the Vaishnava traits, such as abstinence from meat eating. Whatever the origin of the Jains and the Bhatias, in popular imagination, they are associated with the Vaishya stock no less than the Vaishnava Banias. Among the non-Hindu groups the most important were the Muslims and the Parsis.

Except for the Parsis perhaps none of these categories, whether Hindu or non-Hindu, constituted a cohesive cultural group. The Bhatias, were distinctly different in habits and mores of behaviour from the Vaishnava Banias in spite of their adherence to a common religion. For instance, while foreign travel was considered taboo by the latter, the former never suffered from this inhibition. Perhaps because of this, the Bhatias found it easier to develop trade links not only with far-off regions in India but also with the ports of Muscat and Arabia. In fact a large number of them settled down in these flourishing ports.[15] The cultural traits of the Jains and Vaishnava Banias also differed in many respects, and for a long time, these two groups looked at each other with suspicion and even hostility.[16] The Muslims were divided among the Khojas, Bohoras, Memons etc. who formed separate socio-cultural groups of their own.[17] Perhaps the only elements of non-economic character which were common to all these categories of merchants was that they spoke a common language (though the Bhatias claimed Kutchchi as their mother tongue rather than Gujarati which they spoke fluently) and belonged to a common geographical region.

Because of the cultural ties being strong, various categories of businessmen depended on their social rather than occupational linkages to further their business interests. In other words, merchants belonging to a particular socio-cultural background had, by and large, much closer business connections with one another than with their counterparts whose socio-cultural backgrounds were different. But they were by no means averse to making common cause with other categories to avert a crisis, meet a common threat, or promote such business interests which transcended the narrow interest of a single community.

An action of the Surat merchant in 1669 provides an excellent example. As a result of Aurangzeb's policy of religious persecution, the nephew of Tulsidas Parekh, a prominent broker of Vaishnava Bania stock, converted to Islam. In protest, the Hindu merchants gave a call for a general strike. Responding to this appeal, about 8000 persons migrated *en masse* to the neighbouring town of Broach. The effect of this action on the business life of Surat can best be stated in the words of Gerald Aungier, the President of the English factory in the city:

> Ever since the flight of the Banians, the trade of Surat hath suffered great obstruction and it's the opinion of many wise men that it will prove of fatall consequences to the utter ruin of all. . . . The people in Surat suffered great want, for the Banians having found themselves under severe penalties not to open their shops without order from their Manager, or general Council, there was not any provisions to be gott, the Tanksall (mint) and custom house shut, no money to be procured soe much for house expenses much lesse for trade, which was wholly at a stand and soe it will continue till their return.[18]

There is little doubt that the Banias who reacted against Aurangzeb's bigotry belonged to different castes, as a servant of the East India Company remarked only three years later. Referring to the Hindu population of Surat as comprising Rajputs, Brahmans, and Banias he added: "These are the principal tribes or as (we) call them castes . . . and these are generally their professions, but that several of them are one anothers and many of them of other profession. . . . as there are Brahmans that are soldiers and merchants soe well as Priests, and there are Banians that are Labourers, Handicraftsmen (and soe as Merchants) and curers of Herbs, and there are weavers of all sects, Moore Hindoos, and Parsees."[19] That the protesting group consisted of persons belonging to a variety of socio-cultural backgrounds is also clear from a letter that Bhimji Parekh, one of their leaders, wrote to the authorities of the English East India Company in 1673. Expressing the desire of his fellow merchants to settle down in Bombay, he emphasised that they would do so only if religious liberty was guaranteed to *every sect* to which they belonged.[20]

The instrument of the Surat protest was, as Aungier mentioned, the *mahajan.* Reminiscent of the ancient trade guilds, such *mahajans* were an essential element of the business life in every urban centre of Gujarat in the 17th and the 18th centuries. If Aungier is to be trusted, Surat probably had an apex body of merchants or a general assembly, as he calls it. This body must have been composed of persons belonging to or claiming to represent various segments of the business population. It is probable that it was some kind of a federation of various *mahajans* or trade associations in which the merchants were organized. They were different from the caste Panchayat, called *Panch*, which was not concerned with business matters alone; practically all aspects of life, social as well as economic, of the members of a caste came under the purview of its *panch.* Most of the *panchs* represented the artisan castes whose members carried on their business on the basis of skills handed down from one generation to the other, such as goldsmith, carpenter, blacksmith etc., perhaps because there was no real cleavage between the social and professional matters among these castes. Practical difficulties in acquiring the craftsmanship, that characterised these castes, must have made entry into their professions by other castes extremely difficult. This, coupled with low expectancy of economic reward in their profession and their low position in the caste hierarchy, helped the artisan castes to retain their homogenous character in social as well as occupational spheres.[21]

In contrast to the *panchs*, the *mahajans* were predominantly occupational bodies representing those who were engaged in a particular occupation. Much more heterogenous in character, they had little to do with the socio-cultural problems of their members; they were mainly concerned with the problems facing the occupation in question. The Soni Panch, for instance, would address itself to the problems of the goldsmith caste in general, as all those who were engaged in this specialized craft belonged to this caste, but if a Soni developed into a jeweller, not concerned with the craftsmanship as much as with transactions in precious jewels, his professional matters came under the control of the Jewellers' Mahajan whose members belonged to diverse social backgrounds.[22] The head of the Jewellers' Mahajan in Ahmedabad in the first half of the 17th century was Shantilal, a jain merchant, who traded in various commodities, and also acted as a broker to the Mughal emperors and banker to the English East India Company.[23]

That the *mahajans* represented occupations rather than castes is clear from a somewhat later example. In the middle of the 18th century, a large number of Gujaratis migrated to Poona to set up banking business with a view to financing the Peshwas and other Maratha sardars. The emigrants included some of the most prominent businessmen of the times such as Haribhakti, Dullabh Govindji, Dayaram Atmaram Shah, Vishundas Harikishandas, Purshattam Morli, and Dalaram Keshavji. Belonging to different castes, they carried with them the tradition of *mahajan* to their new headquarters and set up a "*mahajan* of twelve castes" to promote and safeguard the interests of their banking business.[24]

The *mahajan* organization did not run on similar lines in all the cities. Unlike Surat for instance, Ahmedabad never had a city wide organization contrary to the suggestion of some scholars.[25] Not less than 53 organizations of this kind existed in the city in the first quarter of the 18th century as the signatures of the representatives of "all the *mahajans*" appended to a document of 1725 indicates.[26] The capital city of Gujarat also had a *nagarsheth* ever since the middle of the 17th century, a position which developed in Surat and other urban centres much later. The *nagarsheth* was the link between the city and the state, used his influence to settle disputes between various *mahajans*, and on occasions conferred with the heads of other *mahajans* with a view to evolving a commons trategy towards specific problems facing the city or the businessmen in general. In short, he was a sort of father figure to the city.[27]

The *nagarsheth* did not owe his power and authority to any formal action on the part of the civic population or the state. He was neither appointed by the ruling power nor was he elected by anyone. The position evolved gradually. The most influential merchant began to be looked upon as the leader of the city through popular sanction and began to be recognized as such by the public as well as the state. In due course the position became hereditary.[28] Under his leadership the Ahmedabad *mahajans* on several occasions worked in unison to safeguard their own interests or those of the city. One such example is provided by the action of Khushalchand, a descendant of Sheth Shantidas, at the time of the Maratha raid in 1724. The Jain Sheth paid a handsome ransom to the greedy invaders to buy off the safety of the city and its inhabitants and ensure stability and peace so much valued by businessmen. To reward their leader for his noble sacrifice, "all the *mahajans*" of the city representing every segment of the business population resolved to assign in perpetuity a small percentage of the town cess to the Sheth and his descendants.[29] Another occasion when the *mahajans* led by the *nagarsheth* represented to the ruling authorities with the plea to ensure peaceful environment was when the Marathas occupied Ahmedabad in 1753. They did so once again when General Goddard took possession of the city in 1780.[30] The Surat example of 1669 indicates that merchants were capable of uniting against a common threat even if they did not have a common leader or hereditary head. And there was at least one occasion when a Gujarati businessman joined his counterparts in another part of the country to safeguard their common interest. In 1795 Shri Krishna Travadi of the Travadi banking family personally went to Calcutta to represent to the Governor general against the incidents of piracies and robberies jointly with the famous bankers of Bengal including the illustrious Jagatseths.[31]

None of our examples, except perhaps the last one, indicates that the merchant groups united to safeguard what may be considered purely commercial or business interests. Business life was much less complex and the interests of various occupational groups were much less intertwined. The result was that occupational linkages between various groups of businessmen were limited so that few developments could threaten the interests of all the groups together. But what is significant is that all were willing to collaborate to ensure healthy market conditions lest commercial transactions suffered to their common detriment.

British occupation of Gujarat intensified the process of occupational mobility. The new rulers introduced a series of changes to safeguard their imperial interests but a welcome and wholly unintended byproduct of these measures was the expansion in the business horizon. The establishment of a liberal legal framework and a better enforcement of law and order than heretofore promised greater security to people, the impact of English education and India's contact with European liberalism resulted in the rise of a number of reform movements and the dogmas and prescriptive sanctions began to loose their grip on occupational choices. The result was that many who had kept away from business partly because of the prescriptive system, reinforced by relatively weak economic stimuli, began to perceive new avenues of economic gain.[32] A large number of Kanbis. for instance, who had all along been engaged in agriculture, trekked to the urban centres like Ahmedabad where they took to weaving, trading and money-lending. Some of them, as we shall see later, invested their profits in industrial enterprises.[33]

Whether the so-called "social revolution" generated by the intervention of Britist colonialism, without which no progress according to Karl Marx[33] was possible, was sufficient to effect significant change in the time-honoured mode of production and business operations is doubtful. Perhaps the most decisive influence in this respect was that of a new technoloy which the Indians could hope to avail of because of the new colonial linkages. The emergence of the factory-based textile industry was a direct outcome of this development. It is Significant that the pioneering role in promoting textile production both in Bombay and Ahmedabad was played by those who had gained sufficient understanding of the production processes in England through their contacts with English merchants and administrators in India, and experienced the impact of new social ethos.[34] Ranchhodlal Chhotalal and Bechardas Laskari, the founders of the first and the second mills in Ahmedabad respectively, belonged to non-business castes; the former was a Nagar Brahman and the latter a Kanbi. As a civil servant, Ranchhodlal developed interest in textile manufacturing through his interaction with British officials some of whom had close links with machinery manufactures in England. Bechardas' connection with the British circles was due to his family having been suppliers of provisions to the British army in India.[35]

For almost two decades after the birth of the Ahmedabad textile industry, these were the only two families in the field. With the rate of interest ranging between 12 to 19 per cent in the city,[36] investment in uncertain industrial ventures would have appeared to be an opportunity loss to the traders and moneylenders. Since the Nagar and Kanbi pioneers could not hope to compete with the established houses in the traditional lines, they found it easier to express their entrepreneurial urge in the new field. It was only after the profitability of the textile manufacturing had been established beyond doubt that the Jains and Vaishnava Banias entered the field. With their hold on enormous capital, they soon emerged as the most dominant social groups on the industrial horizon of Gujarat, but the significance of the rise of Ranchhodlal and Bechardas—and a number of other less visible and less successful non-Vaishya mill-founders—should not be lost sight of.[37] Instead of being exceptions, they symbolised a trend.

Census figures testify to this trend eloquently. Unfortunately, the reports of the first two censuses in the Bombay Presidency do not provide information about the occupational affiliation of various social groups in the Presidency or the Gujarat region. We, however, have detailed statistics about the Baroda territories from the report of 1881. According to it, 9369 persons in a total population of 21,85,005 were engaged in commercial and trading professions.[38] Persons in these professions have been subdivided into bankers, money-changers, ordinary moneylenders, brokers, and general dealers and shopkeepers. The following table gives the detailed breakdown of persons belonging to various Hindu castes placed in each of these categories:

OCCUPATIONAL AFFILIATION OF HINDU POPULATION IN BARODA (1881)

	Bankers	Money-exchangers	Money-lenders	Brokers	Shop-keepers
Banias & Jains	782	422	1125	N.A.	1586
Brahmans	128	58	659	N.A.	193
Kanbis	69	12	139	N.A.	39
Others	24	32	102	N.A.	471*
Total	1003	524	2025	414	3060

Source: *Census of Baroda Territories* (1881), 217-221.

*We have left 771 Macchis out of count who seem to have returned themselves as general traders.

Leaving the brokers out of our analysis, since we do not know the caste breakdown of this category, we find that out of 6612 persons engaged in some kind of business, as many as 1926 or about 30 per cent did not belong to the traditional business castes. We should also remember that these categories are not mutually exclusive (a banker, for instance, could have been a money-changer and a moneylender as well) and thus the number of persons mentioned in each category in the above table would be somewhat inflated. But since this would affect the total number in each caste group, this problem should not bother us unduly. It is necessary to remember, however, that the possibility of inflation would be somewhat proportionate to the actual number in each caste group. The larger the figure the greater will be the possibility of upward distortion. In actual terms, thus, percentage of persons belonging to non-Vaishya castes in business was, in likelihood, higher than simple arithmetical calculation would indicate. Even if we do not resort to this statistical hairsplitting, it is obvious that the participation of non-business castes in business was by no means unimpressive. And if this was the state of affairs in a princely state, where the environment offered more limited business opportunities,[39] conditions in British Gujarat would have certainly been better.

If we had similar data for the earlier period, we could have established more convincingly that occupational mobility in the region was increasing. But the census of 1872, the first ever taken in the Presidency, does not give the occupational affiliation of people according to caste. Unfortunately, we do not have these figures separately for the Gujarat region from the later censuses also. There is enough in the general description given in these reports as well as other official literature to indicate that caste affiliation was becoming a less significant factor in occupational choices. The *Gazetteer of theB aroda State* published in 1923 clearly states that the castes had abandoned the narrow limits of their special occupations laid down for them by the scriptures and tradition.[40] That this was applicable to the whole of Gujarat is clear from the Census Report of 1911 which states in clear terms that caste had ceased to be a factor in the choice of profession in this region. A case in point is the example of the Kanbis. By 1911, as many as 65 per cent of them had abandoned agriculture, their traditional occupation, and taken, among other professions, to trade and industry. Similar occupational changes are indicated in other castes as well.[41] And new entrants in business were partaking of opportunities not only in the commercial field but also in the industrial sector. Two prominent examples of this trend are Mafatlal Gagalbhai, a Kanbi who branched off into textiles in 1905, and B.D. Amin, a Patidar who initiated, in collaboration with two scientists, a venture which resulted into today's Alembic Chemical Works.[42]

Perhaps more significant was the fact that various caste groups following a particular occupation began to take more concerted action to safeguard their occupational interests than seems to have been the case before. The new entrants in business, who crossed the barriers of tradition, did not sever their links with their social or religious groupings or abandon the caste rituals or practices; but in occupational matters they identified themselves with their new profession. The most telling example of this trend is provided by Ranchhodlal Chhotalal. On the occasion of the opening of his first mill in 1861, the founder of the Ahmedabad textile industry, declared that he "could not have succeeded without the cooperation of my partners (Jains and Vaishnavas Banias) and the full confidence they have reposed in me."[43] It is well known that it was the lack of cooperation from the bankers and merchants that delayed by several years the consummation of the Nagar industrialist's dream. But aware of the importance of establishing meaningful links with the financial circles, the Nagar industrialist preferred to look at the positive side of their behaviour rather than lament over what was now inconsequential.

Perhaps a more significant example of Ranchhodlal's desire to strengthen his ties with the Jain and Vaishnava banias was his reply to a group of social reformers. Approached by them for contribution to promote the cause of widow remarriage, he expressed his inability on the ground that "most of my millowning colleagues are Jains and Vaishnavas and they do not look with favour the promotion of widow remarriage. I have to work with them and I can't afford to displease them."[44] The Nagar brahman sympathised with the cause of reform and some of the prominent reformers belonged to his caste, but he did not wish to jeopardise his business connections just to help some unfortunate widows. His millowning friends reciprocated in full measure his desire to cultivate them. They looked upon him as their leader who was called upon to perform the opening ceremony of each and every mill that was established in the city following his initiative. When the Ahmedabad Millowner's Association was formed in 1893 he was elected to be its first President even though the textile industry by that time had come to be dominated by the Jains and Vaishnava Banias. A few years after his death his grandson Chinubhai Madhavalal was elected to this august office.[45] The new-comers' identification with the business occupation was indelibly registered in the popular mind also. The honorific epithet of Sheth began to be attached to their names in the same way as it had been done to those of Vaishya merchants from times immemorial.

What does this survey bring out? First, it is clear that by the beginning of the present century, the business profession had already ceased to be the sole monopoly of the Vaishya castes. When the European trading companies started their operations in India, the caste groups associated with business under scriptural dispensation and by tradition understandably dominated the scene, but the signs of a certain degree of occupational mobility were already visible. In later years, increasingly large number of people belonging to other castes were lured into business as the opportunities expanded. In fact, some caste groups such as the Bhatias, though theoretically out of the Vaishya category, began to be associated with the latter because of their participation in commercial pursuits. Industrial opportunities that unfolded themselves shortly after the establishment of the British power in Gujarat strengthened this trend still further. Consequently, caste barriers in the choice of profession practically broke down under the impact of economic stimuli and business in Gujarat came to be characterised by the presence of a variety of socio-cultural categories.

Secondly, collaboration based on occupational affiliation rather than purely socio-cultural ties became much more visible among the Gujarati businessmen as the centuries rolled by. This trend was represented in the earlier stages by the *mahajans* which operated in their respective spheres but occasionally came together to ensure peace and stability necessary for the common economic interests of their members. As the business life became more complex, more sophisticated business associations, cutting across caste and community barriers, came into being. These associations operated as economic interest groups; socio-religious matters affecting their members were attended to by other organizations. The Jain mill magnates, for instance, used the Millowners' Association as an instrument of concerted action with regard to the problems affecting the textile industry but the purely religious issues were taken care of by the Anandji Kalyanji Pedhi in which Jain members of the Association were equally active. Even the artisan *panchs*, which regulated social as well as occupational matters in earlier years, began to loose their occupational roles as their members joined professions in which other castes also participated.[46]

The two characteristics mentioned above—occupational affiliation transcending socio-cultural barriers and collaboration to safeguard economic interests as distinct from socio-cultural concerns—are essentially those of a class. We do not intend to discuss in this paper the developments after the First World War. But there are sufficient reasons to believe that these characteristics continued to gain strength in later years, as business opportunities expanded in response to a series of stimuli. To view the Gujaratis as a business community, thus, is to ignore the historical process of its development, to minimise the importance of the socio-cultural varieties that enriched the business life in Gujarat, and to underestimate the impact of economic interests in diluting the socio-cultural differences. Seen in a proper historical context, the Gujarati business community possessed some characteristics of a business class. There are reasons to believe that historical insights into the evolution of other so-called business communities would provide a similar understanding of their class character. And if that is so, each of these communities may be seen as proto-business classes which together contributed to the emergence, in due course, of an Indian business class.[47] The Gujarat experience, at any rate, suggests the need for a significant modification in the Gadgilian approach.

NOTES

1. D.R. Gadgil, *Business Communities in India* (mimeo, New York, 1951), Preface.
2. See for instance Helen B. Lamb, "Indian Business Communities and the Evolution of an Industrial Class", *Pacific Affairs*, XXVII (June 1955), 101-16 and "Business Organization and Leadership in India Today" in *Leadership and Political Institutions in India*, ed. by R. Park and I. Tinker (Princeton, 1959), 251-67; P.B. Medhora, "Entrepreneurship in India", *Political Science Quarterly*, LXXX (Dec. 1965), 558-80, and T.A. Timberg, *The Marwaris : From Traders to Industrialists* (New Delhi, 1978) are also tilt towards the community view. V.I. Pavlov, *The Indian Capitalist Class : A Historical Study* (New Delhi, 1964), which presents a Marxist perspective has not been able to extricate itself from the community framework.
3. Pavlov, *The Indian Capitalist Class*, n. 2 refers to "The Gujarati, Marwari, and other castes of merchants", p. 44. For the differences among the sociologists and anthropologists about the definition of the term "community" see B.E. Mercer, *The American Community* (New York, 1956), 25-27; also *Encylopaedia Americana* (New York, 1963), VII, 420; *Encylopaedia of Anthropology* (New York, (1976), 84.
4. H.H. Gerth and Wright Mills (eds.), *From Max Weber: Essay in Sociology* (New York, 1958), 412-13. Among the recent works on

Weberian lines is K.W. Kapp, *Hindu Culture, Economic Development and Economic Planning in India* (New York, 1963).

5. Some of the works that throw light on relative economic prosperity of Gujarat are Michael Pearson, *Merchants and Rulers of Gujarat* (Delhi, 1976); Surendra Gopal, *Commerce and Crafts in Gujarat, 16th and 17th Century* (New Delhi, 1975); Ratmanirao, *Gujaratnun Paatnagar Amdavad* (in Gujarati, Ahmedabad, 1928); B.G. Gokhale, "Ahmedabad in the 17th Century", *Journal of the Economic and Social History of the Orient*", XII (April 1969), 187-97; "Merchant Community in the XVII Century India", *Journal of Indian History*, LIV (April 1976), 117-41; and "Capital Accumulation in XVII Century Western India", *Journal of the Asiatic Society of Bombay*, XXXIX—XL (1964/65), 51-60. On the rise of factory industry in Gujarat, see S.D. Mehta, *Cotton Mills of India, 1854-1954* (Bombay, 1954).
6. Kautilya in the *Arthasastra* declared that the businessman was a thief but was not called so. A Rajasthani proverb echoes the feeling in the following words "The Jain bania does not drink water unless it is filtered but does not mind sucking the unfiltered blood of the poor".
7. Kenneth Gillion, *Ahmedabad: A Study in Indian Urban History* (Berkeley, 1968), 3.
8. Abbe J.A. Dubois, *Hindu Manners, Customs, and Ceremonies* (Oxford, 1943), 292.
9. *Khatpatras* nos 96 and 105, B.J. Institute of Research and Learning, Ahmedabad. For value of these documents for historical research see Makrand Mehta, "Khatpatras as a Source of Urban History", *Indian Archives*, XXX (January-June 1981), 22-29.
10. Makrand Mehta, "Some Aspects of Surat as a Trading Centre in the 17th Century", *Indian Historical Review*, I (September 1974), 249; also Govinddas Gopaldas Shah, "Punana Gujarati" in *Shri Pune Gujarati Bandhu Samaj Suvarna Mahotsava Smrutigranth, 1913-63* (in Gujarati, Puna, 1964), 129.
11. *Bombay Gazette*, Sept. 10, 1881; also see B.A. Saletore, "*Forgotten Gujarati Brahman Banker, 18th Century*", Indian Historical Records Commission, *Proceedings*, XXX (Hyderabad, 1964), 157-60.
12. B.G. Gokhale's assertion, "The *Bania* was a *Vaishya* and the ordained occupations for him were commerce and money-lending", is typical of this belief. "Merchant Community of India", n. 5, p. 140.
13. Edwin F. Gay, quoted in Arthur H. Cole, "An Approach to the Study of Entrepreneurship : A Tribute to Edwin F. Gay", *Explorations in Enterprise*, ed. by G.H. Aitken (Cambridge, Mass., Harvard University Press, 1965), p. 31.
14. For a good example see Dwijendra Tripathi, *The Dynamics of a Tradition : Kasturbhai Lalbhai and His Entrepreneurship* (New Delhi, 1981), 9-39.

15. Government of Bombay, *Gazetteer of the Bombay Presidency: Gujarat Population, Hindus* IX-1 (Bombay, 1901); R.E. Enthoven, *The Tribes and Castes of Bombay* (Bombay, 1920), I, 133-44; James MaCmurdo, "An Account of the Province of Cutch and of the Countries Lying between Gujarat and the River Indus with Cursory Remarks on the Inhabitants, Their History, Manners and State of Society", *Transactions of the Literary Society of Bombay* I (London, 1820), 243-44; *Times of India*, 1 February, 1862; also Christine Dobbin, *Urban Leadership in Western Indian Politics and Communities in Bombay City* (Oxford, 1972), 137.
16. For detailed discussion see Dwijendra Tripathi and Makrand Mehta, "The Nagarsheth of Ahmedabad : History of an Urban Institution in a Gujarat City", Indian History Congress, *Proceedings*, 39th Session (Hyderabad, 1978), 481-96.
17. For details see S.C. Misra, *Muslim Communities of Gujarat* (Bombay, 1964).
18. Original Correspondence, 3373, Vol. 30, 26 November 1869, India Office Library, London.
19. Henry Yule (ed.), *The Diary of William Hedoes* (London, 1888), II, 304.
20. Original Correspondence, 3921, Vol. 341, 12 January 1674, India Office Library, London.
21. Government of Bombay, *Gazetteer of the Bombay Presidency*, Vol. IV, *Ahmedabad* (Bombay, 1879), 111-13. Also, Tripathi and Mahta, "The Nagarsheth of Ahmedabad", n. 16; Sushil Chaudhary, "The Gujarati Mahajans", Indian History Congress, *Proceedings*, 41st Session (Bombay, 1980), 357-65.
22. *Ibid.*
23. Tripathi, *Dynamics of a Tradition*, n. 14, p. 22-30.
24. Govinddas Gopaldas Shah, *Punana Bar Nat Mahajanno Itihas 1740-1956* (in Gujarati, 1956), 4-21. Pearson holds that the Mahajans were occupational in character while Das Gupta thinks that their character was essentially social. See M.N. Pearson, *Merchants and Rulers in Gujarat* (New Delhi, 1976), 123-31; Ashin Das Gupta, *Indian Merchants and the Decline of Surat, C. 1700-1750* (Wiesbaden, 1979), 86-87.
25. Pearson and Misra among others think that Ahmedabad had a city Mahajan. M.N. Pearson, "Political Participation in Mughal India", *Indian Economic and Social History Review*, IX (June, 1872), 122-23; S.C. Misra, "Some Aspects of the Self Administering Institutions in Medieval Indian Towns," in *Studies in Urban History*, ed. by J.S. Grewal and Indu Banga (Amritsar, 1981), 80-90. That this was not so has been discussed in Tripathi and Mehta, "The Nagarsheth of Ahmedabad", n. 16, p. 490-91.
26. A copy of the document has been reproduced in Tripathi, *The Dynamics of a Tradition*, N. 14, facing page 36.

27. Tripathi and Mehta, "The Nagarsheth of Ahmedabad", n. 16, pp. 490-91.
28. *Ibid.*, 483-90.
29. *Ibid.*, 489.
30. H.G. Briggs, *The Cities of Gujarashtra* (London, 1849), 211-13.
31. Imperial Record Department, *Calendar of Persian Correspondence Being Letters which Passed Between Some of the Company's Servants and Indian Rulers, and Notables, 1794-95*, pp. 314-15, National Archives of India, New Delhi.
32. For a fuller discussion on the impact of change in environment see Tripathi, "Occupational Mobility and Industrial Entrepreneurship in India: A Historical Analysis", *Developing Economies*, XIX (March 1981), 52-64. Maganlal Vakhatchand, *Amdavadno Itihas* in Gujarati, (Ahmedabad, 1851), 115, refers to the migration of Kanbis to Ahmedabad.
33. Karl Marx and Frederick Engels, *The First Indian War of Independence, 1857-1859* (Moscow, 1959), 20.
34. For a fuller discussion see Dwijendra Tripathi and Makrand Mehta, *Business Houses in Western India; A Study in Entrepreneurial Response, 1850-1956* (Mimeo, Indian Institute of Management, Ahmedabad, 1981), 282-302.
35. For the career of Ranchhodlal Chhotalal see Bhagwanlal Badshah, *The Life of Rao Bahadur Ranchhorelal Chhotalal C.I.E.* (Bombay, 1899); N.N. Parikh, *Directory of Ahmedabad Mill Industry, 1929-56* (Ahmedabad, 1957), 38-39 gives a brief life sketch of Bechardas Laskari.
36. Foreign Political Department Proceedings, Consultation nos. 7-10 of November 9, 1840; no 152 of June 28, 1841; no. 153 of June 28, 1841, no. 43 of June 9, 1857, National Archives of India, New Delhi.
37. Makrand J. Mehta, "Ranchhodlal Chhotalal and the Ahmedabad Cotton Industry : A Study in Entrepreneurial History", Ph.D. Thesis (Gujarat University, Ahmedabad, 1979), 212-251.
38. *Census of Baroda Territories* (1881), 217-221.
39. Opportunities of business in Baroda state began to develop only after 1886 as a result of the progressive policies of Maharaja Sayajirao Gaekwad III. For discussion on the earlier period see Gita Bajpai "Baroda in Transition, 1860-1886", Ph. D. Thesis (M.S. University of Baroda, 1980)
40. *Gazetteer of the Baroda State*, (Bombay, 1923), I, 253-54.
41. *Census of India 1911, Vol. XVI: Bombay Presidency*, 345-46.
42. B.D. Amin, *The Rise and Growth of the Alembic Chemical Works: A History* (Baroda, 1939); Tripathi and Mehta, *Business Houses in Western India*, n. 34, pp. 148-166; 167-193.
43. *Buddhi Prakash*, July 1861, 156-57.
44. Badshah, *Life of Ranchhorelal Chhotalal*, n. 35, p. 22.
45. *Prajabandhu*, 5 March 1916, 12-23.

46. The case of the Panchals, as referred to in Shirin Mehta's paper offers a good example (see chapter 10 in this volume).
47. For Gujarati contribution in forming trade associations involving various social groups see Stanley Kochanek, *Business and Politics in India* (Berkeley, 1974), 131-196; Rajat K. Ray, *Industrialization in India; Growth and Conflict in the Private Corporate Sector, 1914-47* (Bombay, 1979), 292-366; H. Venkatasubbiah, *Enterprise and Economic Change—50 Years of FICCI* (New Delhi, 1977).

10

The *Mahajans* and the Business Communities of Ahmedabad

Shirin Mehta

Ahmedabad was the centre of guild life in Gujarat. These guilds were often named as *mahajans* in case of merchants and traders and *panchs* in case of artisans. These *mahajans* or *panchs* were corporate bodies or self administering institutions which existed in Gujarat since ancient times.[1] Though they had no legal standing, both the state and the society recognized them as an integral part of the system.

Our knowledge of the *mahajan* system in Ahmedabad is much more satisfactory than in other towns in Gujarat. The city was founded in 1411 by Sultan Ahmed Shah and was made capital of Gujarat. In due course it developed into a major city. It was not merely the administrative headquarter of the state but also a centre of trade, commerce and industry. As a result a large section of its population consisted of merchants and artisans organized into identifiable communities. The guilds regulated the occupational and social life of these communities. They had horizontal as well as vertical character i.e. the guilds pertaining to a single social group and those which belonged to different social and economic stratifications. In addition to their role in the business and social life, they performed many of the functions of modern government and municipality.

The purpose of the paper is to examine the guild organisations in a historical perspective and to study their typological classification, behaviour and modes of interaction with state, society, other guilds and their individual members. The task is not easy as the materials available are sketchy and fragmentary. The only available studies are of F.S.P. Lely, the compiler of the district gazetteer of Ahmedabad, and of E.W. Hopkins, an American professor who visited Ahmedabad around the turn of the present century.[2] Both had little knowledge of the actual operation of these micro institutions. Moreover these studies belonged to the nineteenth century. The source materials of the sultanate period (1411-1573) which constituted the formative years of the guild system, have precious little information about the *mahajans*. By 1573 when the Mughals occupied the city the guild system had consolidated itself and had become a prominent feature of the urban setting. There are frequent references to them in a number of imperial *farmans*, *Ain-i-Akbari* and travellers' accounts. After the disintegration of the Mughal empire, the *mahajan* system experienced several ups and downs because of political social changes, but it did not suffer a total eclipse. Even today there are as many as sixty guild associations in Ahmedabad.[3] This study is based, among other things, on the survey of the existing *mahajans* and interviews with their functionaries.

I

In the fifteenth century Ahmedabad developed a peculiar residential pattern known as *pols* which contributed to the growth of self-governing local units like guild. The Bhadra fort, the administrative headquarter, the Jama Masjid and the Tin Darwaza which were situated near one another formed a pivotal complex around which the city expanded radially like concentric circle rings representing successive zones of urban extension within a circumference of six miles.[4]

The patron-client relationship that characterised social relationship influenced the pattern of settlement. As a result the fort area was inhabited by nobles, government officers and armymen. Around their residences there developed the localities of merchants and artisans in *pols*. Each *pol* was exclusively occupied by a single caste of merchants. They might be either Jains, Vaishnav or Shrimali Banias, Brahmans, Lohanas, Bhatias or artisan castes of goldsmiths, Gandhi (oilpressers),

Chhippa-bhavasar (printers and dyers), silversmiths, ironsmiths or carpenters. Many *pols* in Ahmedabad even today bear caste or community names like Zaveripol of Jains, Gandhipol, Kagdipol (paper manufacturer who were muslims), Chhippapol (printers), Soniwada (goldsmith) etc.[5] The relationship between the guild system and *pol* federation was intimate indeed. This facilitated united action on the part of various communities. For instance in 1546, it was easy for the merchants of Ahmedabad to come together to present a common front against the arbitrary valuation of coinage by the Portuguese authorities at Diu.[6]

The guild system secured firm footing and achieved multilateral growth during the Moghul period. Abul Fazal in his *Ain-i-Akbari* has referred to the *mahajans* while enumerating the duties of Kotwal. He writes that Kotwal while recording a case should enter the name of guild master (*sar-i-giroh*) of every guild (*juki*) of artisans.[7] Many *Khatpatras* or sale deeds of property especially of the seventeenth century frequently mention terms like "*Mahajan*", "*Shresta*" *and* "*Nagaradhyaksha*".[8] The Mughals realised the importance of the organizations of businessmen and sought support from them. On 1C August 1658 for instance, Aurangzeb issued a *farman* to Sheth Shantidas, a very influential Jain merchant, asking the latter to convey his message of goodwill and amity to all merchants, *mahajans*, common inhabitants and general residents of Ahmedabad.[9]

The above evidences give ample proof of the growth of the *mahajan* system. By the beginning of the 18th century, the institution of *nagarsheth* had developed fully. The occupant of this office, normally the principal merchant in the city, acted as a kind of opinion leader of the entire population. There were no less than fifty-three *mahajans* in Ahmedabad when Aurangzeb died in 1707. In the face of political instability, frequent occurrences of natural calamities, and Maratha raids, the institution of *nagarsheth* became mature and crystallised into the life of the city. The *mahajan* system by this time was so firmly rooted in soil, that they could survive the misrule, shattered economy and heavy exactions during the sixty-four years of Maratha rule, following the disintegration of the Mughal rule.

When the British took over the city in 1817 they quickly recognised the value of self-governing institutions in their bid to win popular acceptance, create the support network and stabilise administrative machinery. They extended courtesy to the then Nagarsheth and looked upon him as an important leader in the city. They granted him an annual pension of Rs. 2130 from public treasury.[11] They also recognised the Kazi as the head of the Muslim community who registered marriages and deaths and settled disputes.[12] Some of the changes wrought by the British rule had unsettling effect on the traditional structure but the guild system showed signs of adaptability and transformation and not dissolution. When F.S.P. Lely made a survey of the city *mahajans* in 1877, he found that only twenty-nine such bodies were in operation. This represented a drastic reduction from the figures in the first quarter of the 18th century. Perhaps the Maratha rule that preceded the British occupation had something to do with the eclipse of a large number of them. The number registered gradual increase after 1817. For, by the end of the 19th century, there were not less than 40 *mahajans* in the city as Hopkins who visited Ahmedabad in 1896 testifies. In the present century, the number increased still further as we have already seen.[13]

II

The guilds were of two types. Those of the merchants and financiers were known as *mahajans* and their heads were called Sheths. The *panchs* or the artisan guilds had Patels as their heads.[14] The *mahajans* dealt solely with occupational matters. Social and religious matters were outside their purview though a clear distinction between the two kinds of functions was not always possible. The social base of the *mahajans* was broad. They cut across castes and communities. As a result a *mahajan* could have persons of many castes as its members. Social and religious problems were handed by the respective caste panchayats which represented homogeneous caste group.[15] The membership of a *panch* was usually coterminous with a caste.

Both types of organizations performed definite and sometimes overlapping functions. Both regulated trade, kept up standards, controlled prices, determined wages, controlled admissions of new members and restricted competition. They protected the interest of their members against the government, other guilds, and outsiders. The right to arbitrate vested in them and their decision on matters falling under their purview was considered as final.[16] If a member went against the decision of a *mahajan* or the *panch*, as the case may be, it resulted into his social ostracism. For instance, the cloth merchant *mahajan* expelled a Shrimali Bania who offended his caste by marrying a widow. The power of guild was absolute and generally coercive. They sometimes discouraged initiative and innovation. The indolent and the industrious were treated alike.[17] The Gazetteer of Ahmedabad characterised the system as "blind communism". But the coercion by the guilds had a general acceptability. As Hopkins remarked: "Even the victims regard themselves as martyrs in a good cause, and think themselves protected where they are tyrannized over". No doubt guilds provided shield to their members in difficult times Especially in the case of petty artisans their *panch* could discuss matters on equal footing with higher castes. The *panchs* invested their members with a sense of dignity.

The title of the head of the mahajan, Sheth as he was called, was hereditary. He was the highest executive authority. He usually sought advice from some influential elderly men who acted as an informal inner council of the *mahajan*. These men were the links between individual members and the Sheth.[18]

The Sheth was a spokesman of his members. The state treated him as an intermediary between his community and state. He was also used as a convenient agency to collect taxes. The merchants paid to the state custom duties, inland transit duties and market taxes. The government allowed complete autonomy to *mahajans* in commercial matters. The *nagarsheth* of Ahmedabad belonging to the Jain community maintained the dominance of Jains in the city. The people looked upon him with great respect. He could call the meeting of all *mahajans* to collect funds in adverse circumstances. In case of draught he performed puja ceremony to please the gods and perform several other sundry functions.[19] The position of the Patel, as the head of *panch* was lower in comparison to that of the Sheth. In matters of dispute Patels usually acted through the Sheths.[20]

There was a variety of organisational patterns in the case of the artisan *panch.* There were intermediate artisans between great merchants and petty artisans. The artisan *panchs* were obviously divided into sub-types—the intermediate artisan craftsmen *panchs* and petty artisan *panchs.* The intermediate artisan *panchs* were of goldsmiths, silversmiths, clothdyers, printers, Chippas and Bhavsars, gold-threaders and borderers. The profession of an intermediate artisan required high skill and technical knowledge. Each of such *panchs* tended to belong to a single caste since skilled workmanship precluded the entry of outsiders into a specialized[21] profession.

There was close relationship among the guilds. Three different modes of interaction between the *mahajans* and the *panchs* existed. (i) The artisans often worked on their own. They bought raw material and sold their products either to the local markets or to wholesale merchants. In such cases transaction remained advantageous to artisans. (ii) The merchants would advance money to artisans to buy raw material. The artisan had to deliver products to the merchants at an agreed price. (iii) The merchants would provide raw materials to the artisans and the latter would be paid at piece-rate for their labours. In this case artisan was reduced to the position of wage labourers.[22]

But the merchants could not exploit the artisans beyond a point. The latter could always act through the powerful mechanism of *panch.* Even if they were scattered they maintained close contact and continued to feel primordial attachment to their group. An example of 1860 illustrates how the *panchs* functioned in relation to merchants. The weaver *panch* decided to sell handloom fabrics to be sent to foreign markets only through their agents—the *karidias.* The merchants were required to deal only with the individual weavers.[23] A marked feature of the artisan guilds was that they retained their separate identities for a longer time than the merchant *mahajans.* For instance the workers in silk and gold in the late 19th century formed two distinct *panchs* in brocade trade.

Below the cluster of guilds representing merchants and manufacturers were the *panchs* of petty artisans, though in their structure and mode of interaction, they were in no way different from the *panchs* of upper class artisan. The work of petty artisans demanded less skill, more manual work and needed simpler tools. They catered to the requirements of residents. Their products had limited markets. The petty artisans were masons, brick makers, potters, tile makers, tailors, oil pressers, carpenters, etc. The tile maker *panch* was perhaps the most powerful among them. It controlled the potters *panch* as well. Though their guilds fell outside the perimeter of merchants manufacturers nexus, they were very powerful since they satisfied the basic need of the community. In 1895, one Ahmedabad banker developed differences with a tile maker. The result was that his roof remained uncovered for months. The tile makers *panch* gave a tough fight and the banker had to settle his differences on amicable terms acceptable to the other party.[24]

The class conflict between merchants *mahajans* and artisans *panchs* was frequently visible. Once in Ahmedabad in the second half of nineteenth century the potters raised the price of their wares. The merchants and bankers *mahajans* picked up the issue on behalf of the public. They decided to use copper utensils in place of earthen-ware wherever possible. The potters did not relent until the merchants purchased the land from where potters dug clay. Similar tactics were resorted to by the *mahajans* though with less success, when the barbers and carpenters raised their rates. The *panchs* were such close-knit organizations that the entry of anyone in the profession represented by a *panch* would be resented and resisted. In the closing years of the 19th century some masons from outside came and settled in Ahmedabad; to secure customers they reduced their rate. The masons' guild aligned itself with the potters *panch* and decided to sell sands only through their agents. As a result the outsider masons found it difficult to get sand for their mortars. Though the *panchs* were much weaker than the *mahajans*, they on occasion showed their strength to deal with the authorities. In 1846, the Ahmedabad municipality decided to levy one pie tax on each donkey-load of bricks entering the city walls The brick makers *panch* refused to deliver goods except at kilns, thus throwing the cess as well as the cost of carriage on customers.

In addition to being a home of big financiers and bankers,[25] Ahmedabad was the chief emporium of textile trade. The *mahajans* of textile merchants were divided according to the varieties of cloth. Thus there were separate *mahajans* of merchants selling cotton, silk, silk mashru, handloom, brocade, etc. The cloth *mahajan* dominated the city. The sahukar, bankers or saraf *mahajan* was second in hierarchy. There were printers' *mahajan*, *mahajans* of grain-dealers, grocery dealers, and tobacco dealers..[26]

The *mahajans* were heterogeneous in character. Each *mahajan* represented more than two castes or communities. Ahmedabad cloth *mahajans* for instance, had Jains, Vaishnav Banias, Meshri Brahmans, Lohanas and Bhatias as members. The bankers or Sarat *mahajans* were dominated by the Banias but some shroffs were also Nagar Brahmans. The silk mashru *mahajan* contained both Patidars and Banias castes. The grain business was mostly run by Lohanas, Bhatias as well as Vaishnav Banias. Many of them also controlled timber business of the city. Muslims and Hindus of Bhavsar caste were good printers of cloth.[27]

Hopkins was wrong in observing that guilds in Ahmedabad were predominantly Hindu or Jain bodies and that the muslim guilds were in "weak imitation of Hindu models".[28] Muslims belonged to diverse social groups. They were Syeds, Pathans, Arabs, Shaikhs and Sunni Bohoras. Sunni Bohoras were rich and were engaged in mercantile venture. Many muslims were artisans, manufacturers and workers. In Ahmedabad the paper industry was mostly patronised by muslims whose *mahajan* was known as *Kagdi ni Jamat*.[29] In addition to the purely occupational groupings the Muslims also had organizations which, like the *panchs* regulated the social life of their members. Kazi was perhaps comparable to the *nagarsheth* who acted as the most dominant spokesman of the muslim communities. The office of Kazi also became hereditary like the office of the *nagarsheth*.[30]

III

In the nineteenth century, the *mahajans* and *panchs* experienced structural and functional transformation The new infrastructural measures introduced by the British undermined the traditional structure of the society. This naturally affected the guilds. Their tight social bond was loosened. The *mahajans* now were less able to enforce penalties against individuals, who could resort to laws and courts for redress. Social groups which dominated certain *mahajans* had to accommodate other groups which emerged on the commercial scene. For instance, the position of the Jains was impaired by the Vaishnav Banias, the Patidars and some Parsis in cloth *mahajans*. In 1927, Vaishnav Banias refused to appropriate their share in the common fund to maintain the Jain *panjrapol* meant for disabled animals. They insisted that a part of the common fund must be transferred to their own temples.[31] The hereditary office of Sheths and Patels were now subject to election. Sheths of old *mahajans* now began to be called presidents. The Ahmedabad Maskati Mahajan founded in 1906 as an offshoot of the old Madhupura Sutar Mahajan used to have a Jain as the head but now the Vaishnav Banias also got elected as presidents.[32]

Similarly *panchs* and caste panchayat lost some of its restrictive and coercive aspects. As a result of new changes in the economic sphere the traditional artisan industry lost its past significance and the artisans began to gravitate towards new industries. For instance, the blacksmiths began to make small parts needed by the factories. Some of them turned entrepreneurs and started their own factories. In due course these part makers joined Ahmedabad Factory Association which was more secular, democratic and occupational than the traditional *panch*.[33] Similarly the goldsmiths joined the Choksi Mahajan which consisted of banias, patidars and of goldsmiths.

The historical survey presented above indicates how resilient and enduring was the guild system in Ahmedabad. Max Weber was of the opinion that "the guilds of merchants and the hereditary caste system of Indian society with its ritualistic segregation of professions excluded the emergence of citizenry and urban community."[34] True, the *mahajans* and the *panchs*, with their horizontal expansion, were more powerful than vertically integrated institutions. But there are sufficient evidences, as we have seen above, that underline the role of guilds in furthering the corporate feeling and spirit. There were town councils in small cities; in big cities *mahajans* and their heads presented common fronts to meet common threats. The experience of the Ahmedabad guilds also run counter to the prognosis of Karl Marx who envisaged the dissolution of traditional micro-institution. Rather than dissolving themselves, the *mahajans* and *panchs* transformed themselves into organizations consistent with the needs and aspirations of changing times.

NOTES

1. Many inscriptions referring to mahajans are available in Kathiawad. For instance, one inscription dated 1146 at the Deguvar stepwell at Mongrol in which the contribution of mahajan of Chorwad in constructing the stepwell is mentioned. *Bhavnagar Collection* (Bhavnagar Government Press, 1885), Part I, p. 2.
2. James M. Campbell, *Gazetteer of the Bombay Presidency : Ahmedabad* (Bombay, 1879), Vol. IV.
3. Ravishanker Vyas (ed.), *Amdavadna Vyapar Udyogo* (in Gujarati) (Ahmedabad, 1851), p. 40.
4. Maganlal Vakhatchant, *Amdavad na Itihas* (in Gujarati) (Ahmedabad, 1851), p. 40.
5. Harish Doshi, *Traditional Neighbourhood in Modern City* (New Delhi, 1974), pp. 30-40.
6. M.N. Pearson, *Merchants and Rulers in Gujarat* (California, 1976), p. 121.
7. Ali Muhammad Khan, *Mirat-i-Ahmadi*, tr. by M.F. Lokhandwala (Baroda, 1965), p. 145.
8. Dwijendra Tripathi and M.J. Mehta, "The Nagarsheth of Ahmedabad: History of an Urban Institution in a Gujarat City." Indian History Congress, *Proceedings*, 39th session, (Hyderabad, 1978), pp. 482-483.
9. M.S. Commissariat, *Imperial Farmans in Gujarat* (Bombay, 1940), p. 17.
10. Tripathi and Mehta n. 8, p. 484; *Ahmedabad Gazetteer*, n. 2, p. 113; Commissariat, n. 8, p. 10. Also see D. Tripathi, *The Dynamics of a Tradition : Kasturbhai Lalbhai and His Entrepreneurship* (New Delhi, 1981).
11. *Ahmedabad Gazetteer*, n. 2, p. 90.
12. Kenneth L. Gillion, *Ahmedabad : A Study in Indian Urban History* (Ahmedabad, 1968), p. 52.
13. Vyas, n. 3, p. 90.
14. H.G. Briggs, *the Cities of Gujarashtra* (Bombay, 1849), p. 18.
15. Ratnarao Bhimrao, *Amdavadnu Patnagar* (in Gujarati) (Ahmedabad, 1929), pp. 545-562.

16. Gillion, n. 14, p. 49.
17. S.C. Misra, "The Self Administering Institutions in Medieval Indian Towns", J.S. Grewal and Indu Banga, (ed). *Studies in Urban History* (Amritsar, 1981), p. 81.
18. *Ahmedabad Gazetteer*, n. 2, p. 111.
19. Hopkins, n. 2, p. 186.
20. *Ahmedabad Gazetteer*, n. 2, p. 113.
21. Hopkins. n. 2, p. 178.
22. A.K. Bagchi, "Merchants and Colonialism", Occasional Paper no. 38, Centre for Studies in Social Sciences, (Calcutta, mimeo, 1981), p. 11.
23. *Ahmedabad Gazetteer*, n. 2, p. 110.
24. Hopkins, n. 2, p. 183.
25. *Ahmedabad Gazetteer*, n. 2, pp. 108-110.
26. Ratnamanirao Bhimrao, n. 18, p. 455.
27. *Ahmedabad Gazetteer*, n. 2, p. 108. *Census of India 1961 : Special Report of Ahmedabad City* (Ahmedabad, 1967), p. 41.
28. Hopkins, n. 2, p. 178.
29. M.J. Mehta, "Indigenous Paper Industry and Muslim Entrepreneurship", *Indian National Science Academy*, February 1982, p. 32.
30. Pearson, n. 6, pp. 136-137.
31. Hiralal Bhagvati (ed.), *Maskati Kapad Markit Mahajans Bhaddharan futha Niyamo.* (in Gujarati) (Ahmedabad, 1955), p. 13.
32. Author's interview with Chandulal C. Dave, The Secretary of Maskati Mahajan, 20 January 1982.
33. Author's Interview with Ramanlal Motilal Panchal, Secretary of Panchal Yuvak Mandal; Ramanlal Motilal Panchal (ed.), *Shri Panchal Yuvak Mandal Rajat Jayanti Ank* (in Gujarati) (Ahmedabad, 1949), pp. 7-9.
34. Quoted in Llyod L. Rudolph and Susanne H. Rudolph, *The Modernity of Tradition* (Chicago, 1967), pp. 30-32.

11

The Marwaris: Economic Foundations of an Indian Capitalist Class

G.D. Sharma

The politico-economic set-up of Rajasthan in the late 18th and the first half of the 19th century reflects the emergence of the traders and merchants in the mid-eighteenth century so much so that the Jaipur State was described as *baniya rajya* in the popular lore. This rise of the trader-merchant class was due to large scale use of money capital in the commercial transactions—a practice in which the money accumulation of this class was favourably employed. The policy of the Rajput rulers towards commerce and taxation in the preceding century had allowed a multiplication of the capital assets of the business class; the political edifices at the turn of the 18th century ensured them a greater participation in state affairs particularly in the formation of the commercial policy. Therefore, one is not surprised at James Tod's expression that "none of these states were without traffic; each has a mart of entrepot and while Mewar boasts of Bilwara; the Rathors claim Palli, which is not only the rival of the places just mentioned, but many make pretension to the title of emporium of Rajputana. The pretensions, we may the more readily admit, when we recollect that nine-tenth of the bankers and commercial men of India are native of Maroodes, and these chiefly of the Jain faith".[2] Even if an element of exaggeration could be seen in Tod's statement, the importance of the traders and merchants in the economy of Rajasthan, as realised by a knowledgeable

English administrator of the early 19th century, can hardly be denied.

The study of the economy and society of the erstwhile native states of Rajasthan has drawn considerable attention of both historians and social scientists. Research in this area falls broadly under two levels.[3] Scholars studying contemporary society at the micro level have focused on isolated problems, while the macro level efforts have been concerned with the potentialities of the growth of money economy in Rajasthan on the eve of the establishment of the colonial system in India.[4]

An examination of the historical material reveals that the term Marwari dates back to the establishment of Marwari business houses outside Rajasthan, particularly in Bengal, Bihar and Orissa, since the time of Akbar and Shahjahan. It is said that some members of the Vaishyas class first came to Bengal along with the Rajput army. These *Modis* and *Potedars* besides serving the army engaged themselves in conducting private business. Some of them settled there permanently and participated in local trade and money-lending. These *Vaishyas* belonged to the Marwar region of Rajasthan and hence began to be called as Marwaris by the local population. With the passage of time, these Rajasthani immigrants into Eastern India, particularly in Bengal, established their credibility in commercial enterprises and emerged as the leading merchants and traders. Soon, friends and relatives joined them to help and open new firms. It seems that since they were either associated with the Marwaris or introduced by them, all of them came to be known as Marwaris outside Rajasthan irrespective of their original homes. Possibly, the credibility attached to the Marwari businessmen would have also influenced other Rajasthani traders and merchants to introduce themselves as Marwaris. So these economic entrepreneurs of the 19th century Rajasthan were termed as Marwaris outside Rajasthan. Interestingly, inside Rajasthan, the appellation still has a purely regional as opposed to occupational connotation.[5]

The following discussion proposes to examine the factors responsible for the growth of Marwaris as a capitalist class and the sphere of their activities beyond Rajasthan. It seeks to suggest that although the politico-economic structure of the 18th century Rajasthan was favourable to the growth of merchant capital, the internal contradictions proved detrimental to the economic interests of the business community. Further it would also be seen that this capitalist class did not at any stage lack practical knowledge, useful for the growth of liquid capital, and the capacity to divert that capital to non-traditional sectors if circumstances permitted.

I

The fiscal policy of the Rajput rulers and its implementation, particularly in the case of land revenue, as well as the increase in the cultivation of cash crops provided conditions for the growth of merchant capital in the 17th century. These merchants were known as *mahajans*, *shahs* or *sahukars*, *vohora*, and *sarraf* in Rajasthan. The emphasis of the state on the realization of the revenue in cash and its need for advance payment against the revenue as also the practice of transmitting funds through *hundis* can be considered as some of the important factors which necessitated the presence of men with liquid capital.[6] This helped the merchant capitalist to establish his dominance. Thus, the growth of this class can be traced to this revenue policy and commercial practices of the Mughals.

The Rajput rulers of Rajasthan followed the practice of appointing moneylenders—mahajans or shahs—in the office dealing with the revenue both at the pargana and the state levels. Although this was not a new practice, it became more widespread during the 18th century. A study of the documents belonging to *Diwan Hazuri* of Amber State and *Jama-bandi* of Jodhpur state makes it clear that mahajans or shahs were occupying the offices of Potedar, Amil and Amin almost in all the parganas of Amber and Jodhpur. Some of them also worked as Modi (supplier of provision to the army). It is also revealed that the transfer or dismissal of these officers was quite frequent and sometimes such changes could be made even within six months. Apparently these offices were treated as a source of profit and were awarded to the highest bidders. It was the usual practice that the incumbents should furnish the security of the local mahajan who would take the responsibility of the payment of revenue regularly to the state treasury in case of a default by the officer. The mahajan and sahukar thus had a dual role and as such they established their monopoly on the major sources of the surplus. It may be noted that even in the 17th century the pargana revenue officer had to rely on the mahajan to fulfil the state demand for advance revenue.[7]

Indeed, the traders had found yet another way of making profit i.e. through *ijara* (revenue-farming). Taking ijara of land revenue was prevalent even during the 17th century, although its wide scale use in all the spheres of revenue, including the *khalisa* territory, was a new phenomenon in the revenue system of the Rajput states during the 18th century.[8] This practice originated as a result of political instability in the Rajput states and was repeatedly followed as the Marathas' demand for cash went on increasing. It was not the land revenue alone which was given on *ijara* but also the right of mining, *rahdari*, *kotwali* and *mapa-dan*. Recent studies make it clear that the mahajans and sahukars as a class enjoyed an outright monopoly on the *ijara* practices. Taking *ijara* was considered a profitable investment. There was always a keen competition among the *ijaradars* to secure *ijara* of land and other revenue resources. Since the state had instituted this practice to get ready money without risk, it always favoured the person who used to bid the highest.[9] Apparently under this system both the state and the *ijaradar* remained interested in exploiting each other at the cost of the peasantry. Whatever be the incidence of the revenue, this practice and involvement of the businessmen inevitably put more money into circulation for profitable gain. It has generally been presumed that the mahajan's involvement in *ijara* practices was a result of the declining trade and commerce in the state of Rajasthan. The assumption misses the fact that both the *ijara* practices and trade were complimentary to each other.

The merchants carried on with the traditional profession of usury and banking. It is now fully acknowledged that the practice of usury and banking was quite common in the native states of Rajasthan. While usury was practiced by all classes of merchants both in the rural and urban sectors, the operation of banking was mainly an urban phenomenon penetrating into the countryside through banker's agencies.[10] It was through the practice of employing accumulated money in usury that the growth of capital started—a favourable situation created due to the state revenue policy and increase in cash crops. Some 18th century documents belonging to Marwar, Amber and Bikaner throw sufficient light on the credit and banking operations.[11] The mahajans or sahukars in their capacity as financiers, besides advancing loan to the peasants, also gave advances to the pargana officials and looked after the payment of bills at pargana, town and village level.[12] It is worth-mentioning that in a state of emergency, which was fairly frequent, the pargana officers collected the land revenue in advance to fulfil the state demand.[13] Apparently, in such a situation the peasant had no other alternative but to secure a loan from the mahajan and pay the state demand of land revenue. Similarly the pargana officers, who could hardly be in a position to collect the assessed revenue were compelled to borrow money from the pargana mahajan or sahukar to meet the balance of the amount to be paid to the state. Mahajans and sahukars also worked for bankers and earned commissions.

We come across a large number of bankers in these Rajput states. They got special treatment from the rulers as the latter were always in need of money—a need which increased during the latter half of the 18th century. Since the bankers got their return mostly in the form of revenue, they always received more than what could be stipulated in the form of interest. Such practices also enabled them to purchase crops on favourable terms. The 18th century Rajput states gave enough encouragement to the traders and merchants. The latter were granted free trade facilities and reduction in the taxes levied under the name of *sair-dan*, *mapa* and *rahdari*.[14] Prominent traders were granted permission to conduct trade without paying transit duties and sales-tax.[15] However, their number was very small and generally they were those who had advanced money on credit to the state. Some of the traders and merchants were granted exemption to the extent of 50 per cent and 25 per cent of taxes payable by them in the name of *dan*, *mapa and rahdari*.[16]

Favours were also granted in other ways. They were given the contracts for providing better amenities at big *qasbas* or villages. Some examples could be cited from Jodhpur State where Bikaneria Kanha, Radha, etc. were asked to open shops at Nagor with necessary requirements.[17] Rathor Amar Singh and other mahajans were assured of concessions if they started business in Marwar.[18] Similarly Bhatt Ramchandra Roop Chand was asked to open a shop at Pali and was assured concession from the *darbar*.[19] Bania Viney Chand Santokhchand was granted permission for opening a shop of *pashmina* (cloth) at Jalor.[20] Besides the permission to the merchants to conduct business in Marwar, the state provided them facilities for constructing *havelis* (mansions) and starting cultivation on *mukata*.[21] The mahajans and choudharis of village Ahuwa, a patta village, were allowed to purchase fields, shops and *arhats* and to sell them to others if they desired to do so.[22] Parwanas were also issued to the effect of providing *havelis* to the leading mahajans of the town.[23] The concessions given, thus, to the mahajans were of immense significance in the light of the political situation faced by the State of Marwar. Similar practices prevailed in Amber and Bikaner States also.

The Rajput states also encouraged the merchants of the neighbouring territories to participate on a large scale in the fairs held in their own states. In the case of Marwar references are made to the holding of an annual fair at Mundawa (near Nagor) where merchants of Jaisalmer, Fatehpur, Nawalgarh and Churu (Bikaner State), Bikaner, Kishangarh and Bhilwara and Ghaneroa (Udaipur State), were invited to participate. They were assured of the reduction of one-fourth of the duties levied in the fair normally.[24] In the case of Marwar this attempt was quite successful during the time of Maharaja Vijay Singh and shows that there were a large number of participants from the five neighbouring states in the fairs held in Marwar. It is worth-mentioning that the *parwanas* issued by the Maharaja were always addressed to the *mahajans* and *vyaparis* of the towns and not to the state. This might imply an inter-State trade contract under which the merchants were free from interference of their rulers.

Since such *parwanas* were addressed to the *mahajans* and *vyaparis* it can be safely maintained that in each of these cities and big towns, the associations of businessmen were institutionalized. Such institutions were fairly noticeable in the first quarter of the 19th century and therefore it can be said that the business associations were an important feature of the commercial towns of Rajasthan—a characteristic which we notice in Gujarat also.[25] The merchants with their powerful associations conducted trade and commerce within and outside Marwar.

II

In spite of state patronage and the favourable condition enjoyed by the traders and merchants, they could not free themselves from the hurdles created by the changes introduced in the politico-administrative structure of the Rajput states in the 18th century. In fact, changes were detrimental to the progress of trade and commerce in all the Rajput states. The *ijara* practices had become quite common and were spread in all the branches of administration concerning state revenue. Another change instituted was the practice of fixing a lumpsum on the *pattadars* (holders of *jagirs*) who as a result of this, had become semi-antonomous.[26] In a state of political uncertainty each one of them was eager to exact taxes in the name of the *rahdari* and *mapadan* on the goods passing through or from their territory. These *jagirdars* had a tendency of levying taxes frowned upon by the state authority.

Apparently, the state's aim was to increase revenue from commercial taxes by providing facilities to the traders and merchants. This had become more important as land revenue fell considerably. In the case of Rajput states the taxes levied on sale, import and export and transaction of goods from the territory could broadly be categorised into three headings: *Mapa*, *Dan*, and *Rahdari*. The term *mapa* was often employed as a generic term for various taxes imposed on the sale of local produce. The *dan* was in fact the same as *mapa* but was calculated *ad valorem* The term *margvahin* is synonymous with *rahdari* used in Mughal documents. The state had set principles for levying duty on different categories of merchants and fixed the rate of the taxes imposed on them. Significantly, the local traders who operated between the pargana town and its villages enjoyed the largest concessions and paid only *dan* as soon as they entered the jurisdiction of the town. The traders engaged in supplying articles to the other pargana towns and carrying articles from the other towns of the state paid duties at higher rates. Many of those traders who had their establishments in the pargana towns kept a link between the town and its rural sector on the one hand and between various towns on the other. There was another category of traders who carried articles from neighbouring states. They paid *dan* and *mapa* and *rahdari*, the latter two being the additional taxes levied only on this category of traders.[27]

An examination of the nature of taxes levied on inland trade in Rajput states shows that apart from traditionally recognized taxes such as sales-tax, entry tax and transit duty, there were a number of imposts borne by the internal and external traders during the 18th century. Thus we notice that in Marwar, about twenty taxes were levied under different names on the sales, imports and exports of goods. Many of them were exacted by the state,[28] while others were charged by the *thikanadars*, *ijaradars* or *jagirdars*.[29] An almost similar trend has been noticed in the State of Amber where the number of commercial taxes was more than those in Marwar. It has also been seen that the merchants paid a variety of taxes in the form of duties levied in the territories belonging to the *bhomia* and *thikanadars*. Reference has already been made to the taxes levied by the various official authorities in Jaipur State.[30] These were the recognised duties which prevailed along with illegal taxes and perquisites imposed by the *bhomis*, *jagirdars* and the state officials.[31] However, it should be mentioned that neither the imposition nor the rate of these taxes was uniform and they varied according to the status of the traders and authority exercised by the local zamindars.[32] Moreover, the payment of additional taxes was dependent on the time and space also. On the basis of the number of taxes it is really difficult to infer the total incidence on the traders. However, there was definitely an increase in the revenue from *sair* which could be attributed to the increase in taxes and the volume of trade. The table on pages 194-95 exhibits this trend clearly.

From the data recorded in the table it is clear that on an average the *sair* income comprised between 20% to 30% of the total *jama* of various parganas. It is safe to conclude, therefore, that the loss incurred in land revenue was replaced by the *sair* revenue. It is noteworthy that in spite of the heavy burden of taxes and illegal extortion and harassment, trade was brisk and flourishing as well as quite lucrative. One of the reasons given in favour of this trend is an upward tendency in prices from the middle of the 17th century onwards.

On the whole, reviewing the practices of *ijara* of commercial taxes, the increasing power of the *jagirdars* and the tendency of local officials to levy illegal taxes, it seems that the orders issued by the State sanctioning the various concessions to the mahajans began to fell by the wayside as political instability increased. Because of general disorder the *jagirdars* began to assume more powers and the state began to lose its foothold in their areas. Under these conditions, both the privileged and unprivileged merchants had to bear the burden of taxes levied on them by *ijaradars* and *jagirdars*. Consequently, the gap between those who had less capital and those who had more widened considerably during this period.[33]

III

During the 18th century, thus, merchants and traders continued their business operations within and beyond Rajasthan despite the oppressive nature of taxation. As has been shown above, the families posted at the offices of Potedar (Poddar), Modi, Amil and Amin had an advantage of accumulating liquid capital through engaging in moneylending and tradting activities within and outside the region. Under such circumstances they had no hesitation in shifting their centre of operation to place which provided them relief in the form of concessions in taxation. Did such relief really influence the venue of their activities? How for did the Rajasthani traders have the potentialities of spreading their trade? What type of relations did they have with the original venue of their activities? And finally what was the nature of their business firms? These are some of the questions which require a deeper investigation and which will help us in understanding the growth of capital in the hands of the Marwaris and the expansion in their trade operations after the establishment of colonial rule.

In an attempt to seek answers to the above questions, I have undertaken to study the history of two business families, belonging to two different Rajput states and who developed their trading operations on two different economic fronts.

THE REVENUE FROM SAIR

	PARGANA NAGOR			PARGANA MERTA			PARGANA SOJAT		
	Total Revenue Rs. A. P.	Sair Revenue Rs. A. P.	Percentage of total	Total Revenue Rs. A. P.	Sair Revenue Rs. A. P.	Percentage of total	Total Revenue Rs. A. P.	Sair Revenue Rs. A. P.	Percentage of total
1822	149136.07.02	44735.01.03	30.01%	260038.08.02	22224.01.03	8.55%	55257.04.00	7488.03.01	23.55%
1823	—	—	—	—	—	—	41710.14.01	7000.06.03	16.78%
1824	—	—	—	147088.02.03	27069.12.02	28.40%	38078.06.03	10886.13.03	28.59%
1825	133320.10.03	44821.09.01	33.62%	129686.04.01	25573.09.01	19.41%	61034.11.02	7548.10.03	12.37%
1826	158960.07.00	60538.14.03	37.85%	167859.06.00	35881.13.01	21.38%	32024.12.02	6045.07.02	18.88%
1827	—	—	—	—	—	—	38549.01.03	7057.00.01	18.31%
1828	147175.11.02	56108.00.03	38.12%	129683.04.00	39325.08.01	30.32%	43663.08.02	10380.03.02	23.77%
1829	160038.10.02	51638.02.03	32.27%	—	—	—	50699.11.02	10444.02.01	20.60%
1830	214138.12.01	55864.12.00	26.08%	—	—	—	56813.09.02	11836.03.01	20.19%
1831	—	—	—	—	—	—	—	—	—
1832	126811.04.02	57586.08.03	45.41%	—	—	—	—	—	—
1833	137044.10.01	70690.04.03	53.66%	86856.12.02	12277.07.03	14.13%	—	—	—
1834	191667.07.01	58329.15.03	30.43%	N.A	N.A	—	N.A	N.A	—

Contd.

1835	N.A	N.A	—	110156.09.03	12146.14.03	11.20%	—	—	—
1836	188217.06.01	35811.11.00	19.03%	—	—	—	—	—	—
1837	183764.02.02	63416.05.03	34.51%	—	—	—	—	—	—
1838	241862.06.01	74384.06.03	30.75%	160585.00.00	32799.03.03	20.42%	—	—	—
1839	—	—	—	135776.02.00	20346.09.02	14.99%	25831.10.00	7952.08.00	30.78%
1840	—	—	—	—	—	—	—	—	—
1841	162435.12.03	55543.08.01	34.19%	—	—	—	—	—	—

Source : The figures shown here are tabulated out of the data available in the *Jama-bandhi sair* of the parganas of Nagor, Sojat and Merta available at the *Rajasthan State Archives Branch Jodhpur*.

One Seth Bhagoti Ram belonging to the Poddar family of Fatehpur (Shekhawati) left his native place and settled at Churu sometime in the last quarter of the 18th century. He had three sons and grandsons; one of his grandsons Seth Mirzamal emerged as a big trader in the next century. One member of the family went to Punjab and established his operations in Bhatinda in the latter half of the 18th century.[34] Others stayed at Churu, but due to bitterness in their relations with Shivji Singh, the Thakur of Churu, they shifted in 1791 to (known as Setho-ka-Ramgarh), an area falling in the territory Ramgarh of Sikar.[35] Although later on the Thakur tried his best for their return to Churu, he did not succeed. In revenge, Thakur Shivji Singh, increased the custom duties on the goods carried through his territory from Ramgarh.[36] It was after settling at Ramgarh that Poddar Seths expanded their trading activities.[37] The trade reached its height with the establishment of firms in different parts of the country. Their headquarter remained at Ramgarh till they returned to Churu in 1823 on the persuasion of Surat Singh (1787-1820), the ruler of Bikaner.[38] By now Mirzamal had accumulated a huge capital and expanded his trade to all the leading towns in Rajasthan, and also engaged in the inter-regional trade, Punjab being his main external trade link. The account papers of years 1816-18 (v.s. 1872-74) record that during this period the goods (groceries, cloth, elephant tusks, canvas, indigo and lac) worth Rs. 1,18,019 was received in Ramgarh after paying Rs. 1632.90 as taxes on weighing, commission, custom duties and *rahdari.*[39] Between the years 1821-24 A.D. (v.s. 1877-80) the goods worth Rs. 1,37,652.75 were received and Rs. 1,657.53 was paid as *mapa, arhat, rahdari* in the parganas of Jodhpur, Nagor and Merta.[40]

This account, besides furnishing information on the quantum of trade in terms of money, makes it clear that these articles were carried from the trading centres of Marwar (which received them from Gujarat) and therefore indicates highly developed trading practices undertaken by Poddar Mirzamal in the beginning of the 19th century. It seems that Mirzamal had his agents in these towns of Marwar. He had established branches of his firm in Ajmer, Bikaner and Jaipur. He had at least two agents in Bikaner. The capital employed by Mirzamal in the above-mentioned trade was related to not only the western part of Rajsthan, he had much larger operation in north-eastern India. A *bahi* belonging to the firm of Nanagramji Mirzamalji of Calcutta of the year 1826-1831 records the fact that Mirzamal achieved a tremendous success in his business in Calcutta. During these years he recieved transfers of money worth Rs. 80 lakhs or more from his Calcutta firm. His business included the insurance of goods, credit and import-export of goods.[41] Besides trading, Mirzamal was engaged in advancing money on credit He had employed a considerable capital with the ruler of Bikaner even before shifting to Churu from Ramgarh in 1823. It is known that Mirzamal gave Rs. 4,00,000/- on credit to the ruler of Bikaner in 1827.[42] As per practice, the rulers returned the credit through assigning revenue of the various territories or commercial duties to the creditors.[43] The Churu and Ramgarh operations helped the Poddars to increase their capital tremendousiy by the end of the 1830s.[44]

The Company Government, in the meantime, was opening up new vistas of trade, promising better commercial opportunities out of Rajasthan. The British ensured safety of goods beyond the Sindh and the Sutlej. In view of the heavy burden of taxation that the traders had to bear in the Rajput states during the 19th century, the new situation was quite favourable, though it needed initiative and confidence to avail of the new openings. The Rajasthani merchants had enough experience in distant trade and thus they undertook this task, engaging their capital for multifarious operations at far-off places. *A parwana* dated May 23, 1835 issued by Captain Wade records that Seth Mirzamal of Churu dispatched his articles in a big cargo to Shah Bandar under the charge of his gumasta Mulasiram. The *parwana* carried the signature of Captain Wade, and the representatives of the court of Lahore and Bahawalpur. The *mahsool* subject to the payment at various places was charged in the beginning except *rahdari* at Loodhiwa. In fact Seth Mirzamal's enterprise was not restricted to the trade transaction with Sindh and Multan. He had already established his firms at Hissar, Hansi and Ludhiana in Punjab after his return to Churu.[45]

Mirzamal did not stop there. By the middle of the 19th century a broad network of his firm had been established in various parts of the country including Bombay, Calcutta,

Amritsar and Delhi. These firms were named after his own name or those of other members of the family such as, Chaturbhuj Jindaram, Nagogram, Joharimal Ramlal, Tarachand Ghanshyamdas, etc. A study of the documents—*bahis* and *chittis*—belonging to various branches, reveals that these firms were usually engaged in import-export trade, banking (*hundis*), insurance and money-lending.[46] Documents relating to Jindamal Mirzamal's firm at Bombay indicate that this particular firm was mainly interested in import-export. The firm exported fine quality Kashmiri shawls to England. Among the other articles cotton and opium figured on the top of the list.[47] It may be noted that together with this expansion of trade Mirzamal's firm continued its operations in Rajasthan with branches at Ajmer, Jaipur, Bikaner, Jodhpur and Nagor. It seems that in the rise of Mirzamal the concessions and patronage provided by Maharaja Suraj Singh of Bikaner was an important factor, although the Maharaja did so to fulfil his monetary requirement from the Seth. There had been continuous disturbance and looting in the area around Churu during the time of Surat Singh which increased after his death in 1820 A.D. However, the effect of this disturbed state of affairs on Mirzamal was minimal owing to his secure position. A number of other mahajans, however, were forced to leave the territory. It seems that after the establishment of his trade operations in Punjab on a firm footing, particularly after 1834 by which time he had become a financier to the court of Ranjit Singh, his interest in Churu and Bikaner had declined. This was more noticeable after the division of his wealth in 1840 among his brothers and sons. Henceforward he paid greater attention to his trade in Punjab and ultimately died there in 1848.

In contrast to Mirzamal's firm, the history of another firm records the picture of achievement by a Marwari merchant in a different condition. The firm originated with Seth Moti Shah. His father who had been *Kamdar* in a village of Phalodi left Marwar soon after the accession of Maharaja Vijay Singh (Jodhpur) when the state was facing a great famine.[48] It seems that after leaving Phalodi, Amichand stayed for sometime in Pali and then settled in the city of Khambat (Cambay) in 1757.

There he started business in the name of Amichand Sarkarchand. However, he did not stay there for long and arrived in Bombay which was gradually developing into a big commercial centre. He seems to have established his *arhatia* business at Bombay but it collapsed with his death in 1800. His son Nemichand worked as a *dalal* of Seth Hormasji Bananji Wadia, a Parsi family, and after great struggles earned enough money to start an independent business. After his death in 1812, his brother Moti Shah who had acquired enough business experience under Nemichand continued to operate as Amichand Sakarchand. He was engaged in ship-building as well as in import-export trade with countries such as Bagdad, Madagaskar, Muzambique, and China. It is stated that Moti Shah got a small ship built for himself and this facilitated his trade with inland ports as well as with south-eastern countries.[49] It seems that by the end of the third decade of the 19th century Moti Shah had established himself as one of the leading businessmen in Bombay. The Jain temples and other public buildings which he constructed in Bombay and Marwar bear witness to his abundant wealth and capitalist enterprise which he had followed for almost 20 years.

IV

Some significant points emerge from the foregoing discussion. Our study makes it clear that the leading merchants and traders served the financial need of the Rajputs and other ruling houses. The increasing demand of the Maratha sardars and reduction of revenue due to administrative changes had made the Rajput rulers increasingly dependent on the merchants. It has been generally argued that the employment of merchant capital on credit by the Rajput rulers was in the nature of a non-commercial investment. In this connection it should be noted that money advanced by the merchants to the state was given on interest basis and was thus a form of usury. Further, those merchants who employed their capital in financing the state received various kinds of concession. Thus the patronage received by the favoured merchants and traders helped them in expanding their trade and reduced the possibilities of official harassment generally faced by the non-privileged merchants. However, as we have seen above, the state generally returned the credit with interest not in cash but by assigning the revenue of the various territories or custom duties of the amount equivalent to the demand agreed in writing. Apparently, the collection of assigned revenue from the parganas and customs officials facilitated the claimant merchants to channelise their commercial interest. Thus, the state patronage and concessions, extended to those who helped the state financially promoted the growth of commercial capital in a given politico-economic structure.

Those who were deprived of these concessions were naturally attracted to places where better facilities were available. The merchants, however, did not remain blind to the commercial opportunities elsewhere including the territories belonging to the English or the Marathas. It this way, many of them established branches of their firms in the main commercial and trading centres of the country.

The motives and factors responsible for the emigration of the Marwaris from their homeland have been explained mainly in terms of political and economic situations.[50] While the 18th and the first half of the 19th century witnessed a scene of contradictory opportunities, the trend of migration may rightly be considered in terms of an economic base for those who attempted to shift or start their trade and commercial activities outside Rajasthan. We may recall that some resourceful merchants and traders had established a strong financial position by the end of the 18th century and were in a position to investigate new avenues for their trading operations. They had enough capital and necessary experience to employ their capital in new enterprises at the first favourable opportunity. That these traders were imbued with the concept of mobility may be clearly seen from the remark of Maharaja Surat Singh who once stated that "Calcutta and Bikaner is one".[51] On another occasion it was emphasized that it was not necessary on the part of the sahukar to continue in one place; he could move from one place to another if he so desired.[52] Though these words were expressed in relation to one leading merchant of Shekhawati (viz. Poddar Mirzamal) they may apply to the Rajasthani merchant community in general.

The establishment of business operations out of Rajasthan by the above category of merchants was always welcomed by the Rajput rulers as well as others. Theirs was a class of highly developed capitalists who continued expanding their trading operations beyond Rajasthan, though they kept their business headquarters in it. One of them, as has been stated above, did finally set himself up completely outside, compelled as he was by personal problems (viz. division of property). Others, who had money but faced more competition and enjoyed lesser advantages at the local level were, tempted to move to British or Maratha controlled territories where better opportunities were available. It may be possible that migration amongst this middle or second strata of capitalists was more popular and consequently more numerous than the first category. Many of those who accompanied them as *gumastas* or *arhatia* were also successful in establishing their independent operations after a few decades. Many of them became the bankers of the Maratha sardars and also started trading operations in their capital towns.

The rise of the British power in India further increased their trading activities by opening new vistas for them. It was this class of the middle strata of the commercial enterprises which benefited in the new situation and emerged as 'great firms' in the 18th and 19th centuries.[53] However, this class of capitalists should not be confused with those who enjoyed the reputation of being big merchants during the heyday of the Mughal Empire. It seems that the 'big' of the Mughal period did not change their loyalties in the subsequent period and continued to operate from their original centres. Thus, they declined alongwith the decline in the power of their patrons. The vacuum, thus, created by the extinction of the old capitalist class was filled up by the 'new' which was the creation of the immediate situation and helped the English so as to securely build up their own trading empires in the course of time.

There is a proverb in Rajasthan stating that the Rajasthani mahajan went to *pardesh* (other region) with an empty pot (*lotah*) and returned with the pot full of coins. This is said about those Marwaris who had no means of subsistence in their home towns and, thus, went out in search of jobs to other regions. In the latter half of the 18th and the first half of the 19th centuries, Calcutta, Bombay and Patna were known as places of commercial speculations. In these cities as well as other places the Marwaris started working as *gumasta* or *arhatia* to the firms belonging to other Marwari families. It is noteworthy that established Marwari business families extended a helping hand to persons coming from their native places and belonging to their caste. Thus the economic considerations played a significant role in the process of Marwari emigration to different parts of India.

The study of the firms established by some of the Marwaris reveals that their business operations were multifarious in character. While trade and wholesale business remained their main occupation, they continued practising banking and insurance on a wide scale. Usury had become less attractive outside Rajasthan and was limited only to the known and reputed factors. Only those who exercised political influence could operate usury on a significant scale. Thus, while usury became secondary in importance, banking and insurance came to be practised on a large scale with the increase in the volume of trade and expansion of the trading operations. The development of commercial capital in the 18th century Rajput states was revolutionized with the increase in demand for cotton and opium, and later on tea, in the foreign market. The Marwaris availed themselves of the opportunities to the maximum and with the unorthodox character of entrepreneurship, they succeeded in increasing their capital—though commercial in character as long as industrial development remained out of reach.

The involvement of the merchants in taking *ijara* on a large scale was a significant factor in the process of development of the capitalist orientation of the business class in Rajasthan. It was a new sector of the capital investment and lucrative for gaining profit on large scale. The *ijara*, particularly of land revenue and commercial taxes, was obviously helpful to promote their original profession. Under the existing situation, however, they remained more concerned with collecting as much revenue as possible without bothering to solve the problems of cultivators and encourage agricultural production. The so-called orthodox section of the Bania community, thus, was not orthodox as far as the trade and commercial enterprises were concerned. It seems that agriculture failed to attract the traders and merchants not because they lacked entrepreneurship but because agriculture did not promise as high dividends. On the other hand, if they remained aloof from industrial undertakings, it was because the colonial economic structure offered very little scope for the development of industrial capital—a facility available to the commercial economy of European countries during the same period.

NOTES

1. Brijkishore Bhargava, *Indigenous Banking in Ancient and Medieval India* (Bombay, 1934), p. 233.
2. James Tod, *Annals and Antiquities of Rajasthan* (New Delhi, 1978), II, p. 127.
3. S. Nurul Hasan, K.N. Hasan and S.P. Gupta, "Pattern of Agricultural Production in the Territory of Amber", Indian History Congress, *Proceedings* (Mysore Session, 1966), pp. 224-264; and "Prices of Foodgrains in the Territories of Amber" (1650-1750 A.D.), Indian History Congress, *Proceedings* (Patiala Session, 1967), pp. 345-68; Satish Chandra, "Role of the Local Community, the Zamindars and the State in Providing Capital Inputs for the Development and Expansion of Cultivation in Medieval India", *Indian Historical Review*, Vol. III, No. 1 (1976), pp. 83-98; G.D. Sharma, "Indigenous Banking and the State in the Eastern Rajasthan during the Seventeenth Century", Indian History Congress, *Proceedings* (Waltair Session, 1979), pp. 432-41 and "Vyaparis and Mahajans in Western Rajasthan during the Eighteenth Century, Indian History Congress, *Proceedings* (Bombay Session, 1980), pp. 377-85.
4. Satish Chandra, "Some Aspects of Growth of Money Economy in India during the 17th Century", *Indian Economic and Social History Review*, No. 4 (1965), pp. 321-331; Irfan Habib, "Potentialities of Change in the Economy of Mughal India", *Socialist Digest*, No. 6 (Sept. 1972), pp. 74-137; Iqtidar Alam Khan, "Middle Class in the Mughal Empire", Medieval Section Presidential Address, Indian History Congress, *Proceedings* (Aligarh Session, 1975); V. I. Pavlov, *Historical Premises for India's Transition to Capitalism* (Moscow, 1979), pp. 83-109. Thomas A. Timberg, *The Marwaris* (New Delhi, 1978).
5. Nainsi's classification of Urban population clearly shows the dominance of the *Mahajans* or *Banias* (traders and merchants) over the other communities in the *pargana* towns of Western Rajasthan during the 17th century. However, Nainsi has placed all the communities of commercial enterprises into one category, i.e. *baniya*; G.D. Sharma, "Urban Social Structure : A Case Study of the Towns of Western Rajasthan during the 17th Century," in J.S. Grewal and Indu Banga (ed.), *Studies in Urban History*, (Amritsar, 1981) pp. 70-9, cf Timberg,

The Marwaris, n. 4, p. 10; Balchand Modi, *Deshke Itihas Men Marwari Jati Ka Sthan* (Calcutta, 1940), pp. 222, 365-67; Job Charnock speaks highly of the honesty and faithfulness of the Marwaris in the seventies of the 17th century. Brijkishore Bhargava, *Indigenous Banking*, n. 1, pp. 40-41.

6. Irfan Habib, "Usury in Medieval India", *Comparative Studies in Society and History*, Vol. VI, No. 4 (July 1964), pp. 393-423, cf. G.D. Sharma, "Indigenous Banking ..." and "Mahajans and Vyaparis ...", *op. cit.*
7. Documents pertaining to the *Diwan Hazuri* and *Amber Records* throw sufficient light on this trend. *Diwan Hazuri* documents furnish detailed information, *pargana*-wise regarding the appointments of the revenue officers and the names of the sahukar or mahajan who served as security for the appointment.
8. Maharaja Sawai Jaisingh obtained the maximum advantage of the weakening position of the Mughal rule for, he acquired a large portion of Mughal *Khalisa* and *jagir* territory and incorporated it into his *watan* territory. In the territory controlled by him, Jaisingh adopted the practice of *ijara* on a large scale—particularly in the areas acquired from the Mughal Emperors after the death of Aurangzeb. The Vakid Reports (Rajasthani) furnish useful information on the *ijara* secured by Sawai Jai Singh from the Mughal Emperors. The documents pertaining to *Diwan Hazuri* and *Amber-Records* contain the information on the system of *ijara* as it pervailed in the territory of Amber during the 18th century. The *Jama-bandhi* records of Jodhpur State furnish information on the *ijara* practices during the 18th century. For Jaipur State see C.U. Wills, *A Report on the Land Tenures and Special Powers of Certain Thikanedars of the Jaipur State*, (Jaipur, 1933), pp. 10-14, Dilbagh Singh, *Ijara System in Eastern Rajasthan, 1750-1800 A.D. Proceedings of Rajasthan History Congress*, Vol. VI, (1973), pp. 60-9; S.P. Gupta, "Ijara System in Eastern Rajasthan", *Medieval India—a Miscellany* (Aligarh, 1972) Vol. II, p. 263; G.D. Sharma, "Political Change and the Rajput Nobility during the Eighteenth Century", Paper presented at U.G.C. *Seminar on Political Change and Socio-Economic Structure*, held in April 1980, in the Department of History, G.N.D. University, Amritsar.
9. Dilbagh Singh, "Ijara System ...," n. 8; G.D. Sharma, "Vyaparis and Mahajans ...," n. 3.
10. G.D. Sharma, "Indigenous Banking ...", n. 3. The pattern of the indigenous banking was similar in all the Rajput states of Rajasthan. The records of *Potedar* of Churu and the *Jamabandhi* documents available in the Jodhpur branch of Rajasthan State Archives, Bikaner testify to the similarity in pattern.
11. The abstracts of the *Jama-Kharch bahis* of Potedar family published in the *Marushree* indicate clearly the prevalence of *hundi* system on

a very large scale in the state of Bikaner; for the *mahajans*, and the *sahukar, sarrafs* forming a part of the broad framework of commercial activities, c.f., Govind Agrawal, "Churu ka Potedar Abhilekh Samgrah" *Marushree, Varsh* 9, *Ank.* 2-3 (January-June 1980) pp. 5-36.

12. cf. G.D. Sharma, "Indigenous Banking ...", no. 3
13. *Parwana* issued by Maharaja Sawai Jaisingh to the *amil* and *amin* of Pargana Ajmer dated *Kartik Vadi* 2, 1779 (v.s.) records the instructions issued to the *amils, amins* and *vyaparis* for advancing the money. *Diwan Hazuri* year v.s. 1779. We come across similar information in the letters of the following years, *Jaipur Historical Section*, Rajasthan State Archives, Bikaner (R.S.A.B.).
14. Levies on internal trade comprised, (a) duties on the sale of local produce known as *dan* which was imposed on the local traders; (b) *mapa* denoted the weighing of goods subject to import and export from a *Pargana*. (Different rates were charged according to the weight or quantity of articles). (c) *rahdari* was road police tax or inland transit duty. Formerly it was a right of the state, but was now levied by local officers, *Zamindars* (*thikanadars*), *Jagirdars* and *Ijaradars*. The term *Sair*, although used separately in the *parwanas* and *sanads* includes taxes covered by *dan* and *mapa* or levied on grains in transit from one district to another. cf. *Pargana Sanchor Ki Jamabandi*, year v.s. 1826, and *Pargana Jalor Ki Sair Jamabandhi*, v.s 1826, Rajasthan State Archives, Jodhpur Branch (R.S.A.J.).
15. There are a number of *Parwanas* to the effect of granting such concessions to the internal as well as external traders, *Sanad Parwana bahi* No. 285, R.S.A.J.
16. *Khas Rukka—Parwana bahi* No. 1, R.S.AB. and *Sanad-bahi* No. 285, (R.S.A.B.).
17. *Parwana* dated *Maha vadi* 3, 1827, *Khas Rukka-Parwana Bahi* No. 1.
18. *Parwana* dated *Vaishakh vadi* 6, 1827, *ibid.*
19. *Parwana* date *Vaishakh vadi* 5, 1829, *ibid.*
20. *Parwana* dated *Vaishakh vadi* 5, 1838, *ibid.*
21. G D. Sharma, "Vyaparis and Mahajans", n. 3.
22. *Parwana* dated *Maha vadi* 9, 1822 issued to the *Jagirdar* of Ahuwa, *Khas Rukka Parwana Bahi*, n. 16.
23. *Parwana* dated *Phalgun vadi* 14, 1825 issued to Bhandari Manakchand and Singhvi Sawaimal informing them that Sami Sawaj would be given possession of *haweli* at Didwana and be paid the same respect as enjoyed by him earlier. It seems that Sami Sawaj was the Sahukar recognized by the State, *Khas Rukka Parwana Bahi*, n. 16.
24. In Marwar such *Parwanas* were issued every year by the rulers, *Khas Rukka Parwana bahi, op. cit.*
25. S.C. Misra, "Urban Structure and Change : A Study of the Impact of Tradition on Indian Towns with Special Reference to Ahmedabad and Surat", in J.S. Grewal and Indu Banga (ed.), *Urban History* (Amritsar, 1981), pp. 80-90.
26. G.D. Sharma, *Rajput Polity*, (New Delhi, 1977), conclusion.

27. The *Jamabandis* of *sair* pertaining to the various *parganas* of Marwar of the years 1769-1800 A.D. furnish details regarding the rates of taxes levied on all the categories of traders, according to the nature of articles they carried. Similarly, the documents such as *Diwan-Hazuri, Yaddashti, Amber Records*, etc., throw considerable light on these problems regarding Eastern Rajasthan.
28. The *Sair Jama Kharach bahis* of Marwar records the prevalence of the taxes such as *Pesar-Nikal, Bohlawa, Vatwai, Tulawat, Parkhai Chhapa* and *Mohari, Chungi-Mosli, Arhat, Delali, Padava, Tehbazari*, etc. For definition and explanation, see, Prince Salim, "Nature of Commercial Taxes in Marwar and the Role of State in Promoting the Trade in the Latter Half of the Eighteenth Century", Paper presented at the Bodh Gaya Session of the Indian History Congress in December 1981.
29. Apparently the references to such taxes are not recorded in the official papers. But the complaints received by the Diwan Office from the merchants and traders indicates that these land-holders and *ijaradars* collected the forbidden taxes from the traders and merchants.
30. V.S. Bhatnagar, *Life and Times of Maharaja Sawai Jai Singh*, (Delhi, 1974), pp. 297-303; Dilbagh Singh, "Nature and Incidence of Taxes Levied on Inland Trade in Eastern Rajasthan during the 17th and 18th Century", Indian History Congress, *Proceedings* (Bhubaneshwar Session, 1977), pp. 311-26.
31. cf. Dilbagh Singh, "Nature and Incidence ...", n. 30.
32. An example is of a trader of Churu (Chaturbhuj) who was forced to pay heavy taxes on the goods passing through this territory because he had shifted to Ramgarh and was not keeping good relations with the *Thakur* of Churu, cf. Govind Agarwal (ed.) *Potedar Sangrah ka Aprakashit Kagjat* (Churu, 1976), p. 7 and *Potedar Samgrah ke Farasi Kagjat*, (Churu, 1978), p. 2.
33. cf. G.D. Sharma, "Mahajans and Vyaparis...," n. 8.
34. It is said that Chaturbhuj, one of the sons of Bhagotiram went to Punjab and engaged in trading and commercial activities keeping his headquarters at Bhatinda, cf. Govind Agrawal, *Farasi Kagjat*, n. 32, p. 2.
35. Govind Agrawal, *Aprakashit Kagjat*, n. 32, p. 7.
36. *Ibid*., p. 7.
37. *Ibid*., p. 9; Balchand Modi, "Desh Ke Itihas me ...," n. 5, p. 464.
38. Govind Agrawal, *Farasi Kagjat*, n. 32, p. 2. Maharaja Surat Singh of Bikaner secured his control on Churu as a result of the treaty concluded in 1818 A.D. with the English, for detail, see Karni Singh, *The Relations of the House of Bikaner with the Central Powers*, (New Delhi, 1974), pp. 125-132.
39. *Hisab-Kitab ke Kagjat*, cited in Govind Agrawal, *Aprakashit Kagjat*, n. 32, p. 14.
40. *Ibid*.

41. *Bahi* No. 8, years v.s. 1883-1887, *Marushri*, *Varsh* 9, *Ank.* 2-3, (Jan-June 1980), p. 8.
42. Govind Agrawal, *Aprakashit Kagjat*, n. 32, pp. 21-34.
43. *Ibid.*, pp. 40-41. The *Parwana* dated *Bhadra Sudi* 4, *Samvat* 1884 issued under the signature of Diwan Muhta Rao Abhai Singh to Potedar Mirzamal contains the details of the revenue assignment made to Mirzamal against the credit taken by the Bikaner ruler in v.s. 1884.
44. Letter dated May 22, 1834, cited in Govind Agrawal, "Potedar Samgrah Se Unnisvi Sadi ke Vyapar Samabandhi Kuch Mahatvapurna Saksh" *Proceedings of Rajasthan History Congress*, Jaipur Session, 1978, also see Govind Agrawal, *Farasi Kagjat*, n. 32, pp. 18-19.
45. Govind Agrawal, *Farasi Kagjat*, n. 32, pp. 16-20.
46. cf. *Marushri*, n. 41, pp. 8-9, also Govind Agrawal, *Farasi Kagjat*, n. 32, pp. 4-5.
47. Jhabarmal Sharma, *Poddar Abhinandan Granth*, 11.
48. Letter year v.s. 1879, cited by Agarchand Nahta in *Seth Motishah* (Ajmer, 1966). It is generally believed that the father of Seth Motishah was originally from Pali, but the information recorded by Agarchand Nahta has proved that this family was originally from Phalodi (Marwar).
49. Nahta, *Moti Shah*, n. 48, pp. 2-6.
50. Girjashankar Sharma, "Bikaner ke Vyapari Varg ka Nishkraman aur usake Karan", *Proceedings of Rajasthan History Congress*, Ajmer Session, pp. 79-87.
51. Letter dated *Pous Sudi*, 1, 1883 written by Maharaja Surat Singh to Potedar Mirzamal, Govind Agrawal, *Aprakashit Kagjat*, n. 32, p. 33.
52. On the plea of Maharaja Surat Singh of Bikaner, Potedar Mirzamal agreed to return to Churu but Rao Lakshman Singh of Sikar was not ready to leave him. Thus on dated *Chaitra vadi* 5, 1879 Surat Singh wrote a letter to Sawai Jai Singh pointing out the freedom of mobility the traders should enjoy in the country, Govind Agrawal, *Aprakashit Kagjat*, n. 32, pp. 19-20.
53. For a detailed discussion on the 'great firm' theory see Karen Leonard, "The Great Firm Theory of the Decline of the Mughal Empire", *Comparative Studies in Society and History*, Vol. 21, No. 2 (April 1979), pp. 152-61.

12

Business Communities of Punjab

J.S. Grewal

To think of the business communities is primarily to think of towns and cities. Unfortunately, very little attention has been paid to urban centres in the pre-British Punjab. The available evidence on one urban centre, namely Batala, clearly shows that business communities such as the Khatris were its economic backbone, though it was founded as an administrative centre. Within the first quarter of its foundation in the late 15th century, a family of Chauna khatrīs had settled in Batala. The Puri, Bhandari, Khosla and Dhir Khatris too were some of the old inhabitants of the town. The Bhandaris believe that their ancestors had come to Batala in the reign of Akbar. The Julka and their *muhalla* and a Sahdan Khtari find mention in a document of the early 1690s. By the early eighteenth century, the Ohri, Sekhri and Chawinda Khatris *too* appear to have settled in Batala. The number of Khatri subcastes in Batala eventually exceeded thirty. The majority of them were shopkeepers, traders and *sahukars* and owned residential and landed property in the town.

The town provided enough opportunities for the trader. It came to serve as a market for the agricultural produce of the surrounding villages. Its *ghalla-mandī* and *bāzār-i-ghalla-faroshān* are mentioned in the documents of the 18th century. It was connected with the markets of the smaller towns on all sides. Besides wheat, the market of Batala was well known for its *gur* (raw sugar) which came from the rich countryside eminently suitable for the cultivation of sugarcane. In the late 19th century, the commodities sent from Batala to Amritsar included sugar, jaggery, *gur*, paddy, mash and wheat. It may be a safe assumption that these commodities were sent to Lahore before the rise of Amritsar as a commercial city. Similarly much of what Batala received in return from Amritsar in the late 19th century also came largely through Lahore: salt, pepper, cinnamon, muslin, Gujarati *khes*, the double *loi* of Khemkaran, and from Sialkot paper and iron. Through the city of Lahore, it was connected with Delhi and Multan and with cities beyond the Indian subcontinent on the north-west. Raw silk, for example, used to come from Bukhara.

Batala was by no means an exception. It is true that cities and towns had begun to decline with the decline of the Mughal power in the north-west of the Empire. With the establishment of Sikh rule, however, many of the old urban centres were revived, particularly those which were adopted as administrative centres by the new rulers. Some new centres also came up. Rawalpindi grew into a town of considerable size under Milkha Singh. Gujaranwala, Qila Sobha Singh and Qila Suba Singh developed as new towns as did Sri Hargobindpur in upper Bari Doab. Cities and towns expanded with the expansion of Maharaja Ranjit Singh's dominions. Most of the administrative centres were retained as *pargana* headquarters or the headquarters of the governors of the Maharaja. The capital cities like Multan, Srinagar and Peshawar were not allowed to suffer in size or importance. Lahore was actually revived on a larger scale. Similarly, towns like Wazirabad, Gujarat and Sialkot flourished under the Maharaja. Some new towns also came up, like Haripur in the Hazara region. Amritsar became the premier city not only in the dominions of Ranjit Singh but also in the north-west of the subcontinent. Every urban centre was, to a varying degree, connected with the villages around; it was linked up also with some other towns of smaller or larger size. We can look upon urban centres as so many linkages between the various regions of the entire Sikh dominions, and with the outside world. The total number of important urban centres in the territories of the Maharaja exceeded one hundred, while the number of large villages with small markets ran into thousands. They all served as more or less important centres of trade.

Cities and towns served as centres of manufacture as well. The revival of Lahore also meant the revival of its most important industries: metal work and textiles, including silk, cotton and wool. Multan was famous for its silks and cottons and well-known for woollen carpets, glazed pottery and enamelling of silver. In Amritsar, towards the end of Ranjit Singh's reign, there were nearly 2,000 shops and manufactories of shawls. Coarse woollen cloth was also made in Amritsar, particularly for the army. It was well known also for its metal work, wood carving and work on marble and ivory. Many of the smaller towns also manufactured goods for local consumption and export. Woollen textiles were prepared in towns like Dera Baba Nanak and Sujanpur. Batala was known for its silk, woollens and cottons, as also for its saddlery and metal work. Qasur was known for tanning and ornamental work on leather, saddles, bridles and shoes. Wazirabad produced large quantities of coarse cloth for export, besides small tents and *sholdaris*. Jhang was known for cotton cloth. Sialkot, Jullundur and Hoshiarpur were known for *susi*, *lachas* and *lungis*. Sialkot was famous also for the manufacture of several varieties of paper: Man Singhi, Hariri, Damhuri and Jahangiri. Bajwara in the Bist Jalandhar Doab was famous for its turbans, Chiniot was famous for its bows, and Kotli Loharan in the Rachna Doab for its matchlocks. Sahiwal was known for its *salus* and copper-ware. Gujrat produced swords and matchlocks.

We may be sure that every urban centre produced cotton cloth and had its *thathiars* and *kaseras*. Metal work was an important industry. Leather goods were produced in all cities and towns. Gold and silver were used for ornaments and leafing. Copper and brass were used for making utensils and images. Trade and manufacture was a private enterprise. Besides traders and merchants, every urban centre had its own *sahukars* who lent money for personal and commercial use. Not only in the capital cities and in Amritsar, Sialkot, Gujrat, Wazirabad, Gujranwala and Batala, but also in unexpected places there were rich *sahukars*: in a small town like Sambrial near Sialkot, and in Sheikhupura and in Gojra, for example.

Items of trade came from both agriculture and manufactures. In 1838, Ranjit Singh agreed to send merchants towards Bombay by way of the Indus with salt and shawls worth a lakh of rupees. In 1839, the English wanted the Maharaja to encourage export of sugar, *ghi*, oils, drugs, ginger, saffron, cotton, madder dyes and grain, and the import of *pashmina*, opium, indigo, dried fruit, superior silks, muslins and broad cloth, inferior silks, cottons and chintzes through Ludhiana, Ferozepur and Mithankot. There is no doubt that wheat, rice, sugar, cotton, indigo, poppy, pepper and dried ginger were already exported to Afghanistan and Central Asia from the dominions of Maharaja Ranjit Singh. Gold, silver, iron, copper, brass and zinc were among the important items of import besides, silk and wool, dry and fresh fruits, as well as horses. To these may be added dyes and some luxury goods.

Internal trade remained more important than external trade. Amritsar was linked by road with Lahore, and through Lahore with Srinagar, Multan and Peshawar. Every city was linked with smaller towns which in turn were linked up with villages. Wheat, cotton and sugar were sold in large quantities in most of the towns and all the cities. Rice, ginger and dyes came from the hills to the plains while cotton was sent from the plains to the hills. Rice, turmeric and hemp were sent from Sujanpur to Lahore and Amritsar. Turmeric and ginger from Amritsar were sent to Multan. These are only a few examples. The items of trade in every city and towns were quite numerous. Amritsar, for instance, exported wheat, rice, cotton, sugar, poppy, indigo, saltpetre, hides and skins, shawls and salt. The items imported were salt, gold, silver, iron, silk, leather, furs, wool, piecegoods, ivory, glass, spices, dry fruit, dyes and horses, besides agricultural products.

Banking facilities were available through the *hundi* system. *Bima*, or insurance, was also available at cheap rates. The means of transportation were traditional: donkeys, mules, ponies, camels, bullock carts and boats. The coinage in the dominions of Ranjit Singh was not uniform, though the Nanak Shahi rupee served as the standard. There were no standardized weights and measures, though the regional variations were small and the traders were familiar with them. There are indications that the *sahukars* used their capital for getting finished products from the craftsmen who were paid wages or remuneration for their output, though many a craftsmen produced goods in his small manufactory with raw materials purchased by himself. There were no corporate business organizations. In the general pattern of trade, the domestic market was more important than the foreign market. Agricultural produce and manufactures from agricultural produce were more important than manufactured goods. The items of import were largely meant for the royalty, the ruling class and rich individuals. Among the items of export, textiles and some basic necessities formed the bulk. The economy of the days of Ranjit Singh compares well with the economy of the Mughal times. In fact, its pattern was much closer to the medieval pattern than that of British India.

Now the obvious question that we have to ask is about the identity of those traders, merchants and *sahukars* who contributed so much to the economic activity of towns and cities. There is no doubt that an important business community in Punjab was that of the Khatris who found a spokesman in Ganesh Das Wadhera at the beginning of British rule in the Punjab. After a mythical account of creation and the origin of the Brahmans, Ganesh Das refers to the time of Raja Bharat when civilized arts were developed and society was divided into four *barans* (varnas). The Kshtriyas were divided into two major groups: the *surajbansi* (*suryavanshi*) and the *chandarbansi* (*chandravanshi*). They both became degenerate and yielded place to the Rajputs. Many of them accepted a subordinate position. And those who refused to acknowledge Rajput superiority were obliged to leave their homes in 'Hindustan' to migrate to the Punjab. Here they developed interest in service, trade, business, shopkeeping, drapery and banking. The Sultans of Delhi discovered their talents and encouraged them to learn Persian and to accept service with the government. Thus patronized, they attained to high positions in the administration, particularly during the Mughal times. They suffered a setback in the beginning of the Sikh rule but eventually their merit was recognized and they again became increasingly important in the administrative set-up. They became *diwans*, *nazims*, *kardars*, *vakils* and commanders, without losing their traditional position as *qanungos*, *mutasaddis* and *munshis*.

Ganesh Das specifically refers to many Khatri families living in the towns and villages of Punjab : in Kaliana, Rohtas, Bahlolpur, Jalalpur, Daulatnagar, Hajiwala, Gujrat, Herat,

Dinga, Akiya Lakhanwal, Bhagowal, Islamgarh, Makhowal, Waraich, Sialkot, Wazirabad, Eminabad, Daska Nidhan Singh Wala, Pasrur, Buchcha, Pindi Bhattian, Malhian, Shaikhupura, Batala, Kalanaur, Dera Baba Nanak, Patti, Qasur, Jalandhar, Nawan Shahr, Amritsar and Lahore, among many others. There was hardly a town in Panjab where Khatris did not have their houses. In many *parganas* they were hereditary *qanungos*. In many towns and cities they are mentioned as *sahukars*, traders and merchants, and in many villages, as proprietors of land. There are also references to their migration from one town or city to another in search of better opportunities.

Notwithstanding his deep interest in the Khatris Ganesh Das does not give the impression that they were the only rich people in the towns and cities of Punjab. There is no doubt that Aroras and Banias as well as Khatris represented the *sahukars* and eminent citizens of the places described by Ganesh Das. In Shahdara, for instance, Dayal Shah Arora and Raman Shah were two of the most important *sahukars* in the early nineteenth century. Of the many rich *sahukars* of Amritsar in the reign of Ranjit Singh, the most distinguished was Raman Shah Bania. Trade and business in Punjab was by no means confined to the Hindus. In Bera, for instance, Qutbuddin and Imam Bakhsh had a flourishing business. They were Parachas. In Chiniot there lived many Khoja as well as Paracha *sahukars*. Khoja traders were important in Narowal also.

Among these mercantile communities, the Khatris with their numerous genealogical sections were on the whole the most important. Their main occupation was trade but they had long been associated with administration too, occasionally as governors and *diwans*, and much more frequently as *qanungos* and *kardars or 'amils*. They owned land, particularly in towns and cities, and some of them took to cultivation as well. They were most numerous in the Bist Jalandhar and the upper portions of the other Doabs. In the Chaj and the Sindh Sagar Doab, they shared their dominance with the Aroras who constituted the leading mercantile caste in the lower reaches of the rivers. Half of the Aroras of Punjab lived in the former province of Multan and the Derajat. Mostly traders, they could turn their hand to anything, including cultivation. A large proportion of the Aroras in the plains lower of the Chenab were purely agricultural. Like the Khatris, they were divided into a very large number of genealogical sections or subcastes; like them again, they were active, industrious, enterprising and thrifty. The Banias lived almost entirely for and by commerce, but their numbers in the land of the five rivers were very small. They were dominant in the Sutlej-Jamuna divide. The Jains, popularly known as Bhabras, were not very numerous, but they could be found in many urban centres as traders and shop-keepers. The Labanas, originally a salt-carrying and salt-trading community, were the transporters of grain and goods. Numerous in the submontane districts and in Lahore, they were also found in Gujranwala. In the western parts of Punjab, the counterparts of the Labanas were the Banjaras. There were many pedlars among the Banjaras and the Labanas.

The mercantile communities among the Muslims were largely represented by the Khojas and the Parachas. They were generally converted to Islam from amongst the Khatris, the Aroras and the Bhatias. The Khojas of Shahpur, for instance, were originally Arora.The Khojas of Lahore were Bhatia. There were important colonies of Parachas in Makhad, Attock and Peshawar. They traded with Central Asia in cloth, silk and indigo. Many of them kept petty shops and some of them pursued agriculture. Where the Paracha were important as traders, the pedlars were called Khojas and where the Khojas were important as traders, the pedlars were called Paracha. The Khojas were numerous along the hills from Gurdaspur to Rawalpindi, and also in Muzaffargarh and the Derajat. They were fairly numerous in Lahore, Sialkot, Gujrat and the Salt Range. In Jhang they owned a large number of wells. On the whole, they were important as traders. They retained traces of the Khatris organization and rules of marriage, bearing Khatri sectional names in Bhera and Shahpur.

More detailed information is available on the business communities in Punjab during the British period in terms of both numbers and distribution. In 1181, for instance, the Aroras numbered 4.5 lakhs and the Banias of whom more than 3.5 lakhs were Aggarwal numbered only a little less. The Khatris were more than 3 lakhs while the Khojas were nearly 66,000. and the Prachas were about 8,500. The Jains, or Bhabras, were about 14,000. By 1921 the number of Jains was nearly the same, the number of Prachas decreased to about 5,000. The Khojas, however, rose to more than 1.5 lakhs. In 1921 the Khatris also increased to nearly 9 lakhs. The Banias were over 6.25 lakhs while the Aroras were more than 13.5 lakhs. The entire membership of these castes, however, was not engaged in trade. In 1921 nearly 80 per cent of the Aggarwals; 65 per cent of the Aroras, 58 per cent of the Khatris and 50 per cent of the Khojas were traders.

As observed by Ibbetson, the territorial distribution of the business communities was very well marked. The Banias were confined to the eastern and the south-eastern divisions of Delhi, Hissar and Ambala and to the states in the Sutlej-Jamuna divide. They were practically unknown to the west of Lahore. The Khatris constituted the largest proportion of the mercantile classes in the centre and the north-west of the Punjab, being most numerous in the Jullundur, Amritsar, Lahore and Rawalpindi divisions. The Aroras had Multan and the Derajat divisions almost to themselves and extended into Peshawar and Kohat. They met the Banias of the east in Sirsa across the Sutlej. The Khojas and the Prachas were confined to the central and western districts and the Salt Range tract. The Jains were found in the northern districts from Ambala to Rawalpindi.

This broad distribution did not appreciably change in spite of some internal migration. The following table shows the position of the male population of the Khatris, the Aroras and the Aggarwal Banias in 1911:

Division	Khatri		Arora		Aggarwal Bania	
	Hindu	Sikh	Hindu	Sikh	Hindu	Sikh
Delhi	7,812	622	1,639	1,299	105,132	30
Jullundur	37,479	3,645	11,927	2,455	15,333	197
Lahore	65,072	9,133	42,517	19,155	5,403	2
Rawalpindi	35,441	30,405	41,176	30,940	512	0
Multan	24,461	3,232	137,461	38,794	846	5

On the whole the business communities in 1881 constituted 7 per cent of the population of the province. But in the districts of Multan and Derajat divisions and in Bahawalpur the proportion was from 11 to 17 per cent. This was due not to the fact that a larger proportion of the population of these parts was engaged in commerce, but to the peculiar versatility of the Aroras who were traders first no doubt, but after that anything and everything. Throughout the eastern plains the proportion was very uniform, rising highest in the districts which included large cities. Throughout the hills and submontane districts the proportion was low because these tracts included none of the commercial centres of the Punjab. In the central districts and the Salt Range tract the proportion was large, probably because the Khatris like the Aroras by no means confined themselves to commerce as an occupation.

The census reports provide concrete information on some of the other aspects of the business communities in the Punjab. In 1891 there were more than 1,50,000 moneylenders, about 60,000 general merchants, about 45,000 general shopkeepers and over 10,000 merchant-cum-shopkeepers. There were about 35,000 middle-men like the brokers, commission agents and auctioneers. The number of bankers and bank managers was over 400. In 1901 the Khatris are mentioned as having made their mark as bankers and civil administrators. By 1911, 25 per cent of the Khatris were educated. The Aroras and Aggarwals followed the Khatris in education with 21 per cent each. The educated Khojas at this time were less then 6 per cent. Furthermore while the Khatris and Aroras took to English education, the Aggarwals and the Khojas were literate in the vernaculars. Among the Khatris nearly 8 per cent knew English while among the Aroras and the Aggarwals this percentage was about 2 each. In the public services also the Khatris took the lead with nearly 9 per cent, while the Aroras constituted a little over 4 per cent of the administrators and the Aggarwals over 1 per cent. In 1921, the Khatris were dominant in industrial establishments also. They owned 300 establishments and managed more than 300 more. The Aggarwals owned 50 industrial establishments at this time and managed about 65 more. This was attributed to the organising ability of the Khatris and Aggarwals. But it was also a consequence of their commanding a large proportion of the floating capital of the Punjab.

It is possible to know something of the response of the

business communities in Punjab to the changing situation of the province under the British. Their activity is in evidence, first, in the increasing size and number of urban centres. According to the census report of 1855, only Amritsar had a population of over 1 lakh. Within three decades, the population of Lahore also increased to more than a lakh. Towards the end of the 19th century, there were more than 50 towns with a population of over 10,000 and nearly 100 towns with a population of over 5,000. Some idea of the increase in population of larger towns may be formed from the fact that Rawalpindi now had a population of nearly 88,000 whereas in 1855 it had about 16,000. Similarly, the population of Multan rose from 25,000 in 1855 to more than 87,000 at the end of the century. The population of Sialkot rose from about 19,000 to 58,000 during this period, that of Jullundur from about 28,500 to about 68,000 and that of Ambala from about 22,000 to about 79,000.

The increasing size and number of urban centres was a reflection of the increasing volume of trade. The average rate of imports for three years from 1886-87 to 1888-89 was 10.3 million maunds, while that of exports was 13.8 million maunds. For the four years ending 1904-05, the average imports rose to 23 million maunds and the average exports rose to 88.4 million maunds. In 1908-09, the total import amounted to 42.2 million maunds.

The major item of export was wheat. In 1891-92, more than 550 thousand tons of wheat were exported. In 1901-02 this figure rose to about 623,000, and in 1903-04 to 877,000. Raw cotton was also exported on a large scale. In 1901-02, raw cotton worth 127 lakh rupees was exported. In 1908-09 this figure rose to 194. The other important items of export were coarse grains, oil seeds, hides and wool.

Among imports, cotton piece-goods came first. Valued at 218 lakhs in 1890-91, cotton piece-goods fell to 190 lakhs in the last year of the century but rose to 423 lakh rupees in the first year of the 20th century. In 1904-05, the value of cotton piece-goods imported was 517 lakh rupees. The average of the four years ending in 1908-09 was 652 lakh rupees. The other substantial imports consisted of sugar, metals, oils, coal and jute goods. All this trade was largely in the hands of the Khatris, the Aroras and the Banias. The colonial character of the new economy is as clear as the successful adjustment of the trading communities in Punjab to the new pattern of economy.

There is hardly any doubt that the position of the business communities in the grain trade was greatly strengthened. They were able to take the grain directly from the peasant-proprietors who were obliged to pay a fixed amount of money annually as land revenue. This grain was taken at cheap harvest prices and disposed of at higher market prices, leaving a high margin of profit for the traders. This was one example of the advantage which the business communities took of the economic opportunities created by British rule.

Another area in which the business communities in Punjab took advantage of the new economic situation was that of moneylending. The money-lender was fairly well established in towns and large villages even before the annexation of the Punjab in 1849. But he was not so powerful under Sikh rule as under the British. Two restraints were removed, or at least weakened: the existence of a vigorous village community and the indifference of the state towards recovery. Moreover, the moneylender's own objective generally was to get the produce from the cultivators' fields rather than his land. In the early 1870s, the suits for debt were handed over to civil courts in Punjab which were presided over by professional judges who were often allied to the moneylender by caste if not by actual relationship. A rigid application of the law put the peasant entirely at the mercy of his creditor. By 1880, the unequal fight between the peasant-proprietor and the moneylender ended in the victory of the latter. For the next 30 years, the moneylender was at his zenith. The number of moneylenders in 1868 was not much more than half a lakh; by 1911 it rose to nearly 2 lakhs.

Legislation on the alienation of land at the turn of the century did not put a stop to moneylending, but it did weaken the position of the moneylender belonging to the traditional business communities. Malcolm Darling observed that the power of moneylender in Lahore, Amritsar and Hoshiarpur was not "half what it was, and around Jullundur, he is almost extinct. There he has been replaced by village banks and the agriculturist moneylender. Even in Multan, one of his strongholds, his grip is not as firm as it was, and in Rohtak the village gathering no longer finds him always sitting at the head of the charpoy, but more often at the foot—a small but significant sign of the change of the times. Nowhere is he as influential as he was, or the peasant quite as ignorant; and as the position changes, recovery becomes more difficult". Though the battle was not yet over, the moneylender started investing in trade. According to an official estimate, the number of moneylenders in the late 1920s was reduced to about 60,000.

Closely allied with the moneylender was the indigenous banker. In the late 1920s the number of indigenous bankers in Punjab was only about 100. A decline in their number had set in before the end of the 19th century. The increasing number of commercial banks in the early 20th century hastened the pace of decline in the fortunes of the indigenous bankers. They found it impossible to compete with the Imperial Bank in remittance, with the co-operative banks in deposits, and with the joint stock banks in advances. Like the moneylender, the indigenous banker also was quick to see the new signs and began to develop his interest in trade. Earlier also the indigenous bankers had generally combined banking with some other business. Now he turned more and more to trade. In Amritsar, for instance, where there were more indigenous bankers than in any other city of Punjab, only 8 out of 17 lived by banking alone. "In the old days bankers did more banking than business: now the tendency is other way. The businesses are of all sizes and vary in capital from Rs. 20,000 to 20 lakhs."

The response of the business communities of Punjab to changes in the area of manufactures was even more remarkable. Under the impact of the colonial economy some of the old industries died out. Sialkot was famous in Mughal and Sikh times for its paper, but the industry had declined in the face of competition from mill-made paper and the manufacture of paper in the jails. The paper industry of Multan also ceased to exist. Similarly, the shawl industry was facing problems. However, some of the manufacturers of shawls switched over to carpet-weaving. Towards the end of the 19th century weaving was a flourishing and important industry in Amritsar and its products were exported to all parts of the world.

Industrial enterprise was coming into evidence before the close of the 19th century. In 1881 there were six steam factories for ginning and pressing cotton. In 1891, there were 12 and by 1904 there were 114. There were 8 cotton-spinning and weaving mills in the Punjab in 1903-04, more than 475 looms worked by steam and 2 distilleries. There were two iron foundries, one at Lahore and another at Sialkot where an enterprising firm made surgical instruments. Steam power was used in 175 factories. In 1908 there were over 260 factories employing 26,000 persons; 182 looms were engaged in ginning cotton, mainly for export and there were 8 cotton-spinning and weaving mills, 17 flour mills, 5 rice mills, 9 iron and brass works and 10 steam printing presses. The Egerton Woollen Mills at Dhariwal employed about 1000 persons on 264 looms and nearly 7,000 spindles. Much of this industrial enterprise was in the hands of the traditional business communities of Punjab.

A British administrator writing in 1947 observed that the shrewd businessmen of Amritsar had taken advantage of every favourable turn of the economic wind, every advance in mechanism and power, every improvement in the means of communication and transport. Indeed, when the shawl industry of Amritsar seemed almost annihilated by shawls imported from France and Germany, the businessmen of Amritsar revived it by importing woollen yarn from France and Poland and producing shawls which could be marketed in different parts of British India, notably in Bengal and Madras. Some of the shawl manufacturers of Amritsar took to carpet-weaving. A woollen mill for the manufacture of carpet yarn was established in 1924. By 1929 there were 600 hand-weaving carpet looms, employing over 3,000 weavers. The Amritsar carpets found a market not only in India but also overseas. The introduction of woollen spinning and weaving mills in Amritsar enabled the industrialists to manufacture heavy woollens like blankets and serges. Amritsar became a manufacturing centre for woollens. Similarly when the old silk industry was phased out, the Amritsar manufacturers started using artificial silk imported from Japan and Italy. Before 1947 there were a few hosiery factories and a sugar mill in Amritsar. The city also developed a chemical industry to meet the demand of the entire province. The city of the Amritsar was by no means an exception.

This general survey of the business communities of Punjab

makes it quite clear that they were playing an important role in the medieval economy; they were capable of taking advantage of the opportunities offered by the colonial economy and they were resilient enough to meet the demands of the new situation. They contributed appreciably to the growth of capital and the beginning of industrialization in Punjab. If large scale industrialization did not take place in Punjab, a few of the more ambitious among them left the province, to explore greater possibilities in some other part of India. It may now be added that the Khatris and Aroras of Punjab played an important role in the movement for socio-religious reform and in the spheres of education and politics. Their number is not an index of their socio-political importance in the province.

SELECT BIBLIOGRAPHY

I *CENSUS REPORTS*

Report on the Census Taken on the 1st January 1855 of the Population of the Punjab Territories (Supt. Donald Mclead), (Calcutta 1856).

Report on the Census of the Punjab Taken on the 17th February 1881 (Denzil Ibbetson), Vol. I, np., nd.

The Report on the Census, The Punjab and Its Feudatories, (E.D. Maclagan), Part I, *Census of India 1891*, Vol. XIX, (Calcutta 1892).

Census of India 1901, Vol. XVII, *The Punjab, Its Feudatories, And the North-West Frontier Province* (H.A. Rose), Part I, (Simla 1902).

Census of India 1911, Vol XIV, Punjab (Pandit Hiti Kishan Kaul), (Lahore 1912).

Census of India 1921, Vol. XV, *Punjab and Delhi*, Part I (L. Middleton, and S.M. Jacob), (Lahore 1923).

Report on the Census of India 1931, Vol XVII, (Khan Ahmad Hasan Khan) Punjab Part I, (Lahore 1933).

II *GAZETTEERS*

Ambala District Gazetteer 1892-93.

Amritsar District Gazetteer 1892-93.

Attock District Gazetteer 1907.

Dera Ghazi Khan District Gazetteer 1893-97.

Ferozepur District Gazetteer 1888-89.

Gujranwala District Gazetteer 1886-89.

Gujrat District Gazetteer 1892-93.

Gurdaspur District Gazetteer 1891-92.

Gurgaon District Gazetteer 1910.

Hissar District Gazetteer 1904.
Hoshiarpur District Gazetteer 1904.
Imperial Gazetteer of India, Vol. XX, Calcutta 1908.
Jhang District Gazetteer 1908.
Jhelum District Gazetteer 1883-84.
Jullundur District Gazetteer 1853-84; also of *1904.*
Jullundur District Gazetteer 1904.
Kangra District Gazetteer 1904.
Karnal District Gazetteer 1890.
Lahore District Gazetteer 1883-84.
Lahore District Gazetteer 1916.
Ludhiana District Gazetteer 1888-89.
Layallpur District Gazetteer 1904.
Montgomery District Gazetteer 1898-99.
Multan District Gazetteer 1923-24.
Muzaffargarh District Gazetteer 1908.
Peshawar District Gazetteer 1897-98.
Rawalpindi District Gazetteer 1893-94.
Rohtak District Gazetteer 1910.
Shahpur District Gazetteer 1904.
Sialkot District Gazetteer 1894-95.

III *MISCELLANEOUS REPORTS*

Monograph on Silk Industry in the Punjab 1885-86 (Lahore 1887).
Report of the Punjab Provincial Banking Enquiry Commission 1929-30, Vol. I (Lahore 1930).
Annual Report on the Punjab Alienation of Land Act XII of 1900 (Lahore 1902).

IV BOOKS AND ARTICLES

Calvert, H., *The Wealth and Welfare of the Punjab* (Lahore, 1922).
Darling, Malcolm, *The Punjab Peasant in Prosperity and Debt*, (Delhi, 1977, Reprint).
Datta, V.N., *Amritsar Past and Present* (Amritsar 1967).
Dungen P.H.M. van den, "Changes in Status and Occupation in Nineteenth Century Punjab", *Soundings in Modern South Asian History* (ed. by D.A. Low), (London 1968), 57-94.
Gauba, A., "Amritsar 1849-1947 : A Study in Urban History (Ph.D. Thesis, Guru Nanak Dev University, Amritsar 1980).
Grewal, J.S., *In the By-Lanes of History*, IIAS (Simla 1975).
———*The Reign of Maharaja Ranjit Singh*, Sita Ram Kohli Memorial Lectures (Patiala 1981).
Grewal, J.S., and Indu Banga (trs and eds), *Early Nineteenth Century Panjab* (Amritsar 1975).

Hazlehurst, Leighton W., *Entrepreneurship and the Merchant Castes in a Punjabi City*, Monograph Number One, Monograph and Occasional Papers Series, Commonwealth Studies Centre (Duke University, Durham 1966).

Ibbetson, Sir Denzil, *Punjab Castes* (Patiala 1970, Reprint).

Jones, Kenneth W., *Arya Dharm : Hindu Consciousness in 19th Century Punjab* (New Delhi 1976).

Latifi, A., *Industrial Punjab : A Survey of Facts, Conditions and Possibilities* (Bombay 1911).

Rose, H.A., *Glossary of the Tribes and Castes of the West Punjab and North West Frontier Province* (Patiala 1970, Reprint).

Shah, K.T., *Industrialization of the Punjab* (Lahore 1941).

Singh, Harminder, *Industrial Development in the Punjab 1901-1947* (M.Phil Dissertation, Guru Nanak Dev University, Amritsar 1981).

Sykes, Thomas Michael, *Society, Power and Representations in Indian Politics : A Case Study of Haryana State*, Ph.D. Thesis, Duke University (Durham 1974).

Tandon, Prakash, *Punjabi Century* (Delhi 1961, Reprint).

Thorburn, S.S. *Mussalman and Moneylenders in the Punjab* (London 1885).

Trevaskis, H.K., *Land of the Five Rivers* (Oxford 1928).

Wilson, Sir James Recent Economic Development in the Punjab, A Paper read to the Royal Economic Society in February 1910 (Suffolk 1910).

13

Entrepreneurship and Business Communities in Colonial Madras, 1900-1929: Some Preliminary Observations

Raman Mahadevan

While in north India, both in the east and in the west, the industrial capitalists belonged predominantly to the traditional merchant and business communities—the Marwaris, Parsis, Banias, Khatris or others — the pattern in south India was not quite the same. Thus, the most prominent of the traditional business communities of south India and undoubtedly the largest component of south Indian capital in the colonial period, the Nattukottai Chettys are not found to be moving into modern industry in any significant sense until about the 1930s and 40s. Similarly, the Komati Chettys, another important section of the traditional business community from the Andhra region fall short of making a concerted breakthrough into modern industry. In contrast to this situation, very interestingly, one observes the emergence of commercial and industrial entrepreneurship among sections of non-commercial ethnic groups and communities such as the Naidus or Kammas of the Coimbatore region, the Tamil Brahmans, the Vellalas and the Nadars.

Though the above observation tends to oversimplify a rather complex situation, by suggesting that modern entrepreneurship in south India was not the preserve of the traditional business communities alone, it underlines the need to take into account the specificities that inhere in a developing historical situation—a complex situation characterised at certain points of time by the convergence of class and caste or community, and at certain other times by divergence of the two. Over time, the class dimension becomes significantly weighty. This is not to deny the importance and usefulness of the business community typology as an analytical category. Admittedly, it has and does provide insights into the specific characteristics and forms of the evolution of indigenous capital under the conditions of colonial rule. However, in itself it is not an adequate category for, over time caste categories recede into the background.

The process of the formation of industrial entrepreneurship in colonial Madras was uneven, protracted and comparatively considerably delayed. The reasons are not far to seek. South Indian merchant and trading capital, with the possible exception of the Nattukottai Chettys, did not enjoy the special advantages and opportunities, such that came the way of some of the Marwaris, Parsis and Banias of accumulating enormous capital through lucrative trade in opium, yarn, etc. In fact Madras Presidency never assumed the commercial importance of Bombay and Bengal—the nodal centres of international capital. It remained a comparative poor cousin. Moreover, the traditional south Indian merchant and banking capital which had been active in the textile trade of the erstwhile Carnatic region was either eliminated or diverted during the 18th century as a result of deliberate colonial policy.[1] Consequently, the process of capital accumulation had to commence from a rather narrow base. The colonial situation in Madras, characterised by the complete dominance of European capital over the key sectors of the economy viz. foreign trade, organised money market, railways, shipping, insurance and industry, tended to further restrict the rate of indigenous capital accumulation. Paradoxically, the very process of intervention of European capital in the economy through increasing commodity production, especially after the mid 19th century, also created conditions for the emergence of indigenous merchant capital. With the spread of cash crops and the introduction of communication networks there developed a need to maintain an expanding internal credit and trade network. Such conditions facilitated the intervention of indigenous capital, and from the last quarter of the 19th century the

Nattukottai Chettys, Komatis, Marwaris, Multanis as well as sections of the Nadars, Brahmans, Beri Chettys, Devangas, Vellalas and Muslims among others moved in to take advantage of these economic opportunities.

Though comprising one of the largest fractions of indigenous capital of south India, the scale of Chetty operations in colonial Madras was comparatively insignificant. From around the middle of the 19th century there was a steady and significant outflow of Chetty capital from its base in Madras to Burma, Malaya, Ceylon and Indo-China regions which were then in the course of being opened up for colonial exploitation. The emergence of very profitable economic opportunities in these regions, coupled with the lack of such alluring conditions in Madras, tended to draw away Chetty capital from India. The movement of Chetty capital was, as such, highly organised. Thus, in response to the new economic opportunities the Chettys developed a host of institutions and a network of associations. In purely economic terms these facilitated the creation of an extensive 'resource group' and subsequently accelerated the process of accumulation of Chetty capital. The significance of this unprecedented migration of Chetty capital in the development of modern entrepreneurship in this community hardly needs to be stressed. Much of the Chetty capital that was to find its way into industries in South India especially in the 30s and 40s of this century was largely accumulated through years of lucrative money-lending and trade overseas.[2]

By the turn of the century a section of the upper strata of the Chettys, though still primarily engaged in money-lending and trade, began gradually investing part of their surplus capital in certain industries and modern incorporated enterprises. Curiously, the Chettys who invested in industry before the First World War were among those whose principal operations were in the Madras region. The Malabar Spinning and Weawing Co. Ltd. was among the first mills to be promoted with substantial Chetty capital. Established in 1888 at Calicut the capital for the mill was principally subscribed by the A.L.A.R. Chetty family, Zamindars of Devakottah, and the Desamangalam Namboodripad family of Travancore.[3] Around the turn of the century the mill came under the management of P. Somasundaram Chetty. The latter, in partnership with the A.L.A.R.

group, founded the Kaleeswara Mills at Coimbatore in 1906. The paid-up capital of Rs. 6,50,000 "was principally subscribed by merchants, bankers and vakils".[4] During this period a group of Chettys, finding cotton industry as a field of profitable investment, acquired the defunct 'Koilpatti Mills'. Established in 1889 by a group of Rowther Muslim traders the mill was handicapped by the problem of insufficient finances and was eventually taken over by the mortgagee, a Hyderabad sahukar.[5] In 1908 it came up for court sale and was bought up by R.M. M.S.T. Vairavan Chetty and M.L.M. Ramanathan Chetty for nearly seven lakhs.[6] The same group of Rowther Muslims had also promoted the Petai Sugar Refining Co. Ltd. at Tachanalloor in 1895. It had a paid-up capital of Rs. 2,40,100.[7] The sugar mill unfortunately met the same fate as the cotton mill and by 1913-14 was taken over by yet another mortgagee—this time a Nattukottai Chetty—A.R.A.R.S.M. Somasundaram Chetty. Renamed the ARARSM Sugar Mill, the entire paid-up capital of 3 lakhs was subscribed by the proprietor. By the early 20s it would seem the mill was yielding adequate returns for, the paid-up capital was raised to Rs. 4,50,000 and in addition a sum of Rs. 2,50,000 had been raised for a distillery.[8] Taking full advantage of the profitable rice trade with Ceylon the Chettys invested quite a considerable amount of capital in the rice mills in the Tanjore district.[9] Chetty capital was also behind the promotion of the Lakshmi Paper Mills at Punalur in Travancore. Established in 1909, with a paid up capital of Rs. one lakh, the mill was severely handicapped by the lack of good machinery, chemicals and technical expertise and hence was commercially an unsuccessful venture.[10]

In the Andhra region prominent Komati Chetty families—the Nalams, Pydahs and the Motheys—had also begun investing part of their surplus capital in a few industries, principally jute and rice. The Krishna Jute & Cotton Mills and the Guntur Cotton & Jute Mills Co., established in 1904, were essentially the product of prominent Komati capital [11]

Among the Muslim traders only a few of them moved into industry and the most outstanding among them was Hajee Ismail Sait. From a base in the middleman trade and commision agency, Hajee Sait moved on to acquire the vast industrial interests of the Arbuthnots after the latter's collapse in 1906.[12]

This was also the period of relatively aggresive entrepreneurship. Under the influence and impetus of the Swadeshi movement a large number of fairly obscure small and middling entrepreneurs came forward to promote industries. However, lack of sufficient capital proved to be a major hurdle and one which these entrepreneurs were unable to overcome. The case of the illustrious Swadeshi Steam Navigation Co. was only slightly exceptional. Thus, apart from having to face the brunt of very severe competition from the powerful and well entrenched international shipping interest represented by the British India Steam Navigation Co. Ltd., the basic problem of 'Swadeshi' was one of lack of capital.[13] The enterprise was essentially backed by small Vellala, Nadar and Brahman capital. Likewise it was essentially the failure to raise sufficient capital that resulted in the Coimbatore Mall Mills, floated in 1908 by C.V. Venkataramana Iyengar, passing into the hands of the Steves group.[14] Another equally revealing case is that of P. Thyagaraja Chetty, a prosperous businessman from the Devanga community—one of the traditional weaving communities of South India. He had substantial interests in the handloom industry and "was said to have some 2000 weavers under him."[15] However, his attempt in 1910 to float a large textile mill in Madras with a capital of Rs. 12 lakhs floundered as he was unable to raise the necessary capital. His efforts to start a match factory in 1912 with a very modest capital of Rs. 2 lakhs was also infructuous.[16] In a situation characterised by the complete dominance of European capital over industry and the organised money market and the lack of cheap institutional credit for Indian industry, the financial staying power of the entrepreneurs was rather crucial and it was here that the Chettys scored over the others. However, the Chettys could not take full advantage of the situation as the bulk of their investments were outside India where they continued to fetch handsome returns until 1930.

A very significant development in this early period, and one which was indicative of a distinctly new stage in the evolution of provincial capital, was the establishment in 1906 of the Indian Bank Ltd., followed soon after by the Southern India Chamber of Commerce in 1907. It marked an attempt to provide concrete meaning to the rudiments of a new consciousness that provincial capitalists were a distinct class with distinct interests which often came into sharp conflict with those of foreign capital. This is not to suggest that caste and communal categories as an organising principle of indigenous capital disappeared. In the peculiar colonial situation characterised by all manner of constraints and restrictions for the growth of indigenous capital, the caste and communal categories continued to be invoked as it facilitated the process of capital accumulation and as such furthered the interests of the dominant classes within these communities and castes. The Indian Bank Ltd. came into existence in the wake of a severe financial crisis that had overtaken Madras following the collapse of the Arbuthnots. Leading traders and bankers of Madras belonging to the Nattukottai Chetty, Komati, Gujarati and Muslim communities came together to found the first indigenous joint stock bank in Madras.[17] The bank "was intended by its founders to be purely indigenous in its aims, and to . . . afford banking facility to Madras merchants and manufacturers."[18] Among those associated with the bank were Lodd Govindoss, Haji Abdul Aziz Batcha Sahib, M. Krishnaswami Ayyar and the Nattukottai bankers, S.R.M.M.A. Annamalai Chetty and S.R.M.A.R. Ramaswami Chetty.[19] The bank, in fact, was backed by considerable Chetty finances. From Rs. 10,00,000 in 1907, the paid-up capital of the bank shot up to Rs. 17,75,000 by 1908. Two-thirds of this sum had been subscribed by the Chettys.[20]

The Southern India Chamber of Commerce, by bringing together the leading sections of indigenous south Indian capital served as an important forum for safeguarding and furthering Indian commercial and industrial interests. A strong critic of the colonial government, it repeatedly demanded full fiscal autonomy and protection for indigenous industries from foreign competition.

The period after the First World War enabled the fledgling south Indian capital to consolidate the gains it had derived in the pre-war phase. There was during this period a perceptible shift in favour of industry but the process continued to be protracted and uneven. Consequent upon the drastic decline in foreign trade during the war years the domestic market, however limited, was partially available to Indian entrepreneurs. But they were unable to take full advantage of the situation owing to the choking off of the imports of mill mechinery and other accessories. The pent-up pressure for industrial growth found a release only after the war. However, the war years were not entirely negative. There was a tremendous growth of internal commerce and trade in the region. The huge profits which accrued to the traders during these years enabled many of them to invest in industry soon after the war.

The rise of the Coimbatore textile industry, and more particularly, of the Naidu or Kamma entrepreneurs can be traced to this period. Coimbatore, which had emerged as an important cotton producing centre even as early as the late 19th century grew in importance during the war years. As a consequence of the disruption in the import of foreign yarn, the demand for local yarn increased. There was a mushrooming of ginning mills in the villages around Coimbatore. Between 1911 and 1921 as many as 42 ginning units came into being.[21] Many of these were established by substantial landlord-cum-cotton traders belonging to the Naidu and Gounder communities The major thrust in the promotion of the cotton textile industry came essentially from three Naidu families. These were those of G. Kuppuswami Naidu, V. Rangaswami Naidu and P.S.G. Naidu. All of them were large landowners and had moved from cultivation of cotton into cotton trading around the turn of the century.[22] During the war years they made handsome profits, partly through speculation and forward trading. The capital thus accumulated enabled two of the groups to move into industry in the immediate post-war period. Thus the P.S.G. Naidu group established the Ranga Vilas Spinning & Weaving Mills Ltd. in 1922. Almost the entire share capital of Rs. 3,30,500 was raised from within the community. While 38 out of the 45 shareholders were Naidus, 55 per cent of the share capital was controlled by the P.S.G. family.[23] The case of the P.S.G. group was not exceptional. Most of the Naidu mills came to be closely held by individual Naidu families and all possible family and community connections were resorted to for raising the necessary capital for such ventures. Following close on the heels of the P.S.G. group, V. Rangaswamy Naidu established the 'Radhakrishna Mills Ltd. in 1923. By 1926 it had a paid-up capital of Rs. 5,78,229.[24] Though one of the earliest among the Naidus to move into cotton trading, G. Kuppuswamy Naidu delayed entering into cotton industry owing to heavy losses incurred in forward trading and speculative dealings. The Lakshmi Mills Ltd., established in 1910 by this group, was essentially a ginning factory.[25] The major spurt of industrial activity in the Coimbatore region occurred mainly during the 1930s and again it is the established Naidu groups which took the lead.

With the lifting of controls and the gradual resumption of commerce and trade, the early post-war years experienced a boom in company promotion which lasted till around 1922-23. Quite a large number of these ventures were promoted by relatively obscure middle and small capital but most of them collapsed in the wake of the recession. Of the ventures that came to be established during this period, textiles accounted for the bulk of investments. Once again, textiles attracted some Chetty capital. Thus, the A.R.A.R.S.M. Chetty firm (referred to earlier) established a mill in Madras in 1921. A privately owned company the ARARSM Spinning Mill had a nominal capital of Rs. 10 lakhs.[26] Karumuthu Thiagaraja Chetty, who was to emerge in post-independent India as one of the leading textile magnates, made his beginning in this period by establishing the Sri Meenakshi Mills Ltd. in Madurai, in 1921. The paid-up capital of Rs. 15,45,365 was raised almost entirely by a group of Chetty bankers and traders.[27] The Mahalakshmi Mills Co. established in 1925 was also the product of Chetty enterprise. Promoted by S.S.N. Lakshmanan Chetty, it had a paid-up capital of Rs. 6,17,700.[28]

On the whole, the diversification of Chetty capital into industry during the pre-1930 period, was rather marginal. Significantly the major Chetty houses such as the M.C.T., A.M.M. and the Raja Sir groups are not seen to be investing in industry during this period. They continued to channelise their capital into their traditional spheres of commerce and money-lending. A not so inconsiderable portion of their capital went into the purchase of war bonds and into such unproductive spheres as construction and renovation of temples, choultries and educational institutions.[29] Significantly, most of these big Chetty houses had considerable investments in Burma. It would seem, and this is purely hypothetical, that the very nature of the Burma business, with its accent on pure moneylending and the high degree of profits therein, was perhaps a limiting factor in the movement of Chetty capital into industry during this period.

In addition, the income tax policy of the Government of India, by regarding capital repatriated from abroad as liable to taxation as business profit, discouraged the Chettys from transferring their excess capital into India.

The introduction in 1916 of the new principle of taxing income on the basis of graduated scales, followed by the introduction of a super tax and excess profit duty may also have contributed towards retarding the flow of Chetty capital into industry. It can be argued that the entry of Chetty capital in a comparatively big way in the 1930s and 40s, was largely the result of the loosening of the hold of European capital over the Indian economy and the subsequent creation of an environment suitable for investment in industry. Moreover, the changing economic and political conditions in the colonial countries of South and South East Asia made it increasingly difficult for the Chettys to operate on their traditional lines.

This period also witnessed the emergence of industrial entrepreneurs in Sourashtra community. Numbering about 40,000 the local Sourashtrians were concentrated mainly in and around the town of Madurai and had traditionally been associated with the silk weaving and dyeing industry. Over the years the process of differentiation within the community had reached an advanced stage and by the turn of the century a few families through a system of credit advances had come to dominate the entire trade of this prosperous handloom weaving industry.[30] The tremendous profits made during the war years by a section of the community enabled them to shift a part of their capital into organised industry. The war, by disrupting the imports of certain specialised yarn threads, dyes and chemicals encouraged import substitution. Thus we find that K.M.S. Lakshmanaier, a leading Sourashtrian merchant, along with his brother floating the Gold Thread Mills Ltd. Established in 1921, it had an authorised capital of Rs. 3 lakhs.[31] About this time, K.V. Ramachari, another Sourashtra merchant, through his firm of Chari and Ram branched out into the field of chemicals and dyes.[32] Another industrial venture of the Sourashtrian merchants was the Madura Sriram Mills. Established in 1916 it had a paid-up capital of Rs. 5,21,000 and specialised in the production of cotton yarn.[33] Another ambitious venture, which however proved abortive, was the promotion of the Pandyan Mills in

1922. It had an authorised capital of Rs. 50,00,000 of which Rs. 30,00,000 was the issued capital.[34] The mill, however, soon changed hands and was taken over by the powerful A & F Harvey group. For want of evidence, it is difficult to ascertain the precise reasons for this takeover. Given the climate of acute recession, presumably the Sourashtra merchants found it difficult to raise the unusually large capital outlay for this venture.

Another noticeable trend in Tamil entrepreneurship during this period was the association of a number of Brahmans (from relatively obscure middle class backgrounds) with commerce and other modern incorporated enterprises. The early growth of the Seshasayees and T.V.S., two of the leading business houses of South India, can in fact be traced to this period.

The Seshasayees entry into the commercial world began during the First World War when they started mofussil road transport service in Trichinopoly. From this small beginning they branched off into servicing and sale of motor buses, cars and motor cycles. This served as a nucleus for the Seshasayees Brothers Engineering Works, Trichy. Specialising in automobile and electrical engineering, they undertook contract for the design, supply and erection of electrical installation in rice and oil mills and other establishments.[35] By 1923 they began moving into the specialised field of distribution and supply of electricity in the interior towns of certain Tamil districts. Thus the Sree Meenakshi Electric Corporation Ltd., established in 1923 at Devakottai with Chetty capital, had Seshasayees as its managing agents.[36] In 1924 the Seshasayees promoted the Trichy Srirangam Electric Supply Corporation.[37] In the following year again in association with the Chettys they promoted the Sree Meenakshi Sundareswara Electric Power Corporation Ltd., at Karaikudi.[38] The process of capital accumulation, in the case of Seshasayees and other Brahmins from a similar background was rather fitful. The Seshasayees had to constantly rely on Chetty bankers and other merchants and landowners of Trichy for the promotion of their commercial ventures. Thus, it took the Seshasayees almost two decades before they could get into industry, principally chemicals and minerals.

The case of the T.V.S. is almost similar. T.V. Sundaram Iyengar, the founder of the business house, is said to have inherited around the year 1908 a sum of Rs. 25,000 as his share of the ancestral property. He invested this sum in timber business and succeeded in realising a profit.[39] From trading in timber T.V.S. around 1912 or so moved into the field of road transport. With a Muslim merchant as his partner he is said to have invested Rs. 50,000 in this line of business. Alongside, he also took up contracts for road repairing.[40] By the 20s T.V.S. was on his own and had also diversified his business to include trading in imported automobiles spares. By 1925 he had acquired the sub-dealership for Chevrolet cars for the Madura region;[41] and by 1929 he had acquired the sole agency for the products of General Motors, U.S.A.[42] In the same year he established the T.V.S. & Sons Private Ltd.[43] This was to serve as the nucleus for a chain of establishments relating to the sale and servicing of automobiles. His major shift of investment to industry occurs only in the post-independence period.

Another important Brahmin entrepreneur and one who moved into industry comparatively early was C. Rajam Iyer. Around the time of the First World War he promoted the India Company Ltd. with branches in Madras and Calcutta. His company traded in imported steel products as well as those of Tatas. He, in fact, held the sole selling agency for Tata hardware materials in South India.[44] As an ancillary to the hardware business he set up several agencies for the import of automobiles.[45] By 1934, C. Rajam Iyer moved into industry by promoting the Indian Steel Rolling Mills Ltd. at Negapatam.

Though none of the Brahman entrepreneurs cited above had moved into industry during the period, the fact that they had organised their business on the lines of joint stock enterprise is significant. As first generation businessmen, they lacked resource networks and institutions for mobilising capital, and, thus, the process of their capital formation in the context of colonial rule was bound to be tardy and slow.

Taking advantage of the economic opportunities consequent upon the expansion of trade, a section of the Nadars had also accumulated substantial wealth in the course of the 19th century.[46] The rapid expansion of cotton cultivation in the Ramnad and Tinneveli belt—pockets of Nadar concentration—especially after the turn of the century further facilitated the growth of Nadar merchant capital. However, during this period very few Nadars succeeded in branching off into industry. Among those who did so were Ayya Nadar and Shanmuga Nadar. In 1922 they set up a mechanised match factory. From matches these two entrepreneurs moved over to the production of fireworks and thereafter into litho printing.[47]

In relation to other entrepreneurial groups the movement of Muslim capital into organised industry during the 20s was almost insignificant. From the turn of the century a significant number of Muslims of Madras came to be increasingly associated with the hides and skin trade, as middle-men supplying raw hides and skin to the European exporting firms. During and after the war, in response to the growing demand for tanned hides a large number of tanneries were established by Muslim merchants.[48] The bulk of the trade was, however, concentrated in the hands of few leading Muslim merchants such as Jamal Moideen, Moosa Sait, Yakub Hasan, Abdul Hakim, Kudus Badshah etc. During and immediately after the war, these traders succeeded in amassing huge fortunes. It was estimated that by 1919 the firm of Jamal Moideen Sahib had assets of about 80 to 90 lakhs of rupees.[49] However, operating within a highly unstable and fluctuating market and with no control over the price mechanism, the Muslim merchants also incurred heavy losses in this trade. The lack of adequate protection for the indigenous tanning industry, the unfavourable exchange ratio and the lack of cheap institutional credit contributed in accentuating the crisis. This may possibly explain the subdued nature of big Muslim capital vis-a-vis industrial promotion.

This period also enabled the established families of Roche Victoria and Cruz Fernandez of the Bharatha fishing community to consolidate their position. Their foothold in the import-export business passing through the port of Tuticorin was crucial in the initial build-up of the fortunes of these two houses. The firm of Roche Victoria was engaged in exporting hides and skins, senna leaves and palmyra fibre to Europe and U.S.A. They were also the shipping agents for Scindia Steam Navigation Co. for the Tuticorin and Travancore region.[50] By 1919 we find Roche Victoria promoting two proprietary concerns at Tuticorin, namely Bravi Sena Press and the Bravi Tanneries.[51]

Another noticeable feature of this period was an attempt by prominent Vellala landowners and moneylenders to diversify their capital into trade. Thus, A.T. Thiruvengadaswami

Mudaliar V.C. Velingiri Gounder, Ratnasabapathi Mudaliar, T.A. Ramalingam Chettiar, and V.S. Shengottia Mudaliar were among those who had developed significant interests in the Coimbator etextile industry and trade. This connection enabled them tolaunch into industrtal investment in the 1930s.

Madras also had a fair number of immigrant Gujrati merchants and bankers. Prominent among them were Lodd Govindoss Chathurbhujdass, Narayandass Girdhardass, Ramjee Calianjee, P.D. Asher, and C.M. Kothari. All of them were actively engaged in a wide variety of commercial enterprises. Though some of them had managed to invest in the share capital of certain industries, they did not as yet promote industries.

Though the traditional business communities clearly enjoyed certain positive advantages (as the case of the N. Chettys and Komatis clearly demonstrates) in terms of their ability to raise capital, so very crucial for investment in industry, that in itself did not always generate industrial entrepreneurship. The specific historical conditions for investment were also crucial. After all, when a suitable environment for industrial investment emerged in colonial Madras as in the 30s & 40s, entrepreneurs from both the traditional business communities and the non-commercial ethnic groups were not found to be lagging behind. The pre-1930 phase was, however, significant in that it prepared the ground for the burgeoning of South Indian entrepreneurship.

NOTES

1. S Arasratnam, "Trade and Political dominion in South India 1750-1790 : Changing British Indian Relationship", *Modern Asian Studies,*" XIII, I, (1971), pp. 19-46.
2. Raman Mahadevan, "The Origin and Growth of Entrepreneurship in the Nattukottai Chettiar Community of Tamilnadu 1880-1930'. Unpublished M.Phil (thesis, Jawaharlal Nehru University, New Delhi, 1976).
3. Mahadevan, n. 2, p. 228.
4. P. Somasundaram Chettiar, Written Evidence, *Report of the Indian Industrial Commission* (hereafter IIC), Minutes of Evidence 1916-17, Vol. III, p. 443.
5. *Hindu*, 27 Jan. 1908, p. 5; 30 March 1908, p. 6.; 9 Sept. 1910, p. 3.
6. Mahadevan, n. 2, pp. 230-31.

7. Asylum Press *Almanac and Director of Madras and South India* (hereafter APA), p. 1730.
8. Mahadevan, n. 2, p. 238.
9. A. Savarinatha Pillai, Written Evidence, *Madras Provincial Banking Enquiry Committee Report* (hereafter MPBECR), 1929, Vol. III, p. 1178; *Thackers India Directory*, 1923. See under Commercial Industries subsection, Rice Mills in the Madras Presidency, p. 77.
10. APA 1912, p. 2100; Mahadevan, n. 2, p. 239.
11. C.J. Baker & D.A. Washbrook, *South India*. XX, (London, 1975), p. 156. Also D.A. Washbrook, *The Emergence of Provincial Politics*, (New Delhi, 1976), p. 143.
12. *The House of Binny*, (Madras, 1969), pp. 133-34.
13. *Hindu*, Dec. 28, 1908, p. 6.
14. C.V. Venkataramana Iyengar, "Mill Industry in Coimbatore", *Journal of the Madras Geographical Association*, Vol. V, Nos. 2 & 3, July-Oct. 1930, pp. 115-116; S.M. Rutnagar, "Mr C.V. Venkataramana Iyengar", *The Indian Textile Journal*, Vol. XLI, No. 481, p. 11.
15. Washbrook, n. 11, p. 102.
16. P. Theagaraja Chetty, IIC, Vol. III, p. 55.
17. *Swadeshamitran* (Tamil daily) Editorial, 5 April 1907.
18. M.S. Natarajan, "A Study of the Capital Market of Madras Presidency", Unpublished D.Phil Thesis, (Univ. of Madras, 1934), p. 60.
19. *Swadeshamitran*, 5 April 1907. See also *Thackers India Directory*, 1915, Section Madras, p. 52.
20. *Swadeshamitran*, Editorial, 30 Jan. 1908.
21. J.S. Ponniah, "Production and Marketing of Raw Cotton in the Madras Presidency with Special Reference to Six Districts of Bellary, Kurnool, Coimbatore, Ramnad, Madura and Tinnevely"; unpublished D.Phil Thesis, (University of Madras, 1944) p. 4.
22. *Navindia* (Tamil daily), 7 July 1955. Special supplement on the ocassion of the inauguration of the new building of South India Millowners Association, p. 3. Also Nilkan Permal, *The Life of a Textile Pioneer*; (Coimbatore, 1967), pp. 1-15.
23. Memorandum and Articles of Association of Sri Ranga Vilas Spg. & Wvg. Mills Ltd. Coimbatore, pp. 3-4.
24. APA 1926, p. 929.
25. Lakshmi Mill Co. Ltd. '*Golden Jubilee : A Report*, 31st March 1961.
26. Govt Order No. 918., Ms Series, Development Department, Govt. of Madras, Statistics Relating to Cotton & Jute Mills in the Madras Presidency for the year 1921-22. (Tamilnadd Archives).
27. Govt. Order No. 889 Dev. Dept. Industries—Statistics—Cotton & Jute Mills 1931-32.
28. *Ibid*. Also Mahadevann, 2, p. 233.
29. *Hindu*, 18 Feb 1908, p. 3 Letter by T. Narayana Sastri, "Regredtable Waste of Rs. 16 Lakhs."; Also see *Hindu*, May 3, 1917, p. 3;

May 4, 1917, p. 3; 9 May 1917, p. 3; See Washbrook n. 2, pp. 107-8.

30. See L.K. Tulasiram, Oral Evidence, MPBECR, Vol. IV, pp. 296-298.
31. *Hindu*, Nov 5, 1921 p. 12.
32. David Arnold, *The Congress in Tamilnad*, (Curzon Press, 1977), p. 129.
33. Govt. Order No. 918. Dev. Dept. 1922.
34. *Hindu*, 13 Dec. 1922, p. 5.
35. *Hindu*, 14 Jan. 1921, p. 5.
36. *Investor's Encyclopaedia* (Madras, 1948), p. 603.
37. *Hindu*, 17 July 1924, p. 9; Jan 16, 1925, p. 10.
38. *Hindu*, 29 Jan. 1925, p. 3.
39. *Sundaram Iyengar Ninaivu Malar* (Tamil Vol. 7, Issue I, (Feb. 1966), p. 6.
40. *Ibid.*
41. *Hindu*, March 31, 1925, p. 12.
42. *Sundaram Iyengar Ninaivu Malar*, p. 6.
43. *Investor's Encyclopaedia*, p. 838.
44. *Hindu*, 7 April 1934 (advt), p. 4; 28 August 1933, p. 12.
45. These included, The British American Motors Ltd. Madras in 1920 (see *Hindu*, 4 Feb. 1920). The Garage Ltd. (see *Hindu*, 7 Jan. 1921, p. 5).
46. Robert. L. Hardgrave, *The Nadars Of Tamilnad* (Oxford, 1969), p. 97.
47. *Ibid.*, p. 150.
48. Purushotamdas Thakurdas Papers File No. 82, C.M. Kothari's correspondence with Purushotamdas. Letter in Gujarati, dated 30 May 1931. (Nehru Memorial Museum and Library, New Delhi).
49. *Ibid.*
50. J.L. Roche Victoria Co., Oral Evidence, MPBECR, Vol. IV, p. 408.
51. APA, Madras 1920.

14

The *Bazar*: Indigenous Sector of the Indian Economy

Rajat Kanta Ray

Indigenous finance and trade is known to have occupied a large place in India's domestic economy even in the late colonial period. It was also an important factor in India's trading and banking connections with neighbouring countries—the Middle East, Africa, Central Asia, South East Asia and the Far East. The migrations of certain merchant communities played a critical role in forging these long distance trading and banking connections, both within and outside India.

Merchant communities with inherited migrant characteristics have a natural advantage in long distance trade and finance. In India they enjoyed greater caste status than the mass of pedlars and retailers. Often the wholesalers on the one hand and the retailers on the other would belong to altogether different ethnic or linguistic groups. This was not so evident in the Upper Gangetic Valley, Rajputana and Gujarat, the home of the great Bania communities.[1] The Marwari and Gujarati Banias and the Agarwal and Vaish communities of UP were numerous in their native places and were thus to be found at all levels of trade and finance—from the village Bania to the all-India *hundiwal*[2] (bill broker). But away from the heartland of the great Bania communities, caste and ethnic distinctions tended to reinforce the distinction between the top controlling level of the indigenous trading economy and the peddling and retailing levels of rural and urban trade. In Punjab, the ascending scale of caste status distinguished the banking and merchant communities from pedlars, carriers, cattle dealers, green-grocers and liquor and meat sellers.[3] In Eastern India the distinction assumed an ethnic and linguistic form. Biharis, Oriyas, Bengalis and Assamese were overshadowed in the higher levels of indigenous banking and trade by immigrant communities from Marwar, Cutch and Gujarat.[4]

The nerve centre of the indigenous money market in Eastern India, Barabazar (Calcutta's native counterpart of Clive Street), was dominated by Marwari bankers and merchants headed by six great all-India houses (*Kothis*)—namely (in rough order of importance recognized by the *Kothiwals* themselves) Tarachand Ghanshyamdas. Bansilal Abirchand, Sadasukh Gambhirchand, Harsukhdas Balkissendas, *Kothiwals* Daga and Ramkissen Bagri.[5] From Barabazar these great Kothiwals financed the centres of Marwari banking and trade eastwards in Assam and East Bengal—Dibrugarh, Jorhat, Nowgong, Gauhati, Dacca, Chittagong, etc—and westwards to Bihar and beyond—Bhagalpur, Muzaffarpur, Patna, Ranchi, etc.[6] Dealers and pedlars in the Assam valley—Assamese, Bengalis, well-to-do Mymensingh cultivators—were the subordinate instruments of big Marwari firms which financed them and collected their produce.[7] In East Bengal, Saha, Tili and other Bengali merchants had large-scale independent business in their hands,[8] but the top level of jute supply was dominated by European and Marwari firms with Calcutta as headquarters.[9] In Bihar and Orissa the pedlars (*Beoparis*) and larger dealers in the rural marts were local Bihari and Oriya traders—not necessarily of the local Bania castes, but including a wide variety of other local Hindus and Muslims as well.[10] However, here too, large scale trade in the main assembling and distributing towns was not in the hands of local traders. In Bihar and on the Chhota Nagpur plateau *hundi* (bill of exchange) finance and big business in grain, cloth, oil and lac was controlled by Marwari merchants and bankers with Barabazar connections.[11] In Orissa the wholesale trade in rice and spices was dominated by Cutchi Memons with headquarters in Bombay, locally known as Nakhoda merchants.[12] Eastwards their connections extended to Calcutta, where they dominated the nerve centre of the entire rice trade of Eastern India. Jealous local merchants in Orissa held that the Oriya could not flourish in business because the Nakhoda merchant competed with large capital behind him[13]—a charge directed against the Marwari for the same reason in Bengal, Bihar and Assam. Throughout Eastern India the trade in produce in its early stages was mainly in the hands of local traders, but at the stage before export or import through the port of Calcutta it was gathered into the hands of Europeans, Marwaris and Cutchi Muslims.

On the other side of India, too, the city of Bombay exhibited significant caste distinctions at various levels of trade. The wholesale trade, and the more capital-intensive retail business, were the preserve of certain distinct communities, while hawking, peddling and retailing were carried on by all sorts of people. The leading traders, as the Bombay City Gazetteer noted at the beginning of the 20th century, were the Banis, Jains, Bhatias, Bohoras, Memons, Parsis, Jews and Europeans. But the lower levels of trade were filled by a more miscellaneous bunch of people. Marathas from the Deccan, for instance, retailed fruits and vegetables in the city, Kolis supplied the fish, and Muslim butchers the meat. In fact a great variety of Hindus and Muslims hawked fruit, vegetables, eggs, baked meat, bread, sugar, molasses, sweets, oils, cotton and silk goods and other articles on the streets of Bombay. But retail grain shops, which required a capital of up to Rs. 10,000, were mostly owned by Gujarati Banias and Lohanas.[14] The wholesale business in cloth was dominated at the Mulji Jetha market by Bhatias, and the retail cloth shops were also mostly in the hands of Bhatias and Banias.

In general, it may be said that a wide range of local castes participated in the peddling trade for, in addition to the above, there were others such as Farias, Beparis and Paikars. They operated in a single rural locality, or moved through the villages as itinerant traders, connecting rural areas with market towns.[15] Market towns, on the other hand, were connected to each other and to the great indigenous money markets—Bombay, Calcutta, Delhi, Amritsar, Cawnpore, etc.[16] This urban marketing and financial network was integrated by *hundis*, or bills of exchange, and by *arhatiyas*, or commission agents who acted for each other at different centres. The shroffs who discounted the *hundis* and the *arhatiyas* who ensured the movements of goods[17] tended to come from specialized communities.[18] Thus, certain distinct communities with strong migrant tendencies dominated the long distance networks of trade that functioned through bills of exchange and commission agencies. Among these were the great Bania communities which may be classed into three entirely distinct groups: (1) the Agarwals and other Vaish communities of the Hindi-speaking Upper Gangetic Valley, Bundelkhand and Delhi;[19] (2) the Hindu and Jain Marwaris hailing from the native states of Rajputana—mostly from Bikaner and Marwar and from the Sekhawati region of Upper Rajasthan and lower Haryana; and (3) Gujarati Banias, both Mesris (i.e. Hindus and Shravaks or Jains).[20] The Bania communities formed the principal element in the commercial population of the Hindi-speaking heartland, Rajputana and Gujarat, but west and south of these areas, there were other mobile Hindu merchant communities—the Khatris and Aroras of the Punjab, the Lohanas of Sind (among whom figured the 'Multani' bankers of Bombay), the Bhatias of Cutch and the Chettiars and Komatis of the Madras Presidency. Bombay city was, moreover, the base of the Parsees and of three great Muslim merchant communities converted from amongst Hindu merchants—the Bohoras, the Khojas and the Memons (the last two communities being Muslim converts from Lohanas of Sind).[21] It should be noted that these large merchant communities were divided into numerous smaller endogamous groups or sub-communities, some of which—such as the Maheswaris of Bikaner, the Oswals of Marwar, the Agarwals of the Upper Gangetic Valley, the Kapol Banias of Bombay, the Shikarpuri Shroffs (Lohanas known in Bombay as Multanis), the Cutchi Memons, and the Nuttukottai Chettiars—distinguished themselves by their enterprise.

Delhi was the meeting point for the migrant merchant communities from different parts of Northern India: Agarwal, Vaish, Khatri and Marwari.[22] Except for the Khatris, who came from the Punjab, these were all communities from the Bania heartland. Agarwals and Vaishes from the Upper Gangetic Valley and Marwaris from Rajasthan were Bania communities united in one caste cluster by a common claim to Vaishya status. The Khatris, on the other hand, claimed

Kshatriya status, and being Punjabis, they were not indigenous to the Bania heartland. The Bania heartland—i.e. Gujarat, Rajasthan and the Hindi-speaking areas of the Upper Gangetic Valley and Central India—was socially distinguished from the areas to the further west, such as Punjab, Sind and Cutch. The Bania heartland was distinct because of the strict adherence of its merchant communities to the rules of the *shastras*.[23] Thus its merchant communities fitted neatly into the third order of the *varna* system—i.e. the Vaishya order. Membership of this order could not be established without the practice of certain ordained rituals. Despite the fact that many merchant communities outside the Bania heartland followed quite strict rituals too, the Vaishya order itself was not an established part of the *varna* system there, and therefore the merchant communities in the outlying areas were never incorporated historically into the Bania caste cluster which most typically represented the Vaishya category. Part of the reason for the separate growth of merchant communities outside the Bania heartland may be due to the weaker presence of the Rajputs. The Rajputs represented the Kshatriya *varna*, and where they formed a principal element of the population, the merchant communities naturally occupied the next position as the Vaishya *varna*. In the Punjab, the Rajputs had long been wiped out, and the Khatris, the principal trading community, claimed to represent the Kshatriya *varna* there. In UP, Rajasthan and Central India, on the other hand, Rajputs and Banias existed in close juxtaposition, one representing the Kshatriya *varna* and the other the Vaishya *varna*, and thus articulating the full four-fold *varna* order. Beyond this Hindu heartland, however, the *varna* order tended to be only imperfectly articulated—with Brahmans and Sudras preponderating at two poles and the middle *varnas* being weak. No caste represented the Kshatriyas, and no caste the Vaishyas with an absolute certainty since the four-fold *varna* system was but weakly developed in North-Western, Eastern and Southern India. In these areas, the merchant communities developed separately from the Banias. The Khatris and Aroras of the Punjab, the Lohanas of Sind, the Bhatias of Cutch, the Vanis of Maharashtra, the Chettiars and Komatis of the Dravida country, the Suvarnabaniks,

Sahas and Tilis of Bengal—these were all established merchant communities, but they were distinct from the Banias.

That is not to imply that the Banias themselves formed one cohesive unit. In the first place, the Bania communities were embedded in distinct linguistic regional societies. Rajasthan, Gujarat, the Upper Gangetic Valley and Central India, each had its own distinct Bania groups. Secondly, the Banias were divided into various subcastes. Their great subdivisions, such as the Agarwals and the Oswals, were to be found in all the Bania lands and far beyond too. However, a UP Agarwal and an Agarwal of Rajasthan (i.e. a Marwari) would not be of the same community despite the fact that they had a common origin (whether mythical or real). It is interesting to note that the Banking Enquiry Committee in Delhi distinguished the indigenous Agarwals and Vaishes of the city from the Marwaris, despite the fact that Marwaris were themselves Vaishya traders with a prominent Agarwal component.[24] The Agarwals and other Vaish communities of the Upper Gangetic Valley were thus not the same as those of Rajasthan. Throughout the Bania heartland—Hindustan, Bundelkhand, Malwa, Gujarat and Rajasthan—we encounter the same Bania subcastes: Agarwals claiming to hail from Agroha, Oswals claiming to hail from Osian, and so on. But despite this mythological claim of common origin, which might well have some historical basis, the Banias of Hindustan, Gujarat and Rajasthan were linguistically and culturally different groups, and those of them who migrated to Central India—especially Malwa—retained their ties with their Marwari, Gujarati and Hindustani kinsmen.

Is there, then, any justification for treating the Bania communities as one category distinguished from the other merchant communities? Despite the internal divisions among the Banias, both Ibbetson and Russell, early pioneers in caste studies, affirm their underlying unity. Thus, Ibbetson remarks in his study of the Punjab castes : "It is sometimes said that Bania is no true caste at all, but merely an occupational term equivalent to "shop-keeper", and that the great divisions of the Banias, the Agarwals, the Oswals, and the like, really occupy the position of the castes; and this is in a sense true. The great sections do not intermarry and very possibly represent stocks of different origin; and if caste is used in the same sense as tribe, these sections are doubtless separate castes. But if the word is used in its purely Brahmanical sense, I do not think that the Aggarwal and Oswal Banias are separate castes any more than the Gaur and Sarsut Brahmans. . . . The great divisions of the Bania caste occupy identical social and religious positions, and recognise each other, whether rightly or wrongly, as of common origin distinct from the Khatris and other castes whose avocations are the same as their own".[25]

Russell expressed more or less the same view: "There has been much difference of opinion as to whether the name Bania should be taken to signify a caste, or whether it is merely an occupational term applied to a number of distinct castes. I venture to think that it is necessary and scientifically correct to take it as a caste. . . . As a rule the name Bania is used only as a caste name for groups who are considered both by themselves and by outsiders to belong to the Bania caste. . . . That the Banias are recognised as a distinct caste by the people is shown by the number of uncomplimentary proverbs and sayings about them, which is far larger than in the case of any other caste. In all these the name Bania is used and not that of any subdivision, and this indicates that none of the subdivisions are looked upon as distinctive social groups or castes. . . . Certain of the more important subcastes of Bania, such as Agarwala, Oswal and Parwar are, it is true, frequently known by the subcaste name. But the caste name is as often as not, or even more often, affixed to it. Agarwala, or Agarwala Bania, are names equally applied to designate this subcaste, and similarly with the Oswals and Parwars; and even so the subcaste name is applied for greater accuracy and compliment, since these are the best subcastes; the Bania's quarter of a town will be called Bania Mahalla, and its residents spoken of as Banias, even though they may be nearly all Agarwals or Oswals. . . . Thus in the matter of common usage Bania conforms in all respects to the requirements of a proper caste name."[26]

The theory of a common ethnic origin of the major Bania groups need not be dismissed out of hand. There is much evidence to show that the theory is at least partially valid. Many of the subcastes that form the Bania population of

Gujarat and Central India originally migrated from Rajasthan. In the state of Indore in Malwa, for instance, all the leading bankers were Jain Banias from Marwar. The Bania groups of Rajasthan, in turn, seem to have migrated from Hindustan at various times. The Agarwals, Jains and Modis in Bikaner, for instance, were driven from the Gangetic plains and Punjab by the insecurity of life and property caused by constant invasions in Upper India.[27] These very Agarwals and Jains later on migrated from Rajasthan to Gujarat and Central India. Thus, the various Bania groups settled in different parts seem to have been formed by the migrations of single clans. Many of the diverse Bania groups, therefore, could legitimately claim a common ancestry. A series of migrations and settlements during the medieval period undoubtedly contributed substantially to the formation of the Bania communities in Hindustan, Rajasthan, Bundelkhand, Malwa and Gujarat.

On the other hand, the theory of common ancestry will not explain the origin of all the component units of the Bania population of different parts. Many Bania subcastes in Gujarat, Malwa and Bundelkhand were indigenous groups, not migrants from Rajasthan or Hindustan. These groups were obviously incorporated into the Bania caste by a social process. It is this social process that needs to be explained. What was it that led to the emergence of the Bania in those lands which he claimed as his own? What was it that Hindustan, Rajasthan, Bundelkhand, Malwa and Gujarat had in common? The answer seems to lie in certain features of the social structure that these regions shared. This does not imply that the societies in these regions had all similar characteristics; merely that they had some common characteristics which may help explain the formation of the social category of Bania in these and not in other areas.

Historically speaking, Hindustan, Rajasthan, Bundelkhand, Malwa and Gujarat were lands in which the Rajputs held sway. The Rajputs were the one caste which had an undisputed claim to belong to the Kshatriya *varna*. In other places there were groups which claimed Kshatriya status, but never with the same universal acceptance. Consequently, the lands of the Rajput had one thing in common, viz. the ideal Brahmanical social order of the four *varnas* as approved by the *shastras* was more fully realized here than elsewhere. The Vaisya or mercantile *varna* was represented in this orthodox belt by the Bania communities who by their strict religious and social practices established their claim to the Vaishya status. Their position was defined as next to that of the Rajputs, who represented the Kshatriya or royal *varna*. In the outlying areas to the west (Punjab, Sind, Cutch) and the south (Maharashtra and the Southern Peninsula), as well as in the east (Bengal, Orissa and Assam), the *varna* social order was not fully articulated, i.e. it was not four-fold. In these areas no caste had an undisputed claim to represent the Kshtriya *varna*, and by natural association no caste had an undisputed claim to represent the Vaisya varna either. The two middle *varnas* between the Brahman and the Sudra—i.e. Kshatriya and Vaisya—were quite often missing. In Punjab, the Khatris laid an uncertain claim to Kshatriya status and thus they did not represent the orthodox Vaisya *varna* that the Bania typically represented. The Lohanas of Sind did claim Vaisya status, but their unorthodox social habits were repellent to the typical Bania communities. The Bhatias of Cutch, who had originally been flesh-eaters before their conversion to Vaishnavism,[28] were looked down upon as inhabitants of a strange land. The Dravidian south, where the prominent trading castes were the Chettiars and the Komatis, was too far-off from the heartland of the Brahmanical social order for these trading groups to be incorporated as Vaisya Bania groups despite their undoubtedly strict Hindu rituals. In Bengal, as the medieval *puranas* stated it explicitly, there were only Brahmans and Sudras in the Kali age, and no Kshatriyas and Vaisyas in between.[29] Thus, the merchant communities of the outlying areas did not become part of the four-fold *varna* order as Vaisyas. They grew up separately from the Bania communities.

In the Bania heartland on the other hand, the trading groups having pure ritual practices were incorporated in the indisputably Vaisya order of Banias. Thus the Bania order in Upper and Central India and in Gujarat was created by the dual process of migration and incorporation, the process being helped by the fuller explication of the Brahmanical social order in these lands. The Agarwals, descendants of the legendary Kshatriya King Agrasena of Agroha, and the Oswals, Rajput converts to Jainism, were the two most important subcastes of the Banias.

Their widespread migrations made them important elements in the Bania population in all areas—Hindustan, Rajasthan, Central India and Gujarat. Indigenous trading groups in Central India and Gujarat were also incorporated as subcastes of the Banias. The process of incorporation of Bania subcastes, however, was possible only in those areas where a four-fold *varna* order prevailed and where the Rajputs represented the Kshatriya *varna* and the Banias the Vaisya *varna*. In the Dravida country, in Eastern India, and in the Western Punjab and Sind, there was no four-fold order and thus no Banias of Vaisya status. Trading communities in these outer lands were often depressed to Sudra status, though in Punjab and Sind some leading trading communities did successfully claim high status. But whatever their exact status, they remained outside the Bania fold. Among these we must count the Khatris of Punjab, the Lohanas of Sind, the Bhatias of Cutch, the Chettiars and Komatis of the south, the Vanis of Maharashtra and the Suvarnabaniks, Tilis and Sahas of Bengal. By contrast, in the Rajput territory the trader of clean ritual became the Bania.

To put it briefly, the Banias of Hindustan, Rajasthan, Central India and Gujarat were an incorporative category formed by three distinct factors: (1) the common ethnic origin of certain subcastes dispersed through all these regions—especially the Agarwals and the Oswals; (2) the incorporation of several trading communities of diverse local origins into the Vaisya order represented by the Agarwals and the Oswals—themselves originally Kshatriyas and Rajputs; (3) the realization of the four-fold *varna* order in all these regions on account of the indisputable Kshatriya status of the ruling Rajput clans, under whom the Bania subcastes formed a natural and complementary Vaisya *varna*. There were many important merchant communities which had not been enfolded within the cluster of Bania groups and were not elements integrated into a full four-fold *varna* order, some of them being not even Hindu castes as they professed Islam, Jainism or Zoroastrianism. But they, too, were endogamous communities whose customs were similar to those of the Hindu merchant castes and that enabled them to maintain their cohesion and exclusiveness.

Among these merchant communities the Parsis had undergone a high degree of Westernization—and, to a lesser degree, the Khojas.[30] The merchant communities of the Indus basin—Khatris,[31] Aroras[32] and Lohanas[33]—had never been noted for social orthodoxy. But speaking of the other merchant communities generally, strict social rules and strong religious connections marked them out. They regarded English education as worse than useless.[34] Pilgrimages, religious charities, and a pervasive regard for life (reflected in vegetarianism) marked their way of life. The sharing of values was strong enough to knit together the Jain and Vaishnava subcastes of the communities of Gujarat, Rajasthan, the Upper Gangetic Valley, Bundelkhand and Central India.[35] Their gods may have been different, but the Gujarati Shravak Banias, the Vaishnava Bhatias and the Cutchi Memons, to take but three instances, had this in common, that they were frequent pilgrims and large spenders on religious and charitable works.[36] They were in general subdivided into innumerable endogenous subcastes, and they were extremely strict in following the rules of marriage and commensality.

The principal merchant communities possessed strong community organizations which enabled them to help each other out in difficulty and to resolve disputes without going to court. Temples, priesthoods and caste institutions played the key role in knitting together these community organizations. The Parsi Panchayat of Bombay had been strong in the 19th century, but their Zoroastrian priests and their assembled Anjuman no longer had complete sway.[37] The scandal arising from the Maharaja Libel Case of 1861, again, had weakened the control of the Maharajas of the Vallabhacharya sect over the Gujarati Meshris and Bhatia community.[38] But such priesthoods and panchayats had served their purpose in their own time, and among other communities the hold of these institutions was still very strong. The Daudi Bohoras were integrated by the social authority exercised by their Head Mulla at Surat, who levied a tax for charitable and religious works and controlled a priestly hierarchy of deputy mullas stationed in every considerable settlement of the Daudi Bohoras. In any dispute, the local mulla called together a meeting of chief members of the community and gave his ruling, from which a final appeal lay to the Head Mulla at Surat.[39] The Khojas were similarly under the authority of the Agha Khan,[40] and the Cutchi Memons were obedient to their Kadiri head priest at Mundra in Cutch.[41] The Nattukottai Chettiars had a community structure similar in some respects to that of the Daudi Bohoras. They were divided into several endogamous *'kovils'* or temple units and for matters affecting the community they had Kovilvasal Mariyal, or temple councils, each with a manager, an assistant and a footman called the Vairavi. Complaints were heard at the temple, the temple manager recording the evidence and the Vairavi enforcing the ruling given by the council.[42] The Komatis, again, had erected temples to their deified virgin, Kanyaka Parameshwari, all over the Madras Presidency, each temple being a centre for large scale charity. Their caste *guru* was the Bhaskaracharya, whose duties were more religious than social. For social issues, the Komatis had in each settlement a headman called the Pedda Seti, assisted by a Mummadi Seti who assembled the castemen for rulings in disputes which were enforced by fines, excommunication or other sanctions.[43]

The strong community organization of the merchant communities facilitated their migrations along the coast and across the country. The Cutchi Memons, for instance, were aided in their widespread migrations by their method of trading in small corporations or moving companies of a small number of relations and friends. A report on them from the Central Provinces described these moving companies thus : "Some of them will have shops in the great centres of trade, Bombay and Calcutta, and others in different places in the interior. Each member then acts as a correspondent and agent for all the others, and puts what business he can in their way. Money are also employed as assistants and servants in the shops; but at the end of the season when all return to their native Gujarat, the profits from the different shops are pooled and divided among them in varying proportion. By this method they obtain all the advantages which are recognised as attaching to co-operative trading."[44]

The migrations of the merchant communities, which their community links made possible, created long distance networks, partnerships, commission agencies and bills of the exchange in the 19th and 20th centuries. New lines were extended which, though not visible like the railways, were no less important. The creation of these new financial and commercial networks is an important event in the economic history of India and is central to the understanding of the structure of indigenous economy. Broadly, these migrations may be bunched into three great movements on the map of India with significant extensions to neighbouring countries to which the *bazaar* (community markets) exported large amounts of capital.

One of these movements centred on Bombay. Starting from further up the west coast, it focused on that great port city, and then carried its thrust across the Indian ocean to Arabia, Africa and China, round the Indian Peninsula to the heart of Central India. The decline of Surat, the financial and commercial capital of Mughal India, and of its vast trade with the ports of the Red Sea and the Persian Gulf, was followed by the rise of Bombay, and successive wave of migration from Sind, Cutch, Kathiawad and Gujarat—Parsis, Kapol Banias, Bohoras, Jains, Bhatias, Khojas, Cutchi Memons and Lohanas moving one by one into the city.[45] The Parsis, who came to Bombay from Gujarat and moved on to China as brokers to the East India Company and English private traders,[46] graduated from the indigenous money market to the world of modern capital by the end of the 19th century. The Khojas, who like the Parsis moved from Gujarat into Bombay as a principal element of the cotton millowner class, had the same widespread overseas connections with China, Japan, South East Asia, East Africa and the Arabian Peninsula, and had strong colonies in Muskat, Aden and Zanzibar.[47] The Bhatias, the third leading Indian element in the millowner class, were also to be found in fair numbers in the ports of the Red Sea and the Persian Gulf, Zanzibar and as far east as China and Japan, and in addition they had a foothold in the Indian *bazaar* through their control of the cotton piece-goods market in Bombay.[48] The Gujarati Banias, Cutchi Memons and Sindhi Lohanas, unlike these groups, had no large stake in organized industry, and belonged really to the commodity markets. The Banias were the principal Gujarati shroffs in Bombay and had a large stake in Bombay's trade, especially raw cotton,[49] and a sizeable connection with Africa, the Gulfs[50] and Burma.[51] The Cutchi Memons and the Shikarpuri Lohanas were closely inter-related in the Bombay business world, and they took a leading part in extending new lines of indigenous trade and finance round the Indian Peninsula right up to Burma.

Multani shroffs from Shikarpur had also established a special relationship with the Imperial Bank in Bombay which enabled them to provide cheap *hundi* finance. They funnelled this cheap finance principally to the Cutchi Memons who with the funds remitted from Bombay traded in produce all over the Bombay Presidency, the Central Provinces and Central India.[52] The Cutchis also used this finance to extend their business to Calcutta, from which point, along the coast, they moved in a large way into Orissa and Burma.[53] Their Multani bankers followed the same coastal route around the Peninsula and moved in a large way into finance in Madras city and the interior towns of the Madras Presidency,[54] even invading Madurai, the home district of the Nattukottai Nagaratharas.[55] Finally they moved on to Burma, where, however, their banking business was confined to Rangoon. Their principal clients, the Cutchis, moved further, forming settlements extending from Calcutta, Orissa, Madras and the Malabar Coast to South Burma, Siam, Singapore, Java in the east and towards the west, in the ports of the Arabian Peninsula (except Muskat where they were ousted by the Khojas), Mozambique, Zanzibar and the East African coast.[56]

The second large movement of Indian bankers and merchants was a purely external migration of indigenous capital from the Indian Peninsula to the countries of South East Asia. While Multani shroffs were moving into every town of any consequence in the Madras Presidency, the local Nattukottai Nagarathars were pulling out capital in ever greater amounts to Ceylon, Burma and South East Asia. The net result of these massive movements of *bazaar* capital, which were well on their way before the First World War, was that on the eve of the Great Depression Multani capital beyond Sind, and Nattukottai Chettiar capital beyond Madras, was far greater than their domestic investments in Sind and Madras.[57] Furthermore, Multani capital moved to Rangoon largely in response to the strong demand in the *hundi* market exercised by the dense network of Chettiar finance in Lower and Upper Burma, the Multanis acting as the Chetti agricultural financiers' bankers and funnelling Imperial Bank finance to the Nattukottai Chettiars up the Irrawaddy valley. Just as the Shikarpur town of Sind controlled the extended Multani financial wire to Bombay, Madras and Rangoon, the rural tract of Chettinad (consisting of 58 villages in Ramnad and 20 villages in the adjacent Pudukother State)[58] controlled even more extended lines of finance through Madras city to Ceylon, Burma, the whole of the Malay Peninsula, Indo-China and parts of Sumatra.[59] The headquarters of Chettiar capital in Burma was the indigenous money market in Mogul Street, Rangoon. Mogul Street was linked by Chettiar, Multani, Marwari and Gujarati financiers with the main money markets in India, with upcountry offices in Burma, and with the large towns of the Malay Peninsula, Cochin China and Ceylon. Marwaris and Gujaratis had linked Mogul Street with Calcutta; Multanis and Gujaratis had linked Mogul Street with Bombay; and the Nattukottai Chettiars had linked Mogul Street with Madras, Colombo, Penang, Singapore and Saigon.[60] In Burma Marwaris, Gujaratis and Multanis operated mainly in Rangoon while the Nattukottai Chettiars had a network of upcountry connections with Mandalay, Bassein, Henzada, Moulmein and Akyab.[61] In Rangoon, the Nattukottai Chettiars were the dominant element, their operations far surpassing the combined operations of the other Indian banking groups.[62] The large Chettiar houses of Rangoon had in all 295 offices in Madras, Ceylon and the other countries of South East Asia.[63] Chettiar offices in Burma numbered in all 1650; and in the Federated Malay States and Straits Settlements 700, in Ceylon 450, in Cochin China 105, and in Madras itself 243.[64] The aggregate property of the Chettiras (excluding borrowed funds) was estimated to have increased from Rs. 10 crores in 1896 to Rs. 80 crores in 1929 as a result of these foreign operations,[65] and on the eve of the Great Depression their total international working capital, including owned and borrowed funds, stood at an estimated amount of Rs. 120 crores, distributed between various countries as shown in the table on the following page.

Their business in the Malay Peninsula, which was the second largest component in their international operations, was mainly loans on personal security to the native Malayans. According to the findings of a committee appointed by the Government of the Federated Malay States they lent to traders merely on a note of hand, with no security, but as they lived closely with the borrowers, they could lay their finger on the pulse of any man's business.[66] In Burma, their loans were only partially to traders (about 1/3rd of their working

ESTIMATES OF TOTAL WORKING CAPITAL OF CHETTIARS (OWNED AND BORROWED)

Country	Amount (Rs. Crores)
1. Burma	75
2. Straits Settlement and Federated Malay States	25
3. Ceylon	14
4. Cochin China	14
5. Madras	1
Total	120

Source : *Report of the Burma Provincial Banking Enquiry Committee*, Vol. I (Rangoon, 1930), p. 211.

capital), their capital being mainly invested (about 2/3rd) in agricultural loans. Averse in general to acquiring mortgaged property, on which the return was slower and more problematic than the quick turnover in fluid money-lending capital, the Chettiars were, nevertheless, forced by the failure of the borrowers to acquire tea, coconut and areca plantations in Ceylon, rubber plantations in the Federated Malay States and—especially during the Great Depression—peasant lands in Burma.[67] While a lot of their capital was thus forcibly tied up, they incurred at the same time the hostility of the local population. A Karen witness said before the Burma Provincial Banking Enquiry Committee in 1930: "Tersely and pointedly speaking, Chettiar banks are fiery dragons that parch every land that has the misfortune of coming under their creeping".[68] The Burma Provincial Banking Enquiry Committee pointed out the other side of the coin: without Chettiar capital, remarked, "the internal and external trade of the country would break down and the rice crop could not even be produced."[69]

The third great movement of *bazaar* capital issued from the northern and western desert tract of Rajputana (Bikaner, Marwar and Sekhawati).[70] Supplemented by movements of Khatri capital from the land of the Five Rivers, this Marwari capital flowed down the Ganges to its new nerve centre, Barabazar (Calcutta).[71] The Khatri migrations, following roughly the same route, were smaller in scope and confined to the Gangetic valley: from Punjab towns to Delhi, Agra, Lucknow and Patna and moving finally to Barabazar, where Khatri traders acted for Punjab firms.[72] The Marwari migrations reached much further and veered off in several directions, so that the entire Indian subcontinent was affected by this desert diaspora.

In the Central Provinces, Indore and other states of Central India, Marwari Banias were long established and they seemed to predominate over the Bundelkhand and Gujarati Banias.[74] Twelve principal Marwari houses in Indore, including the banking and millowning house of Sarupchand Hukumchand, dominated the grain, cloth and opium trade of Malwa.[75] At a later stage Marwari Banias from Malwa and Marwar penetrated to the Bombay and Madras Presidencies. Jains from Marwar moved at first to Surat district, and though held in contempt by the Gujarati Jains who refused to eat with them, they soon penetrated every corner of the Bombay Presidency by moving into the lower levels of the trade.[76] Marwari Jains from Malwa and Marwar then slowly extended their hold on the higher levels of business in Bombay city, and emerged as big dealers in wheat, linseed and *hundis*, and at a later stage, as cotton millowners.[77] At the same time they moved in large numbers to the interior towns of Madras Presidency and of the Hyderabad state, mainly as traders and moneylenders, with a few banking firms at their head. These banking and moneylending firms got their funds at 6 per cent from their homes in Rajputana or from their new base in Bombay, and lent these funds out at 12 per cent to the Komati traders on the Andhra coast.[78]

It was, however, in the towns of Bihar, and in Calcutta, where the Marwari Chamber of Commerce came to control the piece-goods import trade,[79] that the Marwar*is* established a near complete domination of the higher levels of indigenous finance and trade. The impetus of their migrations carried them further eastwards to Dacca, Chittagong, Akyab (Arakan), Moulmein and Rangoon, and up the Brahmaputra valley to the highlands of Assam, where the British tea garden industry opened up to them an expanding prospect of *hundi* banking and trade.

The advancing Marwaris pushed the economic frontier of the *hundi* to areas where it had never operated, to Assam and to Arakan., In Rangoon about 400 Marwaris, organized into a Marwari Association were engaged in trade and *hundi* banking, 95 per cent of their *hundis* relating to piece-goods imported from Bombay and Lancashire.[80] In Moulmein they were involved in financing the export of timber and rice,[81] most of the Burma teaks exported to Calcutta being in their hands at the Calcutta end.[82] In Akyab they dominated indigenous finance and trade, overshadowing the Nattukottai Chettiars, a monopoly made possible by the large Arakan trade with East Bengal where the Marwaris had established themselves at key points.[83] For instance, the large Marwari firm of Lakshminarayan Rambilash, with headquarters in Akyab, had branches in Calcutta, Rangoon, Khulna, Chittagong and Sandow where they dealt in *hundis* and gave loans to traders and private persons. They also made telegraphic transfers between the places where they had branches.[84]

In Assam, which the British integrated into the Indian economy, the Marwaris broke virgin ground by bringing the valley under the realm of the *hundi*. They reached Gauhati around 1825 establishing the firm Jesraj-Tilokchand-Labchand[85] (*aratdars* and moneylenders), perhaps the oldest suriving Marwari firm in the province. They intruded further up the Brahmaputra valley in 1835,[86] and graduated from mere trading to *hundis* banking in the 1860s. The largest indigenous banking firm of Assam, Chunilal Saligram,[87] was established in 1861 and it started the discounting of *bazaar hundis* and tea garden *hundis*,[88] the late development of *hundi* banking being due to the fact that the European tea garden industry, with which Marwari enterprise expanded, was not consolidated until the 1850s.[89] The Marwaris supplied rice to the tea gardens,[90] and in course of time monopolized the imports of *bazaar* goods from Calcutta, where they had branches or headquarters,[91] moving funds to and fro by telegraphic transfers, bills and *hundis*.[92] The Chunilal Saligram firm of Dibrugarh, which secured a valuable agency of kerosene oil and of other goods, dealt in *hundis* with Calcutta to the extent of Rs. 3 to 4 lakhs per month.[93] The large Marwari firms with Calcutta connections financed the market generated by the European tea gardens but the tea industry and the tea export trade proved beyond their reach.[94]

The migrations charted above indicate an extension of the *bazaar* within the Indian subcontinent, and along the coast to neighbouring countries. In course of the 19th century Indian merchant communities lost some old connections and forged some new ones. The large Surat-Mokha connection had been lost by 1800, to be replaced by new bonds with the African coast, with the Arabian Peninsula, with Ceylon, South East Asia and China. Much of this coastal trade and finance was in a subordinate capacity, Indian trade and finance moving behind the expanding British economic and political frontier and depending on the banking, shipping and insurance facilities provided by British overseas capital. Transhipments also continued, however, on country craft plying as far west as Aden and across the Bay of Bengal towards Burma and South East Asia. On the eve of the Great Depression, about 1000 sailing vessels were plying in and out of the ports of India carrying 178,000 tons of goods.[95] Right down to the Second World War India's shipyards were engaged in producing wooden vessels, the largest of which were as long as 100 feet.[96]

Besides these transhipments on country craft, the indigenous sector also sustained the older overland trade across the Himalayas. The transfrontier trade with Afghanistan, Central Asia and the Himalayan countries received new impetus from two factors—opening up of new overseas markets for the goods brought down by the caravan routes to the frontier rail-heads, and the development of a vast trade in perishables—especially fruits—made possible by the railway network running from the frontier to the port cities and the inland centres.[97] The *hundi*—that characteristic financial instrument of the *bazaar*—thus continued to operate across the North-West Frontier to Afghanistan, Persia and Central Asia. The Khatris and Aroras of the Punjab, and the Lohanas of Sind, who had small colonies as far up as Afghanistan, Khorasan and Turkestan,[98] operated a large network of trade and finance across the frontier in association with Afghan traders,[99] while in the east the Marwaris opened up a new and profitable connection at Kalimpong and Darjeeling with Tibetan wool merchants, baling and shipping the raw wool brought down by Tibetan caravans to the USA, England and Europe.[100] There were four main overland routes through which wool, furs, carpets, silk and fruit were carried by caravans from Inner Asia to the rail-heads on India's border districts : (1) the Iranian caravan route through Seistan and Kandahar to the rail-heads of Chaman and Quetta in Baluchistan; (2) the overland routes from Afghanistan, Iran and Central Asia through Kabul and over the Khyber pass to the rail-head of Peshawar; (3) the highland trade over the Karakoram range from Chinese Turkestan through Kashmir to the trading marts of the Punjab Amritsar, Hoshiarpur, etc; (4) the Tibetan trade route through the Himalayan kingdoms to Darjeeling and Kalimpong.[101]

In the overland trans-Asian trade financed by the Indian informal money market, the largest components were the bulk fruit trade with Kandahar through Chaman on the border of Baluchistan,[102] and the trade through Peshawar with Kabul in dried fruits,[103] carpets from Iran,[104] and furs from Turkestan and Afghanistan.[105] The principal financiers of the great overland trade across the Khyber pass were fifty Shikarpur families in Peshawar headed by the great Multani firm of Naraindas Chelaram.[106] A number of Khatri, Arora and Bhatia[107] moneylenders and traders also financed the trade, as did Peshawari Muslim merchants[108] who definitely knew how to calculate the interest in their *hundi* transactions with Kabul. Colonies of Hindu traders and financiers in Afghanistan and Turkestan, assisted by Peshawari Muslims and Kabuli merchants, operated *hundi* and *arhat* lines through Kabul deep into the heart of Central Asia and Iran.[109] The great banking firm of Naraindas Chelaram, with its headquarters in Amritsar and branches in Peshawar, Kohat, Rawalpindi, Karachi and Bomaby, had been engaged in financing the trade with Afghanistan since the days of Durrani invaders of India.[110] The Peshawar trade was financed by *hundis*[111] from Karachi and Bombay (Rs 2 crores each) and to a lesser extent, Amritsar and Calcutta and in its turn it negotiated bills on the principal marts of Afghanistan, Persia and Turkestan.[112] A large number of Muslim banking firms of

Peshawar had branches in Kabul.[113] Other banking firms which had no branches in Kabul negotiated bills through Hindu merchants settled in Kabul who acted on commission (*arhat*) basis to meet their *hundis*.[114] Neither the First World War, nor its disturbing sequel, the Kabul disturbances caused by Baccha-i-Saku, could disrupt these lines of finance.[115] A brisk business went on in rates of exchange of Mushadi (i.e. Iranian) and Kabuli coins, which sometimes changed hands eight times in the course of a day, in the money-changer's shops in Peshawar (21 shops), Quetta, Chaman, Bannu, Dera Ismail Khan, Kohat, Thal and Parachinnar.[116]

The excellent financial services provided by indigenous bankers and money-changers in Peshawar sustained a long distance fur trade worth Rs 1 crore stretching from Khiva and Bokhara to Liverpool, New York and Shanghai. The principal fur merchant in Peshawar, Haji Allah Baksh Sethi, had connections in Mazar (on the Afghan border with Soviet Turkestan in the north), Kabul, Bombay and Shanghai, and a commission agent in London. To remit money for the purchase of furs from Turkestan, he made extensive use of both *hundis* on Kabul and goods sent via Kabul to Mazar. The *hundis* were drawn on Kabul at a rate previouly fixed, and were given by him on Hindu merchants in Kabul as well as Peshawari Muslims and Kabuli merchants there. The Haji purchased his *hundis* on Kabul from exporters to Kabul in Peshawar (the principal exports being piece-goods, salt, hardware, metals and cement). The exported manufactures reached Turkestan via Kabul and Mazar-i-Sharif. The Haji's office used the *hundis* to claim the proceeds of the exports to Mazar and thus paid the purchase money for furs, which were either sold in Peshawar or sent to London for commission sale.[117] Peshawari *hundis*, in fact, were used both ways, by Afghan fur merchants from Kabul who came down to sell in Peshawar, and by Peshawar merchants who went up to purchase furs in Afghanistan and Turkestan. The Afghan merchant who brought furs to Peshawar would deposit the proceeds of the sale with a commission agent there, and the commission agent would give him in return a *hundi* on a trader in Afghanistan with whom he had dealings. Conversely, when a Peshawar trader went to Afghanistan for purchase of furs, he would deposit the money with a commission agent who would give him the necessary *hundis* to receive the money in Afghanistan.[118] *Hundi* banking and commission agency were inextricably intermeshed in the *bazaar* trade with Inner Asia. The carpet trade with Iran was conducted partly through *hundi* remittances and partly through bank transfers.[119]

The long lines along which money and goods passed in and out of India gave a special advantage to merchant communities which possessed the necessary points along those lines. Thus, the Khatri merchants of the Punjab who had lines into Afghanistan and Turkestan in the trade in furs exported the raw products of Inner Asia down the Gangetic Valley[120] and enjoyed a special position in Calcutta as exporters of raw wool to America and Europe.[121] The Cutchi Memons, who had agents at points all along the coast of South and South East Asia, Bombay city, the Malabar and Orissa coasts, Calcutta, South Burma, Siam, Singapore and Java, easily dominated the enormous rice trade of Eastern India,[122] enjoying a natural advantage as 'nakhoda' (sailor) merchants over the resentful local rice dealers. The Marwaris who had opened lines from Calcutta into Arakan and Burma dominated the import of Burma teaks through Calcutta port and they distributed these teaks on credit along the lines of their settlement in Bihar, U.P., Delhi and Assam.[123]

The migrant merchant communities of India, thus, successfully created new long distance networks of trade and finance in the colonial period. The Indian economy realigned itself along a new *hundi* network in the course of the 19th century, with Bombay and Calcutta as its nodal points, and with new eastwards extensions within and outside the subcontinent—into Assam, Burma and the Malay Peninsula. Westwards, the *hundi* network along the overland routes to Inner Asia continued to operate and now linked up the trans-Asian routes with the railways running from Peshawar and Quetta to Bombay and Calcutta; and new lines of emigration to Aden, the Arabian Peninsula, East Africa and Natal opened up new Gujarati commercial connections across the western Indian Ocean. The older, and grander, trans-Asian trade between the Mughal, Safavid and Ottoman empires, with its financial centre in Surat, was gone for ever; but the catastrophic loss was partially balanced in the long run by some new, and more prosaic, compensations.

NOTES

1. For a descrption of the Bania communities in the Bania heartland i.e. the Uttar Gangetic Valley, Central India, Rajasthan and Gujarat see: W. Crooke, *The Tribes and Castes of the North-Western Provinces and Oudh*. 4 vols (Calcutta 1896); R.E. Enthoven, *The Tribes and Castes of Bombay*, 3 vols (Bombay 1920); R.V. Russell, *Tribes and Castes of the Central Provinces of India*, 4 vols (London 1916); *Gazetteer of the Bambay Presidencey*, vol IX, Part I; *Gujarat Population: Hindus* (Bombay, 1901), *Rajputana Gezetteer*, vol III; *The Western Rajputana States Residency and Bikaner Agency*, by K.D. Erskine (Allahabad, 1909); *Central India States Gazetteer Series: Indore State Gazetteer*, vol II, by C.E. Luard (Calcutta 1908); Denzil Ibbetson, *Punjab Castes* (Lahore, 1916).
2. Ibbetson, n. 1, p. 242.
3. *Ibid.*, pp. 237, 253-254.
4. These ethnic distinction stand out sharply in the evidence volumes of the *Reports* of the Assam, Bengal and Bihar and Orissa Provincial Banking Enquity Committees (1929-30).
5. *Report of the Bengal Provincial Banking Enquiry Committee 1929-30*, vol II, evidence, Part I (Calcutta 1930), pp. 421-425.
6. *Report of the Assam Provincial Banking Enquiry Committee 1929-30*, vol II, passim; *Bengal Banking Committee*, vol II, Part I, passim; *Report of the Bihar and Orissa Provincial Banking Enquiry Committee, 1929-30*, vol. III, passim.
7. *Assam Banking Committee*, vol I, p. 89, vol II, pp. 358-359.
8. *Bengal District Gazetteers, Jessore*, by L.S.S. O 'Malley (Calcutta, 1912), p. 105.
9. H. Sinha, *Marketing of Jute in Calcutta* (no date, no place, Commercial Library, Calcutta entry dated 9 September 1932), pp. 533-539.
10. *Bihar and Orissa Banking Committee*, vol I, p. 61.
11. *Ibid.*, vol. I, p. 61; vol. III, pp. 136, 146-154, 156-159.
12. *Ibid.*, vol III, pp. 16-20.
13. *Ibid.*, vol III, pp. 78-82.
14. *The Gazetteer of Bombay City and Island*, vol I (Bombay, 1909), pp. 453-454.
15. *Report of the United Provinces Provincial Banking Enquiry Committee, 1929-30*, vol I, pp. 47-54, 57-58.
16. *Handbook of Commercial Information for India* (Delhi, 1937), Passim.

17. *Report on Fairs, Markets and Produce Exchanges in India* (Marketing Series no. 45, Delhi 1943), pp. 50.51.
18. *Report of the Punjab Provincial Banking Enquiry Committee, 1929-30,* vol. I, pp. 199-203.
19. Ibbetson, n. 1, p. 244; Crooke, n. 1, vol I, pp. 14-16.
20. *Bombay Gazetteer,* vol IX, Part I, pp. 70-95; Enthoven, n. 1, vol III, pp. 412-442.
21. Enthoven, n. 1, vol I, p. 198, vol III, pp. 52-53; *Bombay Gazetteer,* vol IX, Part II, pp. 36-41.
22. *Report of the Centrally Administered Areas Banking Enquiry Committee, 1929-30,* vol I, p. 337.
23. Crooke, n. 1, vol I, pp. 14-26.
24. Central Areas Banking Committee, vol I, p. 336.
25. Ibbetson, n. 1, p. 243.
26. Russell, n. 1, vol II, pp. 113-114.
27. *Report of the Bikaner Banking Enquiry Committee* (1930), p. 96.
28. *Bombay City Gazetteer,* vol I, p. 169.
29. Especially *Brahma-vaivarta Purana.*
30. *Bombay Gazetteer,* vol IX, Part II, p. 49; *Bombay City Gazetteer,* vol I, pp. 181-182, 192-194; Enthoven, n. 1, vol III, pp. 461-466.
31. Ibbetson, n. 1, pp. 247-250.
32. *Ibid.,* pp. 250-252.
33. *The Gazetteer of the Province of Sind,* by E.H. Atkin (Karachi, 1907), pp. 181-186, Enthoven, n. 1, vol II, pp. 381-384; Russell, n. 1, vol II, p. 442.
34. Edgar Thurston, *Castes and Tribes of Southern India* (Madras, 1909), vol V, p. 252; *Bombay Gezetteer,* vol IX, part II, p. 57.
35. Russell, n. 1, vol II, p. 120.
36. Dwijendra Tripathi, *The Dynamics of a Tradition: Kasturbhai Lalbhai and His Entrepreneurship* (New Delhi, 1981), pp. 198-200; Enthoven, n. 1, vol I, p. 142, vol III, p. 54.
37. *Ibid.,* vol III, pp. 461-462.
38. *Ibid.,* vol III, p. 423; vol I, p. 144.
39. *Ibid.,* vol I, pp. 200-203.
40. *Bombay Gazetteer,* vol IX, Part II, p. 41.
41. Enthoven, n. 1, vol III, p. 54.
42. Thurston, n. 34, vol V, pp. 260-267.
43. *Ibid.,* vol III, pp. 306-348.
44. Russell, n. 1, vol II, pp. 440-441.
45 For details of migrations to Bombay city, see : Parsis, *Bombay City Gazetteer,* vol I, pp. 193-194; Kapol Banias, *Ibid.,* p. 168; Bohoras, Lakshmi Subramanian, "Bombay and the West Coast in the 1740s", *Indian Economic and Social History Review,* April-June 1981; Jains, A.D.D. Gordon, *Businessmen and Politics* (New Delhi, 1978), pp. 42, 50; Bhatias, *Bombay City Gazetteer,* vol I, p. 169 and *Bombay Gazetteer,* vol IX, Part I, pp. 161-211 Memons, Enthovan, n. 1,

vol III, p. 53, Khojas, *Bombay City Gazetteer*, vol I, pp. 180-181 and Gordon, n. 45, p. 59.

46. *Bombay City Gazetteer*, vol I, p. 194.
47. *Bombay Gazetteer*, vol IX, Part II, pp. 36,44.
48. *Ibid.*, vol IX, Part I, pp. 116-121; Enthoven, n. 1, Vol I, p. 144; Gordon, n. 45, pp, 69, 78-79.
49. *Bombay Gazetteer*, Vol IX, Part I, p. 78; *Bombay City Gazeetter*, vol I, p. 293; Gordon, *op. cit.*, p. 69.
50. Nineteenth century Aden had a large settlement of respectable Bania merchants who monopolized the trade with Africa. Mokha, too, had an important Bania colony. *Selections from the Records of the Bombay Government, New Series* (Bombay 1859) No. 49. *A Brief History of Arabia Felix or Yemen from the Commencement of the Christian Era to the Present Times Including an Account of the English Settlement of Aden*, by Captain R.L. Playfair. I am indebted for this reference to Lakshmi Subramanian.
51. *Report of the Burma Provincial Banking Enquiry Committee*, Vol I (Rangoon, 1930), pp. 186, 188.
52. K. McPherson, *The Muslim Macrocosm: Calcutta 1918 to 1935* (Wisbaden 1974), passim; R.K. Ray, *Industrialization in India* (New Delhi 1979), p. 150; *Bihar and Orissa Banking Committee*, Vol III, pp. 16-18.
53. *Report of the Madras Provincial Banking Enquiry Committee, 1929-1930*, vol I, p. 160.
54. *Ibid,*, vol IV, pp. 262-269.
55. *Burma Provincial Banking Committee*, vol I, p. 186.
56. Russell, n. 1, vol II, pp. 440-442.
57. See Table on p. 250 for Chettiar capital migration; for Multanis, *Report of the Bombay Provincial Banking Enquiry Committee, 1929-30*, vol IV, pp. 349-364.
58. *Madras Provincial Banking Committee*, vol I, p. 29.
59. *Ibid.*, Vol III, p. 1102.
60. *Burma Provincial Banking Committee*, vol I, pp. 186-188.
61. *Ibid.*, p. 186.
62. *Ibid.*, p. 186.
63. *Ibid.*, p. 191; *Madras Provincial Banking Committee*, vol I, p. 186.
64. *Burma Provincial Banking Committee*, vol I, pp. 191, 196.
65. *Madras Provincial Banknig Committee*, vol I, p. 186.
66. *Ibid.*, vol III, p. 1103.
67. *Burma Provincial Banking Committee*, vol I, pp. 190-191, 196-199, 221.
68. *Ibid.*, p. 189.
69. *Ibid.*, p. 190.
70. See T.A. Timberg, *The Marwaris: From Traders to Industrialists* (Delhi 1978), for a charting of Marwari migrations.
71. *Bihar and Orissa Provincial Banking Committee*, vol III, pp. 150-154.
72. Ibbetson, n. 1, p. 248.

73. Timberg, n. 70, p. 86.
74. Russell, n. 1, vol II, pp. 119-121.
75. *Indore State Gazetteer*, pp. 55-57.
76. *Bombay Gazetieer*, vol IX, Part I, p. 104.
77. Gordon, n. 45, passim; *Bombay Provincial Banking Committee*, vol III, p. 520 ff.
78. *Madras Provincial Banking Committee*, vol I, pp. 30, 192, vol IV, pp. 69-72.
79. *Marwari Chamber of Commerce Ki Report* (in Hindi), March 1920 to June 1924.
80. *Burma Provincial Banking Committee*, vol I, p. 187.
81. *Ibid.*
82. Bengali article 'Kather Byabsa' (Timber Business), in *Probasi* magazine, vol 40, Part I (1940), pp. 472-476.
83. *Burma Provincial Banking Committee*, vol I, p. 187.
84. *Bengal Provincial Baking Committee*, vol II, Part I, pp. 417-419.
85. *Assam Provincial Banking Committee*, vol II, pp. 530-531.
86. *Ibid.*, vol I, p. 166.
87. *Ibid.*, 167.
88. *Ibid.*, vol II, pp. 273-274.
89. *Ibid.*, vol I, p. 166.
90. *Ibid.*, p. 88.
91. *Ibid.*, p. 99.
92. *Ibid.*, p. 100.
93. *Ibid.*, vol II. p. 274.
94. *Ibid.*, vol I, pp.98-99.
95. *Statistical Abstract for British India from 1922-23 to 1931-32*, pp. 712-713.
96. Grady Mission Repot (unpublished), p. 30.
97. *Report on the Cold Storage and Transport of Perishable Produce in Delhi* (Marketing series no. 2, Delhi 1937), pp. 16-18.
98. Ibbetson, n. 1, p. 247: Russell, n. 1, vol II, pp. 441-442.
99. *Report of the Centrally Administered Areas Banking Enquiry Committee, 1929-30*, vol II, p. 234 ff.
100. *Bengal District Gazetteer, Darjeeling*, by A.J. Dash (Alipore, 1947), pp. 167-168.
101. *Trade Condltions in India* (US Consular Report), p. 28.
102. *British India* (US Consular Report by Banker), p. 394.
103. Central Area Banking Committee, vol II, p. 208.
104. *Ibid.*, p. 209.
105. *Ibid.*, p. 192.
106. *Ibid.*, vol I, p. 351, Vol II, p. 206.
107. *Ibid.*, vol II, p. 222.
108. *Ibid.*, vol I, p. 349.
109. *Ibid.*, pp. 349-355.
110. *Ibid.*, vol I, p. 351, Vol II, p. 206.
111. *Ibid.*, vol II, p. 189 ff.

112. *Ibid.*, vol II, pp. 192 ff, 216 ff; Russell, n. 1, vol II, p. 442.
113. *Ibid.*, vol II, p. 349.
114. *Ibid.*, vol I, pp. 352-355, vol II, p. 192 ff.
115. *Ibid.*, vol II, p. 206 ff.
116. *Ibid.*, p. 205.
117. *Ibid.*, p. 192 ff.
118. *Ibid.*, p. 234 ff
119. *Ibid.*, p. 209 ff.
120. *Punjab Provincial Banking Committee*, vol. I, pp. 210-211.
121. Timberg, n. 70, pp. 51, 209.
122. *Report of the Marketing of Rice in India and Burma* (Marketing Series no. 27, Delhi, 1941), p. 386.
123. *Prabasi*, vol. 40, Part I, pp. 472-476.

Bibliography*

Ahmad A.S.F., *Social Ideas and Social Change in Bengal, 1818-1835* (Leiden, 1965).

Ahmad M.B., *Administration of Justice in Medieval India* (Aligarh, 1941).

Altekar A.S., *Rashtrakutas and Their Times* (Poona, 1934).

Amin B.D., *The Rise and Growth of the Alembic Chemical Works: A History* (Baroda, 1939).

Appadorai A., *Economic Conditions in Southern India* (Madras, 1936).

Arasaratnam S., "Indian Merchants and Their Trading Methods, Circa 1700", *Indian Economic and Social History Review*, vol. 3, No.1 (1966).

——— "Trade and Political Dominion in South India 1750-90: Changing British Indian Relationship", *Modern Asian Studies*, vol. 3, No. 1 (1971).

Badshah B., *The Life of Rao Bahadur Ranchhorelal Chhotalal, CI.E.* (Bombay, 1899).

Bagal J.C., "Rustomjee Cowasji", *Modern Review*, vol. 54, No. 1 (1933).

Bagchi A.K., *Merchants and Colonialism* (mimeo, Occasional Paper No. 38, Centre for Studies in Social Sciences, Calcutta, 1981).

——— *Private Investment in India, 1900-1939* (Cambridge, 1972).

Bailey F.G., *Caste and the Economic Frontier Village in Highland Orissa* (Manchestar, 1957).

———*Tribe, Caste and Nation* (Bombay, 1960).

Bajpai G., "Baroda in Transition, 1860-1886", Ph.D. Thesis (M.S. University, Baroda, 1980).

*Only books and articles are listed here. Official and semi-official documents such as reports, gazetteers etc. have been, by and large, left out.

Banaji K.N., *Memoirs of the Late Framji Cowasji Banaji by His Great Grandson* (Bombay, 1892).

Banerjee T., *Internal Market of India 1834-1900* (Calcutta, 1966).

Banga I., *Agrarian System of the Sikhs* (Delhi, 1978).

Basu S.K., *Managing Agency System in Prospect and Retrospect* (Calcutta, 1958).

Battuta Ibn, *Travels in Asia and Africa*, English Translation (London, 1952).

Beidelman T.O., *Comparative Analysis of the Jajmani Systems* (New York, 1959).

Beidict B., *Indians in a Plural Society* (London, 1961).

Berna J.J., *Industrial Entrepreneurship in Madras State* (Bombay, 1960).

Bhandari S.R., *Oswal Jati Ka Itihas* (Indore, 1937).

Bhargave B.K., *Indigenous Banking in Ancient and Medieval India* (Bombay, 1934).

Bhattacharya J.N., *Hindu Castes and Sects* (Calcutta, 1896).

Bhave V.K., *Peshwa Kaleen Maharashtra* (New Delhi, 1976, reprint).

Bhogendranath N.C., *Development of the Textile Industry in Madras* (Madras, 1957).

Bilimoria B.F., *A Warning Word to the Parsees* (Bombay, 1900).

Blunt E.A.H., *The Caste System in Northern India* (Madras, 1931).

Briggs H.G., *The Cities of Gujarashtra* (Bombay, 1849).

—— *The Parsees or Modern Zerdusthians: A Sketch* (Edinburgh, 1852).

Brimmer A.F., "The Setting of Entrepreneurship in India", *Quarterly Journal of Economics*, vol. 69, No. 4 (1955).

Broomfield J.H., *Elite Conflict in Plural Society: Twentieth Century Bengal* (Berkeley, 1968).

Buchanan D.H., *Development of Capitalist Enterprises in India* (New York, 1966, reprint).

Buckland C.E., *Dictionary of Indian Biography* (London, 1906).

Budhwar S., "Mines and Their Administration in the Suba of Ajmer", Indian History Congress, *Proceedings*, 40th Session (Waltair, 1979).

Bulsara P.P., *Highlights of Parsi History* (Bombay, 1963).

Calvert, H., *The Wealth and Welfare of the Punjab* (Lahore, 1922).

Chakarvarty D. and R. Dasgupta, "Functions of the Nineteenth Century Banian: A Document", *Economic and Political Weekly*, (Review of Mgt.) vol. 9 (31 August 1974).

Chandra S., "Some Institutional Factors in Providing Capital Inputs for the Development and Expansion of Cultivation in Medieval India", *Indian Historical Review*, vol. 3, No. 1 (1976).

Chapekar N.G., *Peshawayichya Savaleet* (Poona, 1937).

Chaudhuri K.N., *The Economic Development of India under the East India Company, 1814-58* (Cambridge, 1971).

Chaudhary S., "The Gujarati Mahajans", Indian History Congress, *Proceedings*, 41st Session (Bombay, 1980).

Coates W.H., *The Old Country Trade of the East Indies* (London, 1911).

Cohen A.R., *Tradition, Change and Conflict in Indian Family Business* (The Hague, 1974).

Commissariat M.S., *A History of Gujarat* (Bombay, 1957).

—— *Imperial Mughal Farmans in Gujarat* (Bombay, 1940).

Cooke C.N., *The Rise, Progress and Present State of Banking in India* (Calcutta, 1862).

Coulson N.J., *A History of Islamic Law* (Edinburgh, 1964).

Crane R.I., "Technical Education and Economic Development in India before World War I", in C.A. Anderson and J.J. Bowman, *Education and Economic Development* (New York, 1965).

Crooke W., *The Tribes and Castes of the North-Western Provinces and Oudh* (Calcutta, 1896, 4 vols.).

Cunningham J.D., *A History of the Sikhs* (Delhi, 1966, reprint).

Dadysett M.D., "Social Intercourse Between Europeans and Natives in India", Paper read at the East India Association (London, 1883).

Darling M.L., *The Punjab Peasant in Prosperity and Debt* (Delhi, 1977, reprint).

Darukhanawalla H.D., *Parsi Lustre on Indian Soil* (Bombay, 1939).

Das Gupta A., *Indian Merchants and the Decline of Surat, CC1700-1750* (Wiesbaden. 1979).

——, "The Merchants of Surat, 1700-1750", in E. Leach and S.N. Mukherjee (ed.), *Elites in South Asia* (Cambridge, 1970).

Dasgupta A.C., *The Days of John Company: Selections from Calcutta Gazette, 1814-1832* (Calcutta, 1959).

Datta V.N., *Amritsar Past and Present* (Amritsar, 1967).

Davar S.P., *The History of the Parsi Panchayat of Bombay* (Bombay, 1949).

David L., *Bankers and Pashas* (Cambridge, 1958).

Davies J., (tr.), *The Voyage and Travels of J. Alberde Mandelslo* (London, 1969).

Desai A.R., *Social Background of Indian Nationalism* (Bombay, 1966).

Desai A.V., "The Origins of the Parsee Enterprise", *Indian Economic and Social History Review*, vol. 5, No. 4 (1968).

Desai M.L., (ed.) *Jain Aitihasik Rasmala* (Ahmedabad, 1912).

Desai N.A., *Social Change in Gujarat: A Study of Nineteenth Century Gujarati Society* (Bombay, 1978).

Desai S.F.A., *A Community at the Cross Road* (Bombay, 1948).

Dimock Jr. E.C., "Doctrine and Practice among the Vaisnavas of Bengal", in M.B. Singer (ed.), *Krishna: Myths, Rites and Attitudes* (Honolulu, 1966).

Diskalkar D.B., "The Parsis in India", *The Indo-Asian Culture*, vol. 5 (April 1954).

Dobbin C., *Urban Leadership in Western India: Politics and Communities in Bombay City* (Oxford, 1972).

Doshi H., *Traditional Neighbourhood in Modern City* (New Delhi, 1974).

Dube S.C., *India's Changing Villages: Human Factors in Community Development* (Ithaca, 1958).

Dubois Abbe J.A., *Hindu Manners, Customs and Ceremonies* (Oxford, 1943).

Dungen P.H.M. Von, "Changes in Status and Occupation in Nineteenth Century Punjab", in D.A. Low (ed.), *Soundings in Modern South Asian History* (London, 1968).

Dutt N.K., *Origin and Growth of Caste in India* (Calcutta, 1965).

Engineer A.A., *The Bohras* (New Delhi, 1980).

Enthoven R.E., *The Tribes and Castes of Bombay* (Bombay, 1920).

Epstein T.S., *Economic Development and Social Change in South India* (Manchestar, 1962).

Evans D.M., *The Commercial Crisis, 1847-1848* (London, 1849).

Fazal A., *Ain-i-Akbari*, English Translation (Calcutta, 1949).

Forbes A.K., *Ras Mala or Hindu Annals of the Province of Goozerat in Western India* (London, 1878).

Fox R., *From Zamindar to Ballot Box* (Ithaca, 1969).

Fryes J., *A New Account of the East India and Persia, Being Nine Years' Travels, 1762-81* (London, 1909).

Furber H., *Bombay Presidency in the Mid-Eighteenth Century* (Bombay, 1965).

Gadgil D.R., *Business Communities in India* (Mimeo, New York, 1951).

—— *Origins of the Modern Indian Business Class: An Interim Report* (Mimeo, New York, 1959).

Gandhi L.B., *Shri Jinprabha Suri and Sultan Muhammad* (Lohawat, 1939).

Gauba A., *Amritsar, 1849-1947: A Study in Urban History*, Ph.D. Thesis (Guru Nanak Dev University, Amritsar, 1980).

Gerth H.H. and C.W. Mills (ed.), *From Max Weber: Essays in Sociology* (New York, 1958).

Ghosh B., "Economic Character of the Urban Middle Class in 19th Century Bengal", in B.N. Ganguli (ed.), *Readings in Indian Economic History* (Bombay, 1964).

Ghurye G.S. *Caste and Class in India* (Bombay, 1957).

Gillion K., *Ahmedabad: A Study in Indian Urban History* (Berkeley, 1968).

Gokhale B.G., "Ahmedabad in the 17th Century", *Journal of the Economic and Social History of the Orient*", vol. 12, No. 1 (1969).

—— "Merchant Community in the 17th Century India", *Journal of Indian History*, vol. 50, No. 1 (1976).

—— "Capital Accumulation in the 17th Century Western India", *Journal of the Asiatic Society of Bombay*, vol. 39, No. 1 (1964-65).

—— *Surat in Seventeenth Century* (Bombay, 1979).

Gopal S., Jains in Bihar in the Seventeenth Century", *Jain Journal* (September, 1973).

Gopal S., *Commerce and Crafts in Gujarat, 16th and 17th Century* (New Delhi, 1975).

Gordon A.D.D., *Businessmen and Politics: Rising Nationalism and a Modernising Economy in Bombay, 1918-1933* (Delhi/Canberra, 1978).

Gore M.S., "The Impact of Industrialization and Urbanization on the Agarwal Family of the Delhi Area", Ph.D Thesis (Columbia University, New York, 1961).

Graham M., *Journal of Residence in India* (Edinburgh, 1812).

Green H., *The Deccan Ryots and Their Land Tenure* (Bombay, 1852).

Grewal J.S., *In the By-lanes of History* (Simla, 1975).

—— "The Reign of Maharaja Ranjit Singh", Sita Ram Kohli Memorial Lecture (Punjabi University, Patiala, 1981).

——and I. Banga (ed.), *Early Nineteenth Century Punjab* (Amritsar, 1975).

——and I. Banga, *Studies in Urban History* (Amritsar, 1981).

Griffiths P., *British Impact on India* (Hampden, Con., 1965).

Guha A., "Parsi Seths as Entrepreneurs, 1750-1850", *Economic and Political Weekly*, vol. 5 (29 August and 28 November, 1970).

—— "Raw Cotton of Western India: Output, Transportation and Marketing, 1750-1850", *Indian Economic and Social History Review*, vol. 9, No. 1 (1972).

Gupta S.P., "Ijara System in Eastern Rajasthan", *Medieval India: A Miscellany*, vol. 2 (Aligarh, 1972).

Habib I., "Potentialities of Change in the Economy of Mughal India" *Socialist Digest* (September 1972).

—— "Potentialities of Capitalist Development in the Economy of Mughal India", *Journal of Economic History*, vol. 29, No. 1 (March 1969).

—— *The Agrarian System of Mughal India* (Bombay, 1963).

Hagen E.E., *On the Theory of Social Change* (Homewood, Ill., 1962).

Hamilton W., *A Geographical, Statistical and Historical Description of Hindustan and Adjacent Countries* (London, 1820)

Harris F.R., *Jamsetji Nusserwanji Tata: A Chronicle of His Life* (Oxford, 1925).

Harry A.M., "The Marwari: A Study of a Group of Trading

Cates", Master's Thesis (University of California, Berkeley, 1954).

Hasan H., *A History of Persian Navigation* (London, 1928).

Hasan S.N. and K.N. Hasan, "Pattern of Agricultural Production in the Territory of Amber", Indian History Congress, *Proceedings*, 28th Session (Mysore, 1966).

—— "Prices of Foodgrains in the Territories of Amber, 1650-1750 A.D.", Indian History Congress, *Proceedings*, 29th Session (Patiala, 1968).

Hazari R.K., *The Structure of the Corporate Private Sector* (Bombay, 1966).

Hazelhurst L.W., "Entrepreneurship and the Merchant Castes in a Punjabi City" (Mimeo, Occasional Paper No. 1, Duke University Commonwealth Studies Centre, Durham, 1966).

Hodivala S.K., *Parsis in Ancient India* (Bombay, 1920).

Hopkins E.W., *India Old and New* (New York, 1961).

Hoselitz B., *The Sociological Aspect of Economic Growth* (Chicago, 1960).

Hourani E.F., *Arab Sea-faring in Indian Ocean* (Princeton, 1951).

Hutton J.H., *Caste in India* (Bombay, 1951).

Ibbetson D., *Punjab Castes* (Lahore, 1961).

Ito S., "A Note on the 'Business Combine' in India with Special Reference to the Nattukottai Chettiars", *Developing Economies*, vol. 4, No. 3 (1966).

Iyengar C.V.V., "Mill Industry in Coimbatore", *Journal of the Madras Geographical Association*, vol. 5 (October 1930).

Jain J.P., *Parmukh Aitihasika Jain Purus Aur Mahilayen* (New Delhi, 1975).

Leejeebhoy J.B.R., "Communal Discipline among the Bombay Parsees in Olden Times", in *Kharegat Memorial* (Bombay, 1953)

Jimwala F.F., "Future of Parsis and Trade Unionism", *Journal of the YMPA*, vol. 8 (June 1927).

Jones K.W., *Arya Dharm: Hindu Consciousness in 19th Century Punjab* (New Delhi, 1976).

Joshi A., *Lala Shri Ram: A Study in Entrepreneurship and Industrial Management* (New Delhi, 1973).

Kannagara A.P., "Indian Millowners and Indian Nationalism before 1914", *Past and Present*, vol. 17, No. 40 (1968).

Kapp K.W., *Hindu Culture, Economic Development and Economic Planning in India* (New York, 1963).

Karka D.F., *History of the Parsis including Their Manners, Customs, Religion and Present Position* (London, 1884).

Katrak S.K.H., *Who are the Parsees* (Karachi, 1965).

Kennedy R.E., "The Protestant Ethic and the Parsis", in N.J. Smelser (ed.), *Readings in Economic Sociology* (Englewood Citts. N.J. 1965).

Khan A.M., *The Mirat-i-Ahmadi*, English Translation (Baroda, 1965).

—— *Mirat-i-Ahmadi, Supplement*, English Translation (Baroda, 1931).

Kling B.H., *Partner in Empire: Dwarkanath Tagore and the Age of Enterprise in Eastern India* (London, 1976).

—— "The Origin of Managing Agency System", *Journal of Asian Studies*, vol. 26, No. 1 (1966).

Kochanek S., *Business and Politics in India* (Berkeley, 1974).

Kulke E., *The Parsees in India* (Delhi, 1974).

Kumar D., *Land and Caste in South India* (Cambridge, 1965).

Lamb H., "Business Organization and Leadership in India Today", in R. Park and I. Tinker (ed.), *Leadership and Political Institutions in India* (Princeton, 1959).

—— "Indian Business Communities and the Evolution of an Industrial Class", *Pacific Affairs*, vol. 28 (June 1955).

—— "The Development of Modern Business Communities in India", in R.F. Aronson and J.P.W. Muller (ed.), *Proceedings of a Conference on Labour Management and Economic Growth: Resources and Labour Relations in Underdeveloped Countries* (New York, 1954).

Latifi A., *Industrial Punjab: A Survey of Facts, Conditions and Possibilities* (Bombay, 1911).

Little, J.H., *House of Jagatseth* (Calcutta, 1967).

Lokonathan P.S., *Industrial Organization in India* (London, 1930).

Lord H., *A Display of Two Foreign Sects in the East India, viz., the Sect of the Banians, the Ancient Natives of India, and the Sect of the Parsees, the Ancient Inhabitants of*

Persia, Together with the Religion and Manners of Each Sect (London, 1630).

Low C.R., *History of the Indian Navy, 1613-1863* (London, 1877, 2 vols).

Mekelvey, W.W., "Environmental Influences on Two Business Communities", Industrial Management Thesis, (Massachussets Institute of Technology, Boston, 1962).

Mcleod W.H., *The Evolution of the Sikh Community* (Delhi, 1975).

McPherson K., *The Muslim Macrocosm: Calcutta 1918 to 1935* (Wiesbaden, 1974).

Mahadevan R., "The Origin and Growth of Entrepreneurship in the Nattukutti Chettiar Community of Tamilnadu 1880-1930", M. Phil Thesis (Jawaharlal Nehru University, New Delhi, 1976).

Mahindra K.C., *Sir Rajendra Nath Mookerjee* (Clacutta, 1962, reprint).

Majumdar D.N., *Races and Cultures in India* (Lucknow, 1951).

Malabari B.M., *Gujarat and Gujaratis: Pictures of Men and Manners Taken From Life*, (London, 1882).

Maltison M., *Muslim Merchants: The Economic Behaviour of an Indian Muslim Community* (New York, 1972).

Masani R.P., "*Banking Castes and Guilds in India*", *Journal of the Anthropological Society of Bombay*, vol. 16 (1931).

——— *N.M. Wadia and His Foundation* (Bombay, 1961).

Mayer A.C., *Caste and Kinship in Central India* (Allahabad, 1960).

Medhora P.B., "Entrepreneurship in India", *Political Science Quarterly*, vol. 80 (December, 1965).

Mehta, M.J., "Indigenous Paper Industry and Muslim Entrepreneurship", Indian {Science Academy, *Proceedings of a Seminar on Science and Technology in the 18th and 19th Centuries* (Calcutta, 1982).

——— "Some Aspects of Surat as a Trading Centre in the 17th Century", *Indian Historical Review*, vol. 1, No. 1 (1974).

——— "Ranchhodlal Chhotalal and the Ahmedabad Cotton Industry: A Study in Entrepreneurial History", Ph.D. Thesis (Gujarat University, Ahmedabad, 1979).

Mehta S.D., *Cotton Mills of India, 1854-1954* (Bombay, 1954).

—— *Indian Cotton Textile Industry: An Economic Analysis* (Bombay, 1935).

Mishra B.B., The Indian Middle Class (London, 1966).

Misra S.C., *Muslim Communities in Gujarat* (Bombay, 1964).

—— "Urban Structure and Change: A Study of the Impact of Tradition on Indian Towns with Special Reference to Ahmedabad and Surat", in J.S. Grewal and I. Banga (ed.), *Studies in Urban History* (Amritsar, 1981).

—— "Some Aspects of the Self Administering Institutions in Medieval Indian Towns", in J.S. Grewal and I. Banga (ed.), *Studies in Urban History* (Amritsar, 1981).

Mode J.J., *A Few Events in the Early History of the Parsis and Dates* (Bombay, 1905).

—— *The Parsis at the Court of Akbar and Meherji Rana* (Bombay, 1905).

Mody J.R.P., *Jamsetji Jeejibhoy: The First Indian Knight and Baionet* (Bombay, 1959).

Moraes F., *Sir Purshotamdas Thakardas* (Bombay, 1957).

Morris M.D., *The Emergence of an Industrial Labor Force in India* (Berkeley, 1965).

—— "South Asian Entrepreneurship and Rashomon Effect, 1800-1947", *Explorations in Economic History*, vol. 16, No. 3 (1979).

—— "Values as an Obstacle to Economic Growth in South Asia", *Journal of Economic History*, vol. 27, No. 4 (1967).

Mukherji S.N., "Class, Caste and Politics in Calcutta, 1815-1838", in E. Leach and S.N. Mukherji (ed.), *Elites in South Asia* (Cambridge, 1970).

Mullick K.M., *Brief History of Bengal Commerce from the Year 1814 to 1870* (Calcutta, 1871).

Mahar P.C., (Comp.), *Jain Inscriptions* (Calcutta, 1918).

Namjoshi M.V. & B.R. Sabade, *Chambers of Commerce in India* (Poona, 1967).

Naoraji D., "The Manners and Customs of the Parsees", *Tracts*, vol. 156 (1862).

Nagvi K.H., *Urban Centres and Industries in Upper India, 1556-1803* (London, 1968).

Natesan M.S., "A Study of the Capital Market of Madras Presidency", D.Phil. Thesis (University of Madras, 1934).

Newton A.P., *Travel and Traveller in the Middle Ages* (London, 1926).

Ovington J., *A Voyage to Surat in the Year 1689*, ed. by H.G. Rawlinson (London, 1929).

Owen D.E., *British Opium Policy in China and India* (New Haven, 1934).

Panase M.G., *Yadavakaleen Maharashtra 1000 to 1350 A.D.* (Bombay, 1963).

Papanek H., "Leadership and Social Change in the Khoja Irmali Community", Ph.D. Thesis (Harvard University, Cambridge, 1962).

Parkinson C.N., *Trade in the Eastern Seas, 1793-1813* (London, 1937).

Pavlov V.I., *The Indian Capitalist Class* (New Delhi, 1964).

Paymaster R.B., (ed.), *Early History of the Parsees in India* (Bombay, 1954).

Pearson M.N., *Merchants and Rulers of Gujarat* (New Delhi, 1776).

—— "Political Participation in Mughal India", *Indian Economic and Social History Review*, vol. 9, No. 2 (1972).

Philip C.H., *The East India Company, 1784-1834* (Manchester, 1940).

Pocock D., *Kanbi and Patidar: A Study of the Patidar Community of Gujarat* (Oxford, 1972).

Prakesh Om, "The Dutch East India Company and the Economy of Bengal, 1650-1717", Ph.D. Thesis (Delhi School of Economics, 1967).

—— "The European Trading Companies and the Merchants of Bengal", *Indian Economic and Social History Review*, vol. 1, No. 3 (1964).

Prasad P., "Jahangir and Jains", *Islamic Culture*, vol. 56, (January 1982).

Ray I., "Of Trade and Traders in Seventeenth Century India: An Unpublished French Memoir by George Rogues", Mimeographed Occasional Paper No. 26 (Centre for Studies in Social Science, Calcutta, 1981).

Ray P.C., *Life and Experiences of a Bengali Chemist* (Calcutta, 1932-35).

Ray R.K., *Industrialization in India: Growth and Conflict in the Private Corporate Sector, 1914-47* (Bombay, 1979).

Redford A., *Manchester Merchants and Foreign Trade, 1794-1858* (Manchester, 1934).

Redlich F., "Business Leadership: Diverse Origins and Variant Forms", *Economic Development and Cultural Change*, vol. 6, No. 3 (1958).

Rose H.A., *A Glossary of the Tribes and Castes of the West Punjab and North West Frontier Province*, (Patiala, 1970, reprint).

Roth C., *The Sassoon Dynasty* (London, 1941).

Roy S.N., "Bengal Traditions of Trade and Commerce", *Journal of the Anthropological Society of Bombay*, vol. 16, No. 1 (1929).

Rudolph L.L. and S.H. Rudolph, *The Modernity of Tradition* (Chicago, 1967).

Rungta R.S., *Rise of Business Corporation in India, 1851-1900* (Cambridge, 1970).

Russell R.V., *Tribes and Castes of the Central Provinces of India* (London, 1916, 4 vols.).

Rutnagur S.M., *Bombay Industries: The Cotton Mills* (Bombay, 1927).

Saberwal S., *Mobile Men* (New Delhi, 1976).

Sahiar G.H., "Social Change with Particular Reference to the Parsee Community", Typed Manuscript, (University of Bombay, 1955).

Saletore B.A., "Forgotten Gujarati Brahman Banker, 18th Century", Indian Historical Records Commission, *Proceedings*, vol. 30 (Hyderabad, 1964).

Sarkar J.N., *Glimpses of Medieval Bihar Economy* (Calcutta, 1978).

Saswadkar P.L., "Brahmendraswami: His Life and Role in Maratha History", Ph.D. Thesis (University of Poona, 1964).

Semmel B., *Rise of Free Trade Imperialism* (Cambridge, 1970).

Sen A.K., "The Pattern of British Enterprise in India, 1814-1914: A Casual Analysis", in B. Singh and V.B. Singh (ed.), *Social and Economic Change* (Bombay, 1967).

Sen S.K., *The House of Tatas, 1839-1939* (Calcutta, 1975).

Shah A.M. and R.G. Shroff, "The Vahivanea Barots of Gujarat", in M.B. Singer (ed.), *Traditional India: Structure and Change* (Philadelphia, 1959).

Shah K.T., *Industrialization of Punjab* (Lahore, 1941).

Sharma G.D., "Indigenous Banking and the State in Eastern Rajasthan during the Seventeenth Century", Indian History Congress, *Proceedings*, 40th Session (Waltair, 1979).

—— *Rajput Polity* (New Delhi, 1977).

—— "Vyaparis and Mahajans in Western Rajasthan during the Eighteenth Century", Indian History Congress, *Proceedings*, 41st Session (Bombay, 1980).

Sharma G.N., *Mewar and the Mughal Emperors* (Agra, 1954).

Sherring M.A., *Hindu Tribes and Castes* (Calcutta 1872-79, 3 vols.).

—— *When a Great Tradition Modernizes, An Anthropological Approach to Indian Civilization* (New York, 1972).

Singer M.B., "The Indian Joint Family in Modern Industry", in B. Cohn and M.B. Singer (ed.), *Traditions and Change in India* (New York, 1968).

—— (ed.), *Traditional India: Structure and Change* (Philadelphia, 1959).

Singh H., "Industrial Development in the Punjab, 1901-1947", M.Phil. Thesis, (Guru Nanak Dev University, Amritsar, 1981).

Singh D., "Ijara System in Eastern Rajasthan, 1750-1800 A.D.", Rajasthan History Congress, *Proceedings*, vol. 6, (1973).

Sinha N.K., "Indian Business Enterprise: Its Failure in Calcutta (1800-1848)", *Bengal Past and Present*, Diamond Jubilee Number (1967).

Spodek H., "Manchesterisation of Ahmedabad", *Economic Weekly*, vol. 17 (13 March 1965).

Srinivas M.N., *Religion and Society Among the Coorgs of South India* (London, 1965).

Sternbach L., "Gujarat as Known to Medieval Europe", *Bharatiya Vidya*, vol. 15 (1955).

Subramanian L., "Bombay and the West Coast in the 1740s", *Indian Economic and Social History Review*, vol. 18, No. 2 (1981).

Suliram R.J.F., *One Hundred Years of Bombay* (Bombay, 1937).

Sykes T.M., "Society, Power and Representations in Indian Politics: A Case Study of Haryana State", Ph.D. Thesis, (Duke University, Durham, 1974).

Tandon P., *Punjabi Century*, (Delhi, 1961, reprint).

Thorburn S.S., *Mussalmans and Moneylenders in the Punjab* (London, 1885).

Thurston E., *Castes and Tribes of Southern India* (Madras, 1909).

Timberg T.A., "A North-Indian Firm as Seen through Its Business Records, 1860-1914: Tarachand Ghanshyamads, A Great Marwari Firm", *Indian Economic and Social History Review*, vol. 8, No. 3 (1971).

—— *Industrial Entrepreneurship Among the Trading Communities of India: How the Pattern Differs* (Mimeo, Harvard University, Cambridge, 1969).

—— "Marwari Merchant Migration: A Study and Discussion of the Relevance of Theory", Paper read at the 29th International Conference of Orientalists (Paris, 1977).

—— *The Marwaris: From Traders to Industrialists*, (New Delhi, 1978).

—— "Three Types of Marwari Firm", *Indian Economic and Social History Review*, vol. 10, No. 1 (1973).

Tod J., *Annals and Antiquities of Rajasthan* (Delhi, 1978, reprint).

Trevaskis H.K., *Land of the Five Rivers* (Oxford, 1928).

Tripathi A., *Trade and Finance in the Bengal Presidency, 1793-1833* (Bombay, 1956).

Tripathi D., "Indian Entrepreneurship in Historical Perspective: A Re-interpretation", *Economic and Political Weekly*, vol. 6 (29 May 1971).

—— "Occupational Mobility and Industrial Entrepreneurship in India: A Historical Analysis", *Developing Economies*, vol. 21, No. 1 (1981).

—— "Parsees and the United States through Some Unused Documents", *Indian Archives*, vol. 30, No. 1 (1981).

—— *The Dynamics of a Tradition: Kasturbhai Lalbhai and His Entrepreneurship* (New Delhi, 1981).

—— "Problems and Sources of Indian Business History", Indian Historical Records Commission, *Proceedings*, 37th Session (Delhi, 1966).

—— "Innovations in the Indian Textile Industry: The Formative Years", in A. Okochi and S. Yonekawa (ed.), *The Textile Industry and Its Business Climate* (Tokyo, 1982).

—— and M.J. Metha, *Business Houses in Western India: A*

Study in Entrepreneurial Response, 1850-1956 (Mimeo, Indian Institute of Management, Ahmedabad, 1981).

—— "The Nagarsheth of Ahmedabad: History of an Urban Institution in a Gujarat City", Indian History Congress, *Proceedings*, 39th Session (Hyderabad, 1978).

—— "The Profile of an Indian Businessman in the 17th Century: Virjivora", (Case No. 1 Eco 1707/R Mimeo, Indian Institute of Management, Ahmedabad, 1977).

Tripathi S.D. *The Kanpur Money Market* (Delhi, 1966).

Tulpule S.G., *Pracheen Marathi Koreev Lekh* (Pune, 1963).

Tyson G.W., *The Bengal Chamber of Commerce and Industry, 1853-1953* (Calcutta, 1953).

Venkatasubbiah H., *Enterprise and Economic Change: 50 Years of FICCI* (New Delhi, 1977).

Verma K.L., (ed.) *Surishwar aur Samrat* (Agra, 1922).

Vicziany M., "Bombay Merchants and Structural Changes in the Export Community, 1850-80", in K.N. Chaudhari and C.J. Dewey (ed.), *Economy and Society: Essays in Indian Economic and Social History* (Oxford, 1979).

Wadia P.A., *Parsi Era: The Shadows Thicken* (Bombay, 1949).

Wadia R.A., *Scions of Lowji Family* (Bombay, 1964).

—— *The Bombay Dockyard and the Wadia Master Builders* (Bombay, 1957).

Weber M.N., "Towards a Definition of the Interest Community", in P. Worsley (ed.), *Modern Sociology: Introductory Readings* (London, 1971).

Wiser W.H. and C.V. Wiser, *The Hindu Jajmani System* (Locknow, 1958).

Yule H., (ed.), *The Diary of Willian Hedges* (London, 1898).

Zacharia K.C.A., *A Historical Study of Internal Migration in the Indian Subcontinent, 1901-1931* (London 1964).

Zohrapurkar V.P., *Bhattarak Sampradaya* (Sholapur, 1958).

Index